LANDMARKS OF ECONOMIC THOUGHT

LANDMARKS OF
ECONOMIC THOUGHT

BY

JOHN M. FERGUSON, Ph.D.
UNIVERSITY OF PITTSBURGH

Second Edition

LONGMANS, GREEN AND CO.
NEW YORK · LONDON · TORONTO

LONGMANS, GREEN AND CO., INC.
119 WEST 40TH STREET, NEW YORK 18

LONGMANS, GREEN AND CO. LTD.
6 & 7 CLIFFORD STREET, LONDON W 1

LONGMANS, GREEN AND CO.
20 CRANFIELD ROAD, TORONTO 16

FERGUSON

LANDMARKS OF ECONOMIC THOUGHT

First Edition January 1938
Second Edition October 1950
Reprinted January 1952
May 1956, June 1959

Printed in the United States of America

EDITOR'S INTRODUCTION

AMERICAN BUSINESS FUNDAMENTALS is a series of practical texts giving, in books of small compass, the distilled essence of each subject. Emphasis is laid on important principles, and only so much detail is presented as may be necessary to illustrate them and suggest a method of approach to the daily problems of commerce, industry and finance. The series meets the need of readers and students who want perspective rather than elaboration. The present book, based in large part upon a careful examination of many original sources, and condensed from over seven hundred pages of typed manuscript, represents the ripe thought of one who has taught the subject for more than a decade.

Dr. Ferguson holds the degrees of A.B. from Harvard University; M.A. and Ph.D. from Columbia University; and Doctor of Jurisprudence from the University of Leipzig, Germany, where he studied under Professors Bücher and Lamprecht. His European training also included work at the Universities of Berlin and Munich. Severely injured while in the United States Military Service during World War I, he was incapacitated for work for some years thereafter. He has been successively *Privatdozent* at Leipzig, Fellow in Political Science at Columbia, Instructor at Vassar College, Assistant Professor at the Universities of Kansas and Pittsburgh, and Associate Professor at Pittsburgh. He has written *Das Deutsche Eisenbahnsystem; State Regulation of Railroads in the South;* and is co-author of the *Social Workers' Handbook.* Recently he assisted in the editing of the third edition of Spahr's *Economic Principles and Problems.* Articles and book reviews in economic journals have made this mature scholar favorably known to specialists.

The author desires to express his deep gratitude to two

student assistants, Miss Helen B. Snyder and Mr. J. Ford Roche, and to the following members of the faculty of the University of Pittsburgh, Messrs. R. H. Scott and R. E. Slesinger, and Professors R. F. Blackburn, Asher Isaacs, F. D. Tyson and V. C. Wright for their critical and helpful reading of various parts of the manuscript.   To Dean Charles S. Tippetts of the University of Pittsburgh special acknowledgment is due for his ungrudging and generous response to a host of questions arising in its preparation.   His obligations to former teachers and to a large number of economists through their published works are so numerous as to preclude adequate recognition in any great detail.

The subject is timely.   The majestic scroll of the world's best thought on economics unfurls in the following pages, uncluttered by detail, impartially presented, so that modern readers may survey with clarity and perspective the slow progress toward an understanding of the forces which sway men in their business activities.   The strange errors and delusions of famed economists, the ray of insight gleaming forth from others less famous, the variegated color of conflicting opinion, and fiery resurgence of issues which do not die, but change and seethe beneath political creeds, — these vivify the pages which follow. Statesmen who proclaim half-truths, demagogues who prate of utopias, schemers who delude the masses with impossible hopes, these might, if they so desired, learn of the measureless harm which comes from unsound economic doctrine.   On the other hand, sober business men, sorely puzzled by the bewildering swirl of post-war economic currents, can find light, wisdom and inspiration from this record of a nascent science.

THE EDITOR.

CONTENTS

CROSS REFERENCE SUPPLEMENTARY READINGS

BIBLIOGRAPHY ON PAGES xiii-xvi

CHAPTERS OF THIS BOOK	I	II	III	IV	V
Boucke			26-27, 56-58	62-72	72-91
Cossa	127-137	138-150	164-210, 233-238	211-221, 239-284	284-298
Gide and Rist				1-50	50-106
Gray	I	II	III	IV	V
Haney	II, III, IV, V	VI	VII, VIII	IX	X
Ingram	I, II	III	IV 79-82	55-79, 82-87	87-110
Patterson				2-30	31-61
Peck		III	IV	V	VI
Scott			II	III-V	VI, VII
Spann	25-27	27-28	II	III-VI	97-106, 109-116, 150-153
SPECIAL REFERENCES	Cannan, II Clark, (J. M.), IV Knight, I Laidler, I, II Laistner Monroe, I, II Trever	Carlyle Monroe, III, IV O'Brien	Cannan, 6-19 Heckscher Johnson, I-V, VII, VIII, XI-XV Monroe, VI-VIII, X, XVI Schmoller Small Viner, I, II	Cannan, 25-34 Commons, III, 140-149 Higgs Johnson, VI, IX Monroe, IX, XV	Bagehot, III Cannan, 8-13, 164-175, 291-311, 338-352 Clark (J. M.), V Commons, V Davenport, II Ginsberg Hollander MacLeod, 73-100 Morrow Patten, IV, secs. 4 and 9 Price, I Rae Taussig, VII Wagner, I

REFERENCE TEXTS FOR SUPPLEMENTARY READING

O. F. Boucke, *The Development of Economics*, Macmillan, 1921.
L. Cossa, *An Introduction to the Study of Political Economy*, translated from the Italian by L. Dyer, Macmillan, 1893.
C. Gide and C. Rist, *A History of Economic Doctrines*, translated by Wm. Smart and R. Richards, Heath, 1915.
A. Gray, *The Development of Economic Doctrine*, Longmans, 1931.
L. H. Haney, *History of Economic Thought*, 3d ed., Macmillan, 1936.

CROSS REFERENCE SUPPLEMENTARY READINGS
BIBLIOGRAPHY ON PAGES xiii-xvi

VI	VII	VIII	IX	X	XI	XII
92-106	113-116	124-128. 147-148	128-142	109-112, 179, 183-184	VI	VII, VIII
300-301, 303-306	311-321	322-329	329-338, 349-351	307-311, 370-381, 402-407	345-349, 354-355, 410-415, 418-423	351-354, 427-432
120-137	138-168		348-375	107-118, 322-348	264-290, 379-407	517-528, 537-544
155-169, 190-198	170-189	272-277	277-292	238-247, 260-272	227-238	XII
XI, XII 381-384, 555-558	XIII	XVI 310-311	XXIII 688-691	XV, XVII, XVIII 558-569	XXVI, XXVII	XXX, XXXI
110-122	122-137	138-142	142-162	162-164, 168-170, 175-180, 184-188	142-146, 191-231, 234-235	231-234
101-190	191-217	218-269, 727-742	270-322	62-88, 414-443	380-413, 479-544	324-378
119-121, 146, 156-158, 176	97-118, 122-130, 133-137, 140, 153, 154		169-170, 174-181		X	VIII
VIII 188-191	IX	X	XI 291-296	101 242-248	199-209 XIII 505-510	XX-XXIV
116-134	134-153		73-74	106-109, 171-184, 209	187-201, 240-247	256-274
Bagehot, IV Bonar Commons, VI, VII Macfarlane, 276-289 Mitchell, X Patten, V, sec. 3 Price, II Taussig, VIII Viner, III Wagner, II, III Wallas	Bagehot, V Cannan, 172-206, 234-249 Commons, 348-366 Davenport, III Gonner Hollander Mitchell, XI North Price, III Taussig, IX Toynbee, 1-27 126-143 Viner, IV Wagner, IV	Davenport, IV Halevy Macfarlane, 172-182 Patten, V, sec. 5 Seligman, III Taussig, X, Viner, V	Cannan, 434-442 Davenport, V, VI Macfarlane, 232-255 Patten, V sec. 6 Price, IV, V Taussig, XI, XII Toynbee, 114-126 Wagner, XVIII	Hasek MacLeod, III-120, 135-138	Hirst Price, VI VIII	Commons, 378-386, 649-677, XI Davenport, XVII-XIX Knight, V, X Macfarlane, 30-79, 183-214 Mitchell, XII Price, VII Seager, 1-30 Smart

REFERENCE TEXTS FOR SUPPLEMENTARY READING

J. K. Ingram, *A History of Political Economy*, Black, 1915.
S. H. Patterson, *Readings in the History of Economic Thought*, McGraw-Hill, 1932.
H. W. Peck, *Economic Thought and Its Institutional Background*, Farrar and Rinehart, 1935.
Wm. A. Scott, *The Development of Economics*, Century, 1933.
Othmar Spann, *The History of Economics*, translated from 19th German ed. by E. and C. Paul, Norton, 1930.

CROSS REFERENCE SUPPLEMENTARY READINGS
BIBLIOGRAPHY ON PAGES xiii-xvi

CHAPTERS OF THIS BOOK	XIII	XIV	XV	XVI	XVII	XVIII
Boucke	264			200-207		
Cossa	357-361	342-344, 387-389	514-543	544-549	460-483	
Gide and Rist		170-198	198-264, 290-321, 407-436, 579-587, 614-642	449-483	338-340, 563-570	
Gray		204-216		XI		
Haney	XXXII 693-696	XX 698-699	XXII 479-486	486-507	XXXV, XXXVI	XXXIII, XXXIV, XXXVII
Ingram		165-168			170-175, 235-238	VII
Patterson		545-577	580-607	608-666	90-100, 444-478, 667-725	
Peck	211, 219	XI	325-334	334-363		XII
Scott	XXVI	250-259	XVI 277-283	283-288	195-199, 232-241 XXV 483-487, 519-522	XIX 522-525
Spann		247-253	210-218, 236-237	218-236	203-208, 237	XII
SPECIAL REFERENCES	Cannan, 274-280, 320-329 Davenport, XX Homan 195-280 Pigou Scott	Homan, 283-374 Wagner, VI-VIII, XXVIII	Laidler, III-XII, XIX Seligman, II Toynbee, 178-221 Wagner, IX-XV	Beer Cole Hook Kautsky Laidler, XIII-XVIII, XX-XXXI Laski Loria Mehring Salter Strachey Wagner, XIX, XX, XXIII-XXVII, XXXII	Boswell Clark (J. M.), XIII, XIV Commons, 649-677 Dorfman Hobson Homan, 15-193, 375-437 Knight, VI Macfarlane, 256-275, 291-304 Teggart Teilhac Turner Wagner, XXXI	Clark (J. M.), I Commons, XI Fraser Homan, 437-469 Knight, IV, XI Korzybski Macfarlane, 305-317 Mitchell, II, IV-VI, XIII, XV-XVII Robertson Seligman, I Soule Suranyi-Unger Tugwell Viner, VI-IX

ADDITIONAL REFERENCE BIBLIOGRAPHY

W. J. Ashley, *An Introduction to English Economic History and Theory*, Part I, The Middle Ages, 4th ed., Longmans, 1909, Part II, The End of the Middle Ages, 4th ed., Longmans, 1906.

Walter Bagehot, *Economic Studies*, 2nd ed., Longmans, 1888.

H. E. Barnes, *The History of Western Civilization*, 2 vols., Harcourt, Brace, 1935.

Max Beer, *Fifty Years of International Socialism*, Macmillan, 1935.

J. A. Blanqui, *History of Political Economy in Europe*, translated from 4th ed., 1860, by E. J. Leonard, Putnam, 1880.

E. Böhm-Bawerk, *Karl Marx and the Close of the System*, translated by A. M. Macdonald, Unwin, 1898.

James Bonar, *Malthus and His Work*, 2nd ed., Unwin, 1924.

J. T. Boswell, *The Economics of Simon Nelson Patten*, Winston, 1934.

O. F. Boucke, *A Critique of Economics, Doctrinal and Methodological*, Macmillan, 1922.

Edwin Cannan, *A Review of Economic Theory*, King (Lond.), 1929.

R. W. and A. J. Carlyle, *A History of Medieval Political Theory*, Putnam, Blackwood, 1903-36.

E. Chamberlin, *The Theory of Monopolistic Competition*, Harvard, 1933.

J. B. Clark, *Economic Essays contributed in honor of J. B. Clark*, Macmillan, 1927.

J. M. Clark, *Preface to Social Economics*, Farrar, 1936.

G. D. H. Cole, *What Marx Really Meant*, Knopf, 1934.

Gustave Cohn, *History of Political Economy*, translated from the German by J. A. Hill, Annals of the American Academy of Political and Social Science, vol. 4, 1894.

J. R. Commons, *Institutional Economics*, Macmillan, 1934.

W. Cunningham, *The Growth of English Industry and Commerce*, 2 vols., Cambridge University Press, 1890, 1892.

W. Cunningham, *Western Civilization in its Economic Aspects*, 2 vols., Cambridge Historical Series, 1898, 1900.

H. J. Davenport, *Value and Distribution*, University of Chicago Press, 1908.

Joseph Dorfman, *Thorstein Veblen and His America*, Viking, 1934.

R. T. Ely, *The Past and Present of Political Economy*, Johns Hopkins University Studies, 1884.

Encyclopedia of the Social Sciences.

A. W. Flux, *Economic Principles*, Dutton, 1923.

L. M. Fraser, *Economic Thought and Language*, Black (Lond.), 1937.

Eli Ginzberg, *The House of Adam Smith*, Columbia, 1934.

E. C. K. Gonner, *Ricardo's Principles*, introductory essay, notes and appendices by Gonner, Bell, 1891.

Elie Halevy, *The Growth of Philosophic Radicalism*, translated by M. Morris, Macmillan, 1928.

C. W. Hasek, *Introduction of Adam Smith's Ideas into Germany*, Columbia, 1925.

Herbert Heaton, *Economic History of Europe*, Harper, 1936.

F. J. C. Hearnshaw, *A Survey of Socialism*, Macmillan, 1928.

E. F. Heckscher, *Mercantilism*, Macmillan, 1935.

H. Higgs, *The Physiocrats*, Macmillan, 1897.

Margaret Hirst, *Life of Frederick List*, Smith, 1909.

J. A. Hobson, *Veblen*, Chapman, 1936.

J. H. Hollander, et al., *Adam Smith*, Lectures to commemorate the sesquicentennial of the publication of *The Wealth of Nations*, University of Chicago Press, 1928.

P. T. Homan, *Contemporary Economic Thought*, Harper, 1928.

Sidney Hook et al., *The Meaning of Marx*, Farrar, 1934.

E. A. J. Johnson, *Predecessors of Adam Smith*, Prentice-Hall, 1937.

Karl Kautsky, *Karl Marx*, Macmillan, 1925.

J. N. Keynes, *Scope and Method of Political Economy*, 4th ed., Macmillan, 1930.

Thomas Kirkup, *History of Socialism*, 5th ed., largely rewritten by Pease, Longmans, 1913.

F. H. Knight, *The Ethics of Competition and other essays*, Harper, 1935.

Alfred Korzybski, *Science and Sanity*, International Non-Aristotelian Library Publishing Co., 1933.

H. W. Laidler, *A History of Socialist Thought*, Crowell, 1927.

M. L. W. Laistner, *Greek Economics*, Dutton, 1923.

Harold Laski, *Karl Marx*, League for Industrial Democracy, 1933.

T. E. Cliffe Leslie, *Essays in Political and Moral Philosophy*, Longmans, 1879.

A. D. Lindsay, *Karl Marx's Capital*, Oxford University Press, 1926.

Achille Loria, *Karl Marx*, Seltzer, 1920.

C. W. Macfarlane, *Value and Distribution*, 2nd ed., Lippincott, 1911.

H. D. MacLeod, *The History of Economics*, Longmans, 1896.

H. L. McCracken, *Value Theory and Business Cycles*, 2nd ed., McGraw-Hill, 1936.

J. R. McCulloch, *The Literature of Political Economy*, Longmans, 1845.

Franz Mehring, *Karl Marx*, Covici, 1935.

W. C. Mitchell, *The Backward Art of Spending Money and other essays*, McGraw-Hill, 1937.

A. E. Monroe, *Early Economic Thought*, Harvard University Press, 1924.

G. R. Morrow, *Ethical and Economic Theories of Adam Smith*, Cornell, 1923.

J. S. Nicholson, *The Revival of Marxism*, Murray, 1920.

C. C. North, *Sociological Implications of Ricardo's Economics*, University of Chicago Press, 1915.

E. Nys, *Researches in the History of Economics*, translated by N. F. and A. R. Dryhurst, Black, 1899.

G. A. T. O'Brien, *An Essay on Medieval Economic Teaching*, Longmans, 1920.

Sir Robert H. A. Palgrave, *Dictionary of Political Economy*, new ed., Macmillan, 1925-26.

S. N. Patten, *The Development of English Thought*, Macmillan, 1899.

A. C. Pigou, *Memorials of Alfred Marshall*, Macmillan, 1925.

L. L. Price, *A Short History of Political Economy in England*, 4th ed., Methuen, 1903.

Michael Prothero, *Political Economy*, Bell, 1895.

John Rae, *Life of Adam Smith*, Macmillan, 1895.

Joan Robinson, *Economics of Imperfect Competition*, Macmillan, 1933.

F. R. Salter, *Karl Marx and Modern Socialism*, Macmillan, 1921.

H. R. Seager, *Labor and Other Economic Essays*, Harper, 1931.

E. R. Seligman, *Essays in Economics*, Macmillan, 1925.

Gustav Schmoller, *The Mercantile System*, Macmillan, 1902.

W. R. Scott, *Alfred Marshall*, Oxford, 1926.

H. R. Sewall, *Theory of Value Before Adam Smith*, American Economic Association, 1901.

O. D. Skelton, *Socialism ; A Critical Analysis*, Houghton, 1911.

A. W. Small, *The Cameralists*, University of Chicago Press, 1909.

Wm. Smart, *An Introduction to the Theory of Value*, Macmillan, 1891.

George Soule, *The Useful Art of Economics*, Macmillan, 1929.

John Strachey, *The Theory and Practice of Socialism*, Random House, 1936.

J. Suranyi-Unger, *Economics in the Twentieth Century*, translated from the German by N. D. Moulton, Norton, 1931.

F. W. Taussig, *Wages and Capital*, Appleton, 1896.

R. H. Tawney, *Religion and the Rise of Capitalism*, Harcourt, 1926.

R. V. Teggart, *Thorstein Veblen, A Chapter in American Economic Thought*, 1932.

Ernest Teilhac, *Pioneers of American Economic Thought in the Nineteenth Century*, translated by E. A. J. Johnson, Macmillan, 1936.

Arnold Toynbee, *Lectures on the Industrial Revolution*, Memoir by B. Jowett, Longmans, 1890.

A. A. Trever, *A History of Greek Economic Thought*, 1916.

R. G. Tugwell and others, *The Trend of Economics*, Knopf, 1924.

J. R. Turner, *Ricardian Rent Theory in Early American Economics*, N. Y. University, 1921.

Jacob Viner, *Studies in the Theory of International Trade*, Harper, 1937.

D. O. Wagner, *Social Reformers*, edited by D. O. Wagner, Macmillan, 1934.

S. and B. Webb, *Soviet Communism : A New Civilization?* Scribner, 1936.

A. C. Whitaker, *History and Criticism of the Labor Theory of Value in English Political Economy*, Columbia University Studies, Columbia, 1904.

Graham Wallas, *Jeremy Bentham*, 1922.

P. H. Wicksteed, *The Common Sense of Political Economy*, Macmillan, 1910.

A. A. Young, *Economic Problems New and Old*, Houghton, 1927.

ADDITIONAL BIBLIOGRAPHY

Leonard D. Abbott (ed.), *Masterworks of Economics*, Doubleday and Co., 1946.

Dudley Dillard, *The Economics of John Maynard Keynes*, Prentice-Hall, 1948.

Joseph Dorfman, *The Economic Mind in American Civilization*, three volumes, 1606–1918, Viking, 1949.

H. S. Ellis (ed.), *A Survey of Contemporary Economics*, Blakiston, 1949.

C. Gide and C. Rist, *A History of Economic Doctrines*, 2nd English edition, Heath, 1948.

Allan G. Gruchy, Modern Economic Thought, Prentice-Hall, 1947.

L. H. Haney, History of Economic Thought, 4th edition, Macmillan, 1949.

S. E. Harris (ed.), *The New Economics*, Knopf, 1947.

Eduard Heimann, History of Economic Doctrines, Oxford University Press, 1945.

G. Hoover, *Twentieth Century Economic Thought*, Philosophical Library, 1950.

John W. McConnell, *The Basic Teachings of the Great Economists*, Garden City Publishing Co., 1943.

Frank A. Neff, *Economic Doctrines*, 2nd edition, McGraw-Hill, 1950.

Erich Roll, *A History of Economic Thought*, 2nd edition, Prentice-Hall, 1942.

G. J. Stigler, *Production and Distribution Theories*, Macmillan, 1941.

Edmund Whittaker, *A History of Economic Ideas*, Longmans, 1940.

Ferdynand Zweig, *Economic Ideas*, Prentice-Hall, 1950.

LANDMARKS OF
ECONOMIC THOUGHT

CHAPTER I

THE ANCIENT WORLD

ECONOMICS, whether the most dismal of all sciences, as Thomas Carlyle and others have asserted, or, on the contrary, a most fascinating subject of study, concerns itself with the greatest of all human dramas — man's endeavor to secure the things he needs for the satisfaction of an ever-growing number and variety of wants. Nature rarely bestows her gifts with a free hand; she baits the trap with limitations upon the amount of food that will grow naturally and provides a natural birth rate higher than the natural death rate. The struggle of humanity to escape from want is thus never ending. Caught between insatiable desires and a niggardly nature, man devotes the greater part of his waking hours to the economic drama in which he inescapably finds himself.

The sphere of economics.— These, then, are the foundation stones upon which the structure of economics rests. From the outset, human beings have lived in some form of social union; hence economic science deals with man as a member of society, and in common with the other social sciences has as its central problem the behavior of human beings in society. However sharp and precise the demarcations of its subject matter, economics is thus closely related to history, to political science, to jurisprudence, to sociology, to anthropology, to ethics, and, most obviously, to psychology. Because of these close relationships, it is often difficult to single out certain problems and to maintain, without fear of contradiction, that they are economic rather than, for instance, political or sociological problems. If, by and large, the four main branches of learning be taken to be the humanities, the physical sciences, the biological sciences, and the social sciences, economics may be said to comprise within its wide border well nigh the entire field of human knowledge, and to justify the employment of every scientific method.

Definitions.— The term "economics" is derived from the Greek *oikonomike* (*oikos* = the sum of one's possessions; *nomos* = management) ; as used by the Greeks, the word came to signify the act of prudent and systematic household management. Aristotle, however, interested primarily in the provision of a revenue for the state, often used the phrase "political economy." Thus, at the close of the Middle Ages, when discussion of the subject was revived on a large scale, and statesmen studied the art of making a people wealthy and self-sufficient through national regulation, "political economy" became a familiar expression. Despite the advocacy by many of other names such as civil economics, national economics, catallactics, chrematistics, and plutology this term continued its dominance until well toward the end of the nineteenth century. By that time the shift in emphasis on the part of thinkers from the political to the social causes which condition the economic progress of the various groups in society brought the older Greek phrase once more into the foreground. With the publication in 1890 of Alfred Marshall's *Principles of Economics*, the tide definitely turned.

The narrower, though longer, designation is still often used, no doubt through force of habit, and it is clearly to be recognized that the brevity and not the clearness of the word is perhaps in great part the responsible factor in the ever-growing employment of the term economics. From the simple consideration in classic antiquity of household economy, has emerged the present differentiation of the science into almost innumerable separate disciplines. Public finance, agricultural economics, international trade, corporation finance, money and banking, transportation and business cycles are but a few of the categories which economists have fashioned in the course of time in their zealous pursuit of the truth.

Ancient economic background.— Reflection as to man's relation to his material environment must be as old as human life itself. Yet economic phenomena existed for century upon century in the relatively simple and static life of primal man before any attempt at analysis explicitly emerged. Ancient communities were organized primarily for war. Economic life rested, in general, upon the basis of slavery. A few large proprietors owned the land, slaves furnished the bulk of the labor in shop and field, the vast majority of the population passed their lives in abject want, custom and caste imposed an almost impassable barrier to individual progress and to the invention of labor-saving machinery; while, as a rule, such thinkers as there were attached themselves to, or were a part of, the dominant class. In brief, the economic life of the ancients was limited and monotonous to a degree beyond the comprehension of the average participant in the thousandfold variety of activities in the modern world. Given the paucity of economic phenomena, minute regulation of everyday life, the close identification of the individual with the state, and the frequent indifference manifested by thinkers, it indeed seems surprising that economic speculation flourished to any extent at all in the poor soil of the earliest cultures.

At the outset of recorded history, reflection and speculation appeared in their highest state of fruition in the civilizations of the Orient. Recent investigations have brought to light much of interest and value to the economist in the ancient literature, customs, institutions and laws of the Babylonians, Assyrians, Chaldeans, Egyptians, Phoenicians, Jews, Arabians, Hindus and Chinese. So diverse were these civilizations, however, that to generalize with regard to them, except on the broadest possible basis, would be to present a most misleading picture. Excavations and researches now in progress, it is hoped, will in the comparatively near future uncover treasures of information in a field all too long neglected by the economist.

Early economic themes.— In a very general way the subjects most touched upon by the poets and philosophers of those days, or implicitly recognized in customs, institutions and laws, or discussed in occasional treatises may be said to have been the ownership and cultivation of land, the merits and demerits of various occupations, the issue of monopoly versus competition, price regulation, labor and wages, poverty, adulteration, weights and measures, money and banking, taxation, and programs of social and economic reform. Thus the Code of Hammurabi, composed roughly about 2000 years B.C., set standard wages for artisans and fixed the price of cattle, among other things, for the Babylonians of those days. Confucius (551-479 B.C.), public official, historian, and noted teacher in early Chinese history, argued in behalf of government regulation of prices, state relief for the aged, equality and universality in taxation, and the abolition of customs tariffs. Chanakya, Hindu statesman, dealt at length in a work of over one thousand pages with numerous economic problems, devoting his attention in particular to matters connected with farm administration. Finally, Old Testament prophets such as Amos, Hosea, Isaiah, Jeremiah and Ezekiel, agonizing over the tyranny and oppression of which they were eye-witnesses, called attention to the evils of the day, and visioned utopias upon earth where justice in the affairs of men would at last prevail.

Economic fatalism.— A more detailed recital of the achievements of Oriental economic thought would reveal an amount of speculation far surpassing in variety and extent the narrow range to which it has traditionally been confined. True, comparatively little scientific analysis arose. Yet to assert that prior to the Greeks all economic thinking consisted of moralizing upon certain virtues and duties, of ethical exhortations on economic and social reform, and of treatises upon agronomy is far too broad a generalization. Poets, philosophers, priests, lawgivers, historians — all these contributed to a stream of thought that expanded in volume and importance as capitalist trade became more and more highly developed, as systems of money and credit grew more complicated, accompanied by strikes, revolutions, the proclamation of socialistic theories and the launching of socialist movements.

In summary, however meagre the attainments of early thinkers may appear to us, the economic theory of antiquity did in fact explain in large measure the economic phenomena of that time. With social life undifferentiated and the individual subordinated to an all powerful church or state, the subject matter of economics was inevitably and inextricably bound up with philosophy, ethics, religion and law. In the ancient world, furthermore, where the base everywhere was some system of caste, almost all kinds of economic activity became symbolic of slavery. Agriculture alone (possibly because mankind seemed to be indissolubly bound to the soil), escaped the disrepute and derision visited by writers upon manual labor in general. And, finally, the worth of existence was not, as all too often today, measured in terms of material progress. Worship was accorded, not to newness and change, but to that which was old and customary. Wealth or poverty was accepted, in the main, without a struggle. Happiness tended to be measured in terms of decreasing, rather than of increasing, wants. The Orient of old is the supreme example of economic fatalism.

Strictures upon Greek economic speculation.— In depth and scope of analysis and in refinement of method the thinkers of classic Greece stand pre-eminent among the scholars of the ancient world. The Athenian writers were the first of modern men in that by dint of hard and disciplined thinking they began that careful analysis, resumed by the scholastics of the Middle Ages, which has led to the development of modern science. With the Greeks scholarship parted company with organized superstition, and planted those sturdy germs of secular thought which in time were to have an incalculable influence upon the civilizations of today.

Certain barriers, unfortunately, ringed themselves around the Greek mind and prevented it from reaching full maturity. Not even Athens was free from the hampering notion, held throughout the greater part of the world at that time, that the institution of slavery was aught but natural. There prevailed a general obsession that the compact city-state was the ultimate in governmental efficiency. This view absolutely ignored the previous course of history. Empire had always succeeded empire. Still more hampering were (a) the woeful ignorance of mankind's past and of current happenings beyond the limited frontiers of Greece, (b) the undeveloped state of any science except geometry, (c) rudimentary means of communication, and (d) a complete lack of apparatus for exact physical measurement.

The immortality of the Greeks lies therefore not in accomplishment but in attempts at achievement. It matters little that they answered but few of the questions which they raised. Their glory is that challenge to the world in which they found themselves — a challenge which still motivates scientific inquiry throughout the civilized globe.

Xenophon and perhaps Aristotle wrote specific economic treatises. Yet these works treated mainly of household man-

agement. A survey of the entire range of Greek economic literature reveals but little analysis of economic phenomena, beyond
certain incidental observations. While Greek scholars went
further than the Orientals in considering the nature of economic wants and the importance of material wealth, they nevertheless wrote disjointedly, and discussed economics as a
subsection of ethics and politics. For reasons already noted,
this was inevitable, notwithstanding the commercial and industrial revolution in Greece from the seventh to the fifth
centuries B.C.— a revolution which brought her to a comparatively high level of material prosperity.

Earliest sources.— Information on the economic views of
the Greeks comes from a variety of sources. Among historians, Herodotus and Thucydides stressed the economic element in history. Hippocrates, famed physician, wrote of the
influence of physical environment on social and economic
life. Works on wealth and on agriculture, in particular, were
composed by such minor authors as Democritus. In the fifth
century B.C. the Sophists, represented by Protagoras and Polus,
broke the sod in new fields of investigation by a thorough and
systematic study of ethics and the theory of the state. Two
centuries later the Stoics and the Epicureans, headed respectively by their founders, Zeno and Epicurus, boldly stated the
ultimate goal of human life, the former maintaining that virtue
is its own reward, the latter that man is made for pleasure.
Each of these philosophers minimized the responsibility of the
individual toward society. Zeno and his followers, furthermore, restated and re-enforced the universalistic conception
of natural law advanced previously by Heraclitus, identifying
natural law with a divinely ordained order to which it was
man's duty to adapt himself. The spirit of inquiry pervaded
even the tragedies of Aeschylus, Sophocles, and Euripides, and
the immortal comedies of Aristophanes.

Xenophon.— Of all Greek writers, however, the most deserving of the attention of economists are unquestionably
Xenophon (444-354 B.C.), Plato (427?-347 B.C.) and Aristotle
(384-322 B.C.). Xenophon, soldier, historian, and author of the
Anabasis, occupied himself in leisure moments with writing
several short treatises upon estate and household management,

two of which are of some moment. In the dialogue *Oecono-micus,* he accorded effusive praise to agriculture, lauding nature as the source of all production and farm work as the most healthful and delightful of occupations. Tradesmen and artisans, he maintained, weakened themselves while at work sitting down, whereas workers on the land grew robust. He commended slave labor, but stressed the need of humane treatment of slaves. Like others before him he looked upon wealth as something which required interpretation from the standpoint of needs. Wealth was accordingly the excess of possessions over wants, its essence being serviceableness. Thus it was possible for a poor man to be more wealthy than a rich man burdened with obligations and unsatisfied ambitions.

In the essay *Ways and Means to Increase the Revenue of Athens* Xenophon briefly discussed public finance. In lively fashion he pointed out the advantages of international commerce, bespoke a more liberal treatment of foreign merchants as a source of increased revenue for Athens, propounded maxims of just taxation, and stated that prices are fixed by the interaction of demand and supply. With odd lack of insight, however, while endorsing the policy of city ownership and operation of silver mines, he declared that the value of silver would always remain constant regardless of the amount produced. Gold, in his opinion, always depreciated in value when mined in excess, but not silver, inasmuch as the demand for silver is unlimited. Xenophon perhaps is first in that long and apparently endless line of champions of free silver.

The law of diminishing returns was but dimly perceived by the ancients, yet there is a glimmer of its existence in Xenophon's works. He discusses certain advantages of the division of labor. His point of view is always that of a practical man, not of a theorist.

Plato.— Wealthy aristocrat, most illustrious of the pupils of Socrates, and witness of the corruption, license and tyranny to which Athens fell a prey following the Age of Pericles (459-431 B.C.) and the death of Socrates (399 B.C.), Plato is famed as the author of the most celebrated dialogues of all history. In these his old teacher usually is the chief speaker. The dialogues are vehicles for Plato's own views on justice, virtue, religion, education, and government. Distrustful of then existing political institutions, he sought to counsel and teach his contemporaries, especially in two immortal masterpieces ; the *Republic* gives a picture of an ideal society, and the *Laws,* written thirty years later, was intended to make feasible an enduring state.

Briefly stating that the origin of the city-state is to be found in the economic needs of mankind, needs which can be satisfied by mutual co-operation alone, Plato concluded that the proper basis of social organization must be division of labor and specialization in every craft. For each man there is some sort of work which it is "natural" for him to do, inasmuch as there are natural differences in endowment among men. Therefore the city-state must be large enough to afford scope for the proper development of this specialization in labor. Neither poverty nor riches, naturally, should prevail.

Believing that democracy is inefficient from the ideal point of view, Plato provided for a grouping of the citizens of his ideal city-state into three classes. The artisans, composing the largest class, were people without capacity for government or warfare. Their function was to produce commodities essential for the whole community. A second, and much smaller class, the warriors, was to defend the city against attack. The third class, called the guardians, were the rulers ; they were very few and included only the wisest men. In their hands exclusively was to be the government of the commonwealth. Members born into one class were to be promoted or demoted to another class whenever differences in their capacities made such a transfer desirable. Thus every man would then be doing the sort of work for which he was best fitted by birth, breeding, and temperament.

For the limited class of guardians, and for that class alone, was prescribed a sweeping communism in not only property but family relations. In defense of this startling proposal Plato set forth the argument that such common ownership would serve both to keep the guardians together in unity of purpose and to make possible the development of the science of eugenics. In other words, the purpose of his communism was not, at least directly, to lessen the injustice and inequality of the world, but to subordinate the natural selfishness of man to the interests of that superior entity, the state. Not otherwise, he believed, could the guardians efficiently discharge their duties.

In advocating a far higher status for women than they then enjoyed, as well as in his plea for a eugenic race, Plato was centuries ahead of his time. And nowhere in the *Republic* did he explicitly make provision for slavery.

Whether the myth of an ideal republic was used to criticize conditions in Athens without danger to himself personally, or whether Plato was replying, either in a serious vein or with tongue in cheek, to contemporary skits on communistic theories, is a mooted question. At all events his picture of a future ideal state, though necessarily limited by his environment, has ever since captured the imagination of the world.

The state contemplated in the *Laws* is a compromise between the lofty ideals of justice enunciated in the *Republic* and existing institutions as they presented themselves to him. Plato here endeavors to present not the best possible of all states, but the most practicable one. Tempering the asceticism so evident in his earlier delineation, he nevertheless proposed the ideal of a self-sufficient community, comprising 5,040 people, and removed by a safe distance from the sea, in which numerous restrictions were designed to bring about a contented condition of life. All economic dealings were to be subject to rigid control on the part of the ruling class. Not only would fraud be thus prevented but likewise the emergence of extreme poverty or excessive wealth ; to the mass of the people would be ensured a proper supply of the necessaries and comforts of life. Accordingly, the limits of the territory were rigidly fixed ; the population was to be kept stationary by the exposure of infants, the establishment of colonies and the prohibition of early marriages ; the currency was to be of such a nature as to be acceptable only in the city-state where used ; no money was to be lent at interest nor were borrowers to be under obligation to repay amounts borrowed. Slaves were to be employed only in agricultural work ; property was to be privately owned combined with some use in common ; commerce and industry were to be placed in the hands of resident foreigners ; no citizen was to engage in the handicraft arts or in retail trade ; advertising was forbidden.

In short Plato held to the opinion, with Socrates and others, that the object of life is self-realization, not the acquisition of wealth. Probably no writer has more thoroughly subordinated economics to political and ethical considerations.

Aristotle.— So-called father of many sciences and keenest of all thinkers of the ancient world, Aristotle, the most distinguished of Plato's pupils, completes the triumvirate. Taking all knowledge for his province, he wrote important works on poetry, history, rhetoric, and metaphysics — all characterized by the collection of as many observable facts as possible and their systematization into trustworthy theory. Contrasting strongly with the abstract method and exaggerated idealism of his master is Aristotle's historico-philosophical approach, prodigious learning, and earnest striving for scientific precision.

Probably none of his numerous treatises is devoted to the specific subject of economics ; some modern scholars, however, ascribed to his authorship a tract entitled *Oeconomicus*. Aristotle gathered together in various writings nearly all the available knowledge of economics up to his time, and surely ranks first among all the Greeks who concerned themselves with this field of learning.

Of chief concern to the economist are the *Politics* and, in much lesser degree, the *Nicomachoean Ethics*. The *Politics*, based on an examination of the constitutions of over one hundred and fifty Greek city-states, is a study of the principles of politics and government. One of the most remarkable books ever composed, it not only anticipated much that was written and achieved in the domain of political science during the succeeding two thousand years but has influenced in many ways the thought and institutions of the twentieth century.

Defense of slavery.— After tracing the origin of the city-state, not to economic necessities (as with Plato), but to a natural social development out of the previous household and village stages, Aristotle proceeded to his memorable defense of slavery. Plato had tacitly accepted the institution ; Aristotle engaged in a philosophical discussion of the issue. Postulating that all forms of society are made up of two parts, the rulers and the ruled, he contended that slavery is a natural phenomenon. Slaves were but "animated tools," possessing no independent will. Just as in the case of an individual, the body must inevitably and properly be subject to a higher element, the soul, so there are persons who are fit to serve society only through their bodies and who are therefore naturally subordinate to those other persons who are endowed with superior minds and spirits. Thus slavery was necessary in order that the ruling classes might have appropriate leisure time for the cultivation of statecraft and the arts. Since most slaves were obtained by conquest in war, he distinguished between natural and legal slaves, vigorously maintaining that only people of non-Hellenic races should be used as slaves, and that if the slave were really not inferior to the master he should be liberated.

Wealth.— Aristotle next turned his attention to the question of wealth, studying it, not as an end in itself, nor as an object of any fundamental importance to either the state or the individual himself, but as a means to be used in the realization of the good life. He excluded from the concept all useless and all immaterial things, and confined wealth to all those useful, material objects limited in extent which are owned by man — much in the vein of modern, orthodox economists. All wealth acquisition, he asserted, is, in the main, of two sorts. The first or "natural" method consists in the appropriation of the means of subsistence supplied to man by nature for the legitimate purpose of meeting the needs of life. Under this heading would fall the activities of hunting, fishing, cattle raising, flock tending, agriculture and (strangely enough) piracy. Property thus secured constitutes the only genuine or "natural" wealth.

With the primary method is contrasted the "chrematistic" or "unnatural" method, characterized by exchange of products and the use of money. To "unnatural" wealth — commodities acquired in the process of making money — he conceded a certain legitimacy, but in general condemned wealth acquisition by means of trade and commerce as tending to inflame the desire for unlimited gains and enrich one party at the expense of another. Whether Aristotle drew this distinction, now looked upon askance by economists, upon moral grounds chiefly, or whether he believed that the extractive industries alone are truly productive, is debatable.

Aristotle's ideas regarding value.— Every commodity, he further maintained, has two uses. There is the proper use, as when shoes are worn, and the improper or secondary use, as when shoes are exchanged for something else. In this connection he is discussing what modern economists have come to call *value in use* and *value in exchange*. Plato and numerous others before him had but scratched the surface, being content, in general, to state that value is something inherent in an object.

With characteristic acumen Aristotle went farther and reasoned that value in exchange is derived from value in use, finding his standard of measure in man's wants. Obviously, today in exchanging goods, we consider primarily the matter of comparative value. Not alone must the cost of production be taken into account but also the power of the goods to satisfy human wants, a power that economists nowadays dignify with the name *utility*. It is therefore greatly to his credit that Aristotle saw that value is not a quality necessarily bound up or inherent in a commodity, but rather something that arises, in general, by reason of cost of production, on the one hand, and utility on the other. In other words, it is the interaction of the forces of demand and supply that determines the conditions under which the exchange shall take place. Though his notion of value was more clearly subjective than objective, his writings set forth the rudiments of both the cost of production and the utility theories, the reconciliation of which has engaged the attention of thinkers even down to the present day.

Ideas regarding money and loans.— In order that goods may be exchanged effectively in a stage of civilization advanced beyond mere barter economy, he pointed out, money is necessary. Money makes commensurable those things which are incommensurable. Besides serving as a medium of circulation and a measure of value, money also performs the minor functions of a store of value and a standard of deferred payments. Although the value of money varies, it tends to be more constant than the value of anything else, aside from the circumstance that the state can at any time make the value of money nil by appropriate changes. Money, he concluded, must not be confused with wealth, since money is wealth but not all wealth is money.

In contrast with Aristotle's reasonably correct observations as to the nature of money, is his erroneous notion regarding the productivity of loans. Money, he asserted, is barren, even as exchange itself is sterile, inasmuch as one piece of money cannot beget another piece; exchange is but the interchange of equivalents. Interest taking, accordingly, he condemned without qualification. The explanation for this point of view lay in the fact that in those early days funds were loaned, as for centuries past, primarily as money and not as capital. Loans were made, as a rule, not for productive purposes but as mere personal loans for the relief of distress. Not until much later, with the rise of industrial capital, did the function of capital come to be more clearly understood.

Aristotle would have excluded from any share in the government of the state those classes in society directly occupied with ministering to its material needs. With Plato he urged that the population be exactly proportioned to the extent of each civic territory, and likewise he favored a simple separation of employments.

Of final interest to the economist is his attitude toward the communism of Plato. With cogent arguments, after quickly disposing of the issue of community of wives, he stated that a general community of property would not work successfully, and that the principle of private property is deeply rooted in man's instincts. Far better that property, in general, be private with some use in common, so far as practicable (as, for example, common meals). Protesting against the excessive individualism then prevalent among the Greeks, though not opposed to reasonable inequalities, he laid down the fundamental proposition that reformation of the evils in society must wait upon correction of the defects in human nature.

Rome.— The history of Greece is the story of a culture that provided the basis, centuries later, for the language and literature, art, philosophy, and democratic institutions of government of modern European civilization. The history of Rome, on the contrary, is the story of conquest — conquest so vast that in time it spread Roman civilization over almost all of the then known world. The Romans, conquering, established law and order. They were the greatest builders of antiquity, — cities, stadia, roads, monuments, ships, fortresses. Their mission was military and political; their character predominately realistic and practical. Of original work in philosophy or in most of the sciences, accordingly, there is scarcely a trace. Their economic views were for the most part pale reflections of the eminent writers of ancient Greece. Where the Greeks created the Romans borrowed.

Aside from stray observations which may be gleaned from the works of the satirists Juvenal and Apuleius, of poets like Vergil, Horace, Ennius, and Ovid, and of historians such as Livy and Tacitus, the fragmentary contributions of Rome to the stream of economic thought come from three groups of writers : the philosophers, the writers on agriculture, and the jurists.

Cicero.— Of the philosophers Cicero, Seneca, Pliny the Elder, Marcus Aurelius, Epictetus and Lucretius were the foremost. Cicero, reactionary aristocrat, student under many masters, much more the lawyer than the philosopher, and probably the most influential figure in all Roman intellectual life, wrote on the respectability of various occupations. He held trade and commerce in utmost contempt unless conducted on a large scale, but esteemed agriculture as worthy of the highest praise. Workshops, he stated, contained nothing befitting a gentleman's status ; petty merchants, to succeed, must lie. In his orations may be found remarks on the factors controlling price, the nature of money, taxes, the inadvisability of free trade, the necessity of slavery, the advantages of division of labor, and the sinfulness of interest taking. Interesting is his championship of private property.

The Stoics.— Seneca, Marcus Aurelius, and Epictetus, representing the Stoic point of view, denounced avarice and luxury, pictured the ugliness of slavery, and enlarged upon the advantages of trade among nations. In his *Natural History,* Pliny the Elder discussed the relative importance of large and small farms, deplored the growing use of slave labor, and expressed a preference for barter rather than for a money economy. Lucretius, chief philosophical poet of Rome, restated the Epicurean attitudes.

The Agronomists.— Chief among the writers on agriculture were Cato, Varro, Columella, Palladius, and the omnipresent Pliny. Living for the most part during the period of decline in Roman history, and at times basing their works upon Carthaginian treatises on agronomy, they wrote upon a variety of topics. In general they strove to restore the healthier conditions which had prevailed in the simple rural life of early

Rome. Concerning themselves both with the technique and the economics of agriculture, they discussed the problems of the self-sufficient estate, called attention to the economic disadvantages of slavery, inveighed against the growth of large estates and of absentee ownership, advised with regard to various methods of farming and the use of crops, and pleaded for the restoration of small farming as the antidote to the moral degeneracy of their time.

Pre-eminence of Roman Law.—Although Rome did little, if anything, to advance the cause of the natural sciences she made enduring contributions in one field of the social sciences of such signal importance that they may be regarded as one of her most considerable gifts to the history of civilization. The Romans, in effect, created both a science and an art of law which became, in later centuries, the foundation of the legal systems of numerous continental countries, and to which even the common law in the United States owes some of its principles. As Rome expanded from city-state to empire, the civil law (*jus civile*) applicable to Roman citizens only, gave place gradually to a more composite and rational law (*jus gentium*) —a body of law common to all nations. From this there developed in due time the *jus naturale*, a law the basic legal ideas of which were thought to be common to all peoples and therefore "natural." During the reign of Justinian (527-565 A.D.) all the sources of Roman law were collected and codified in the celebrated code termed the *Corpus Juris Civilis*, or "Body of Civil Law," containing invaluable information regarding the economic institutions of Rome.

The writings of such jurists as Papinian, Paulus and Gaius contain the greatest measure of strictly original economic thought attributable to Roman thinkers. On the one hand should be noted their unusually skillful use of abstraction and exact formulation of ideas. On the other is a careful, although at times imperfect, analysis of certain economic conceptions. Apart from searching investigations into the nature and significance of money, and conventional remarks upon slavery, interest taking, sumptuary control, population, and the like, the Roman jurists enunciated the theory of the omnipotence of the state, divorced law from religion, founded the modern law of property, and vastly extended freedom of contract. Moving away from the family, clan, and priesthood, they laid down and enforced the doctrine of the superiority of the State to all other rivals.

Probably for the first time in all history, the individual was recognized as entitled to immunity from arbitrary acts upon the part of his superior, the state, and to the right to make such use of his property as he saw fit. Community of property disappeared in favor of sharply-defined individual rights, including not only the right to enjoy, but the right to destroy — private property, in short, with many modern implications, including unfettered privilege of bequest. Local usage thus yielded to imperial law. Freedom of contract, with all that it was to imply for good or evil in the modern economic system, became firmly established as one of the foremost of man-made institutions.

Christianity.— To the economic thought of antiquity Christianity contributed several more or less revolutionary ideas of significance, while at the same time confirming and strengthening other teachings. The philosophy of the Stoics had brought to the attention of a startled Greek world the concepts of the natural equality of men before God and the inherent dignity of toil. Christianity revived and popularized these concepts. Indeed, the very core of Christian theology sprang from Greek philosophy and metaphysics. Holding that slavery and the caste system were unnatural, it condemned them both, and strove earnestly for the greater amelioration of the lot of women. Manual labor was constantly held up as ideal to clergy and laymen alike. Community of property was practiced among some of the early Christians, but, in general, private, and not common, ownership was stressed by the church fathers, as by Jesus himself. The views held on money, usury, and trade continued to be those of the conventional mold.

CHAPTER II

THE MIDDLE AGES

CONSIDERABLE disagreement still exists among scholars with reference to the chronological period which the Middle Ages may properly be said to embrace. The term itself springs from the terminology employed in the seventeenth century by a certain Dutch Humanist who divided all human history into three periods : ancient history, to the end of the reign of Constantine the Great, 337 A.D. ; medieval history, from 337 A.D. to the fall of Constantinople in 1453 ; and modern history, from 1453 onward. Since his day this threefold division of history has won rather general acceptance, and the designations "medieval" and "Middle Ages" have become conventional and arbitrary ones. Very roughly, the Middle Ages covers approximately one thousand years in the history of western Europe from some time in the fifth century down to the fourteenth or fifteenth centuries.

Medieval culture.—Equally confusing is the difference of opinion concerning the nature of the culture which characterized this period. It is more and more being recognized, however, that the cultural development of the Middle Ages must be considered not alone from the standpoint of centuries included, but also from that of the various regions of the world which may safely lay claim to having possessed any sort of culture during this ill-defined period. The so-called Dark Ages, for example, from the fifth to the ninth century, were "dark" for western Europe only, and less so for Britain and Ireland than for that part of the globe directly under the sway of the Germanic conquerors of the former Roman empire. In the Eastern Empire ("Byzantine" from the beginning of the eighth century), of which Constantinople was the capital, there was no corresponding reversion to an immature type of culture. Byzantine learning, though devoted almost exclusively to the recovery and reworking of ancient Hellenic learning, at least prolonged for many centuries the culture of the Greeks, and assisted inestimably in passing it along to western peoples toward the close of the Middle Ages.

Moslem (or Muslim) culture, furthermore, was far superior to anything existing in Christian Europe prior to the fourteenth century. Civilization arose anew in the Moslem world, from Spain in the West to Java in the East, at a time when western Europe was shrouded in more or less dense darkness. Islam, it is true, did little directly to encourage learning, yet, with remarkable tolerance and open-mindedness, opposed but feeble resistance to scholarly efforts and scientific activity. Rivalling the reopening of the University of Constantinople in 863 was the founding of the Moslem Universities of Baghdad in the ninth century, and of Cairo, Egypt, and Cordova, Spain, in the tenth. The followers of Mohammed took over the remains of Graeco-Roman art, science, and literature, merged with these the scientific lore of Carthage, India, and the East, and passed this borrowed and elaborated knowledge on to the Christians of Europe through the gateway, primarily, of Spanish civilization.

Finally, in any extended study of the Middle Ages, account must be taken of still other civilizations that flourished in remote parts of the world : of those in Inca Peru and Aztec Mexico, and more especially of that in China. Until about the sixteenth century, China kept to the fore of all other contemporary states in artistic and scientific activity, holding a supremacy that yielded only to the dawn of modern scientific discoveries.

Influence of Christianity.— If the most significant transformation wrought in the culture of western Europe during the medieval period be sought for, it must be proclaimed to be that which arose by reason of the enthronement of Christianity. Practically all of this territory may be said to have become Christian by the year 1000. By its very nature the Church was a cosmopolitan organization, conferring thus a certain unity upon that part of the world which the Roman legions had for a time reduced to a settled order. In addition, Christianity held to a rigid ethics, to the belief that all human relationships must be so regulated as to secure the eternal salvation of the soul. The economic factor was consequently subordinated to this most important of considerations, and such speculation on economic questions as appeared tended to be related to the much larger topic of private morality. Theology became the science of sciences.

During the first five centuries of the Middle Ages learning all but perished in Western Christendom. With the disintegration of the Roman Empire, the flourishing commercial activity and the comparatively high level of literacy of Rome nearly disappeared under the heel of the invading Northmen. Not only did no new learning of any great significance promptly replace the old pagan learning, but the treasures of Greek and Latin literature and science were in large measure lost through the wilful destruction of untold numbers of volumes.

Historians, philosophers, poets — all fared badly. Of the Greek and Latin poets only Homer, Vergil, Horace, Seneca and Ovid survived in some entirety. Of the Greek and Latin historians hardly one complete work remains. Of the Greek and Latin philosophers very little has come down to posterity. In the few centers of learning (monasteries and monastic schools) occurred the copying and preservation of such of the Greek and Latin masterpieces as escaped the devastation of the medieval era. While the Germanic races were establishing their sway over conquered territory almost the only educated persons in Europe were the churchmen. Here and there a brilliant intellect arose, like Augustine, Erigena and Gerbert (later Pope Sylvester II), and in Italy the small beginnings of universities made their appearance in several towns as Salerno and Bologna. By and large, however, the European peoples slipped back into industrial stagnation and corresponding mental darkness. Slavery, later transformed into serfdom, continued to be the lot of most workers ; man returned to a primitive system of barter ; feudalism, analogous to the ancient city-state, took firm hold ; superstition replaced knowledge.

Growth of trade.— During the eleventh and twelfth centuries a new economy began to emerge, and the second stage in the medieval period made its appearance. Although agriculture continued supreme, towns increased in number and in size ; the social isolation of village communities began increasingly to break down ; handicrafts flourished under the gilds, and trade and commerce revived under the stimulating influence of the Crusades. France and England built up a considerable degree of national solidarity. Serfdom in the towns gradually gave way to freedom. Money came into increasing use. In other words, a simple independent domestic economy yielded ground on an ever wider and deeper basis to a larger economy.

Together with these fundamental transformations in economic life appeared a rebirth in intellectual activity that was to prepare the way for the extraordinary revival of interest in art, literature, science and philosophy in the fourteenth century. Aristotle's *Politics* again found its way into western Europe through a Latin translation; numerous colleges and universities sprang up in Paris, Oxford, Cambridge and elsewhere, until by the close of the Middle Ages there were approximately eighty in existence; and Abélard, Albertus Magnus, St. Thomas Aquinas, Roger Bacon—to name no others—came to the front as master intellects. The Middle Ages, never a consistently static period, became even more dynamic.

Canon law and scholasticism.—Throughout all this long period expression of opinion on economic matters unfolded in western Europe, but rarely, if ever, as a distinct line of thought, and to no great extent prior to the twelfth and thirteenth centuries. This opinion reached its highest expression in two notable bodies of writing, the canon (Church) law and scholasticism. Canon law, worked out by the Catholic Church on the basis of the application of the old Roman civil law to Church problems and procedure, was codified by the legal scholar and monk Gratian in 1142. Scholasticism represented the endeavor of theologians to fuse Greek philosophy, especially that of Aristotle, with Christian doctrine. The scholastics (or schoolmen) sought not so much to explain phenomena as to lay down absolute rules of conduct based on certain religious standards. Their economic thinking rested upon two postulates: that economic considerations are insignificant, inasmuch as the present world is but a preparation for the hereafter, and that economic activity is simply one phase of all human activity, and thus to be judged in accordance with rules of morality. In general, the doctrines of the economists and schoolmen may be regarded as having been in substantial agreement.

Of the mighty host of medieval theologians, indubitably the greatest was St. Thomas Aquinas, (1225-1274), the acknowledged prince of the scholastics. Although minor schoolmen such as Alexander of Hales, Henry of Ghent, Albertus Magnus, Antoninus of Florence, Bernadine of Vienna, Cardinal de Lugo, John Duns Scotus, William of Ockham and Gabriel Biel, the "last of the schoolmen," aided in building up and refining that union of Augustinian theology and Aristotelian logic known as scholasticism, it was in the works of St. Thomas that theology reached its highest stage of development. With extraordinary industry he wrote no less than sixty works during his comparatively short life, of which by far the most important is the famous *Summa Theologica*.

Medieval ethical economics.—Accepting whole-heartedly the principle of Aristotle that "man is by nature a social animal," medieval theology proceeded to assert that all men are by nature equal, that the state exists for man and not man for the state, and that there is a normal limit to the extent of governmental interference with individual effort. The comprehensive conception around which controversy raged came to be, accordingly, the idea of justice. Let no one receive that to which he was not entitled ; let all men treat each other as brothers. Surely no nobler conception has ever been at the base of economic reasoning and teaching.

Medieval economic theory thus concerned itself primarily with the question : what is justice,—justice in the ownership of property, justice in the relationship of employer to employee, justice in trade and the matter of price fixing and usury ?

Despite lip service accorded by the early Christian fathers to the desirability of a communistic mode of life, the weight of evidence seems clearly to indicate that this praise of communism was but praise of an ideal state, of a state which man had long since forfeited by his fall from grace. Private property was looked upon as a necessary evil or even as "natural to man," and thus in no manner contrary to natural law. With Aristotle, moreover, St. Thomas held that although property should be private in possession it should be, to a certain extent, common in use. Thus maintenance of the poor was considered a legal obligation, wealth being solely a means to an end, and that end the attainment of a life of virtue. Neither wealth in itself nor poverty in itself was good. In line with this notion was the almost general condemnation of slavery as incompatible with the immortality of the human soul. None the less there was recognition of the justice of some degree of inequality in wealth possession due to inequalities in inborn talents for money making and of differences in environment.

Prices.— In the early part of the Middle Ages prices tended to be fixed by custom. As had been the case for untold centuries, goods were made mostly in the home, to be consumed in the home. If made for sale they were produced under the jurisdiction of the merchant and the craft gilds. If brought in from the outside they could not be bought at wholesale in order to be resold at retail. Whatever the seller gained by trade was supposed to be at the expense of the buyer. As of old, therefore, trade and commerce were held vastly inferior morally to agriculture and even to the handicrafts.

With the rapid disappearance of slavery in favor of the more transitory condition of serfdom, the enfranchisement of the working classes in the towns and cities, the growth of enterprise from the eleventh and twelfth centuries onward, and a gradual fading of the hoary theory of business as an unnatural pursuit, the influence of custom in price fixing began appreciably to diminish. Local governments, no longer able to rely upon custom, and face to face with the phenomenon of competition, found themselves obliged to intervene and regulate prices. Thus arose the problem of selecting a proper basis for price fixing.

Theory and practice, at least for the time being, here roughly coincided. Labor cost seemed to be the chief consideration in the cost of production, inasmuch as the artisan worked with his own tools in his own home or shop, and the significance of capital was but vaguely realized. With unusual keenness, however, schoolmen and canonists went beyond a mere cost-of-production analysis, and developed a theory of a just price containing the seeds of the modern doctrine of value. They clearly perceived, for instance, that value (the importance imputed to goods, their power in exchange) is something by no means absolute, intrinsic and objective. As St. Thomas remarked, "If men had no needs there would be no exchange." Correctly attributing the origin of value to men's wants, they reasoned further that things are valuable because people want them, and that people want them because they have the power of satisfying wants, and because they are limited in quantity and thus more or less exchangeable for other goods. Thus it was seen that the value of a thing depends not upon the opinion of somebody as to the importance or righteousness of a want satisfied, but rather upon interaction of the forces of demand and supply.[1]

Value.—Not the need of any one individual, accordingly, nor individual cost of production could or did explain the nature of value. On the contrary, value was held to rest upon the estimate of the whole community of the social utility of the product or products exchanged. The common estimate determined value, and the just price was that price which emerged, within limits, by reason of this common estimate. As St. Thomas further noted, the just price could not always be fixed with absolute exactness and accuracy. But at any given time, so the medieval theologians asserted, every commodity had a just price—a price based upon a fair value, and it was with this criterion in mind that medieval legislators proceeded in their task of price fixing.

In line with the principle of just price was the concept of the just wage. The just wage was asserted to be that wage which enabled the workman and his family to live in reasonable decency in the station of life in which they found themselves.

To carry on a trade or business, consequently, for the purpose of recovering the results of one's labor was universally deemed justifiable, whereas for many decades the reselling of unchanged commodities at a higher price for credit than for cash was adjudged a sinful practice. That medieval ethical ideas as to the necessity of the just price and the fair wage still persist is clearly evident when notice is taken of the living wage doctrines of typical labor organizations and the actual

[1] See "Just Price in a Functional Economy," by Bernard W. Dempsey in The American Economic Review for September, 1935.

setting of minimum wages by wage boards and legislatures, together with numerous modern court decisions and statutes promulgating reasonable or maximum charges for services rendered by railroads and other public utilities.

Interest.—A striking feature of the just price dogma was the prohibition of usury, as contrary to the strictures both of Aristotle and of the Scriptures. To the medieval thinker, usury signified originally not excessive interest, as at present, nor even any loan interest, but all violations of the just price. In due time, however, the term came to connote any profit derived from loans of funds. In an age when loans were characteristically made, not for productive purposes, but for the relief of distress, the prohibition of usury, first to clerics and much later to the laity, was understandable and praiseworthy.

A loan of money was viewed primarily as a change in ownership, and an interest charge as involving a tax on the labor of the borrower. On the other hand, it was no part of the medieval notion of justice that the lender, any more than the borrower, should suffer loss. Accordingly, exceptions to the usury doctrine, weakening the full force of the prohibition, became more and more numerous as theorists and legislators strove to uphold the ideal of justice. Where the lender could prove that by reason of his loan he had suffered a definite loss (*damnum emergens*), or had missed an opportunity to profit in an alternative investment (*lucrum cessans*), or had undergone the risk of not being repaid (*periculum sortis*), equity demanded that the borrower indemnify him. Finally, as commercial and industrial capital came into increasing prominence toward the end of the Middle Ages, the Church was obliged to draw a necessary and belated distinction between legitimate interest and illegitimate usury.

Functions of government.—In general the schoolmen espoused the ideal of liberalism or individualism as opposed to the totalitarian state. Holding that the state is a natural society within which many lesser, though co-ordinate, associations function, each autonomous within its own sphere, and all co-operating to serve the interests of the individuals who comprise the state, they urged that the supreme authority confine its regulatory functions, except in times of emergency, to a minimum. In particular, the economic functions proper to government were set down as the care of the poor, the building and safeguarding of free roads, the maintenance of a system of accurate weights and measures, and the provision of an exact and unchanging supply of metal money.

Oresme.— Toward the close of the Middle Ages, the increasing amount of money in circulation and the appalling extent of the debasement of the coinage by princes drew the attention of many writers, lay and clerical, to the important topic of the theory and functions of money. Of these writers the one most entitled to enduring fame appears to have been Nicholas Oresme, who died in 1382 as Bishop of Lisieux. His book was less a treatise on money than a masterly arraignment of all debasements of the currency. In a quasi scientific and most realistic manner he anticipated a great deal of modern orthodox monetary theory. He enunciated the theory — later to be known as Gresham's Law — that bad money, if issued to excess, drives good money out of circulation, and he seems to have been the first scholar in history to have discussed adequately the problems connected with bimetallism.

Chapter III

MERCANTILISM

THAT the transition from medieval to modern times was in no way a sudden or a uniform change has long been recognized by competent scholars. Medievalism still persists in certain backward regions of the world today. In other parts, and especially in Europe, the transition made its appearance at widely different times.

Yet such was the stupendous transformation that swept over the world from the fourteenth, fifteenth, and sixteenth centuries onward that the term "modern times" has taken on a peculiar, though somewhat arbitrary, significance. The political, intellectual, religious, and commercial revolutions which occurred during those centuries constitute the most staggering break with the past that history had known up to that time.

Feudalism gave way to the national state, and serfdom to a wage earning class. Spain, Portugal, France, England, Hungary and Sweden (to name no others) ceased to be mere geographical expressions and definitely emerged as strongly centralized kingdoms. The Renaissance, whether regarded as the last phase of the dying medieval period, or more properly as that rebirth of interest in matters intellectual, the roots of which go far back into the Middle Ages, swept from Italy over the greater part of Europe during the fourteenth and fifteenth centuries. In literature the humanists, led by Erasmus, recovered and edited many of the hitherto lost manuscripts of the ancient Greeks and Romans. Native literatures in the various European vernaculars throve, graced by such names as Dante, Petrarch, Boccaccio and Chaucer. In the fine arts a new style of architecture developed, sculpture came to fruition at the hands of Michael Angelo, and painting (the outstanding art of the Renaissance) reached the summit of accomplishment in Leonardo da Vinci, perhaps the most versatile genius of all time, Raphael, Rubens and Rembrandt.

Beginnings of modern science.—A series of significant inventions in printing, crowned by that of movable type and usually ascribed to John Gutenberg about 1450, wrought an immeasurable revolution in the cultural history of mankind and in the advance of modern democracy. Knowledge of reading spread rapidly throughout Europe at the same time that the appearance of printed books enormously stimulated the development of free discussion. Notable, and at times breathtaking, achievements testify to the progress of science in such diverse fields as mathematics, astronomy, geography, geology, biology, physics, chemistry and medicine. Copernicus, Galileo, Descartes, Newton, Harvey,—these are but a few of that veritable galaxy of illustrious men whose scientific contributions have aided in making the history of the progress in nearly all fields of knowledge in modern times appear almost like an incredible fairy tale.

Emergence of capitalism.—A great historic movement, the Protestant Reformation (or Revolution), initiated by Martin Luther in 1517, ran its memorable course until 1650, plunged a large portion of Europe into bloody religious conflict, and detached from the temporal sway of the Papacy one half of its previous domain. The new Protestantism replaced the international point of view of the Catholic Church with the idea of national independence, lent its support to individualism in economics as well as in religion, and frankly sanctioned the glorification of the profit seeking motive in mankind. The age-old stigma attaching to money making and personal enrichment disappeared in favor of an entirely new way of looking at life. Trade and commerce became socially respectable for perhaps the first time in all history, and achievement and success began to be measured by a scale of pecuniary values.

The concept of the "good" life slowly but surely gave way to the habit of appraising human worth in terms of wealth-getting and wealth-spending activity. The beginning of what is nowadays called modern capitalism made its appearance in private accumulations of capital built up out of all sorts of enterprises — legitimate and illegitimate. Personality was dissociated from business, new business forms and instruments arose, speculation and "bubbles" flourished, and a new banking class assumed leadership. In brief, economic life was transformed as competition triumphed over the socially-minded economic ideals of the Middle Ages.

Geography and metals.— Finally, the Commercial Revolution enabled Europe in due time to discover the rest of the world. The inventions and improvements connected with the art of navigation upon which this revolution rested hastened the discovery of hitherto unknown all-water trade routes and lands, led to a much widened geographic scope of trading operations, vastly increased the total amount of world trade, and transferred the center of that trade from the Mediterranean city-states to the Atlantic seaboard. Extensive colonial empires were built up by Spain, Portugal, France, England and Holland ; a more general use of money developed in place of barter and services ; prices underwent an amazing dislocation.

The scarcity of the precious metals in Europe since time immemorial began to be relieved shortly after 1500 by the influx of bullion from the pillaged treasuries of the Aztec and Inca empires and by the steady working of rich mines in Mexico, Peru and Bolivia. The yearly output of the precious metals soared to unheard-of heights. European coinage increased at least tenfold during the sixteenth century, and from 1550 to 1650 the general price level in Europe rose by 300 per cent, giving rise to the famous "Revolution of Prices."

Out of all these conditions, and in natural harmony with the facts, arose mercantilism, known also in history as the mercantile system, the restrictive system, the commercial system, and Colbertism in France and kameralism (or cameralism) in Germany.

Manorial system.— During the medieval period two economic tendencies or forces existed side by side for centuries. On the one hand what may be termed localism dominated economic affairs for an undelimited part of this era. In the country, where the overwhelming majority of the population resided, the manorial system prevailed. The manor, the unit of medieval agricultural life, was likewise the unit of medieval rural administration. Regulation of agriculture and of most, and at times all, of the trades indispensable to the proper maintenance of the peasantry lay in the hands of the lords of the manors and their subordinates. To the peasant the manor was practically the world itself, for the manors were largely self-supporting and ordinarily the serfs were bound to the soil. Such kings as emerged interfered normally but little in the economic affairs of the manors, although deriving their chief means of support from them through feudal dues of various sorts.

Gilds.— In the towns control was exercised at first by the merchant gilds (or guilds) and later, beginning with the middle of the twelfth century, to an increasing extent by the craft gilds. The revival of commerce created a distinct mercantile class, the members of which grouped themselves town by town into merchant gilds for the promotion of their economic interest and to which for a time craftsmen were admitted. Supervision of the external trade of the towns to the point of monopoly was the economic goal usually sought for. In the town government gild members often assumed the leading role.

As the towns grew in population and area, the crafts more and more set up their own gilds, and sooner or later overthrew in great measure the domination of the merchant gilds. Comprising both masters (employers) and artisans, the craft gilds undertook the regulation of all the industrial processes of the town. In the course of time elaborate codes developed, by which prices and conditions of sale were fixed, wages regulated, hours and relations between masters and men determined, and workmanship and quality attested. Of individual freedom and initiative there was for a while little more, if any, than existed in the country. Representatives of the craft gilds replaced those of the merchant gilds in the governing bodies of the towns. These governing bodies enforced craft regulations, set up customs barriers against other towns and rural districts, and controlled a host of other matters directly or indirectly connected with the interests of the townspeople. Sporadically the king interjected his authority into their affairs, as with the manors. But in the main the economic life of the towns was locally controlled.

Growth of nationalism.— Subordinate to localism, on the other hand, was nationalism, or the national point of view. At some time in the Middle Ages, although it is impossible to state at precisely what time, purely local regulations were felt, or found, to be inadequate and policies transcending local boundaries were inaugurated. From a comparatively early period certain phases of foreign commerce, of industry, and of agriculture were deemed to be of national concern by kings aspiring to ascendancy over their feudal lords. Thus with increasing frequency the king began to collect duties at the frontiers, to intervene in commercial dealings with foreign countries, to grant charters to trading companies and to towns, to adjudicate quarrels between towns and between manors, and to assume exclusive control over the currency. The growth of nationalism, gradual and irregular though it was, took on an even greater importance as generation succeeded generation, until at last localism yielded to the victorious surge of the national economy. New economic and political situations produced the nationalist state, made possible economic theorizing on a national scale, and ushered in the era of mercantilism.

Whatever mercantilism may or may not have been, we may safely affirm that it was never a "system," never the artificial creation of any one individual or group of individuals, never a goal in itself. Much more accurately may it be considered to have connoted the economic policy of European rulers from the thirteenth to the eighteenth, or even the nineteenth century in certain parts of the continent, plus the views of writers who explained or defended that policy. In a certain sense, indeed, mercantilism has never completely died out. Its modern counterpart appeared during the World War in the hasty efforts made in all belligerent countries to mobilize most or all of the human and economic resources available in support of the military program. There are those, furthermore, who maintain that signs of a mighty resurrection were observable in the economic life of several European countries such as Fascist Italy and Nazi Germany, and who even perceive in the New Deal a reintroduction into the United States of many characteristic features of the old order.

Nationalism and the policy of mercantilism.— Mercantilism, in essence, was an economic policy and an economic doctrine bound up with the political doctrine of nationalism. It was never a system, despite certain family resemblances, inasmuch as both policy and doctrine developed over a course of centuries in an unsystematic fashion and still defies accurate generalization; it was never an artificial creation but rather a spontaneous growth of the times, thoroughly symptomatic of vast changes in the economic situation; it was never a goal or end, but rather the means to a desired end.

That end was political — the establishment of a state as independent, self-sufficient, and powerful as possible. Mercantilism was the total of the economic means employed for that objective, together with the theoretical explanation and justification of the nationalistic policy as set forth by hundreds, nay thousands, of writers. There were, in other words, two aspects to mercantilism: the positive side and the doctrinal aspect. First came the policy of nationalism, and later its theoretical exposition. Two kinds of mercantilists, accordingly, may be distinguished: the ruler, turning more and more instinctively to statutory restrictions in the endeavor to promote the material strength of his nation, and the writer, articulate exponent of mercantilistic theory. Needless to say, rulers were at times, though not ordinarily, both sovereigns and writers.

During the medieval period, kings largely depended upon their feudal lords for revenue, administration of justice, and the maintenance of their own prestige. In an economy based chiefly on barter and on a system of payments in kind, the monarch could make but little progress toward the attainment of a permanent ascendancy over his barons. The indigent prince needed and desired nothing so much as an amount of money sufficient to enable him to maintain a large and loyal paid army.

Sources of kingly revenues.— The rise of absolute monarchies was therefore connected in more than one way with the growth of trade and commerce that followed upon the Crusades and that was enormously stimulated by the geographical discoveries of the fifteenth and sixteenth centuries. In the resulting transition from a barter to a money economy the self-interest of both lord and serf replaced their relation of customs and status by one of a pecuniary nature. The requirements of the king in terms of a stable and increasing revenue were more easily met when taxes consisted less and less of payments in kind, but rather, on an ever growing scale, of contributions in money. Independent sources of revenue continued to grow as the king levied toll on trade and colonization by fees for chartering commercial companies and by

granting monopolies. He shared in the booty from privateer-
ing, profited from the coinage and import of precious metals,
and kept for himself the proceeds of customs duties on foreign
trade. To this impetus was added the effort of numerous civil
and religious wars which killed off many of the feudal barons.
The final barrier to nationalism disappeared when the unity
of the Catholic Church was destroyed by the Protestant Revolution and national boundaries became lines of religious demarcation.

Either England under Henry VII (1485) or France under
Louis XI (1461) may be considered to have been the first
modern, national, dynastic state. Soon thereafter followed
Portugal and Spain, the United Netherlands toward the end
of the sixteenth century, Sweden early in the seventeenth century, and Prussia and Russia toward 1700. By the middle of
the eighteenth century nearly all Europe was ruled by strong
monarchies. Only in Germany, Italy and the Balkans did
this transformation wait until the nineteenth century.

The two fundamental bases of mercantilism were the growth
of a money economy and the rise of nationalist states. In this
period of intense international rivalries, all else was subordinated not alone to the maintenance of an independent existence, but also to the extension, so far as possible, of the
nation's holdings in Europe and overseas, more particularly
in the New World. With every state the potential enemy of
every other, and force the only efficient means, apparently, that
could be utilized in the prosecution of this objective, monarchs
and nations bent their energies to making the nation as strong
as possible. Absolutely necessary were powerful armies and
navies, a centralized administration, a large and growing population, and the development of the material prosperity essential to their support.

Bullion from the new world.— To the precious metals,
meanwhile, had come an amazingly new importance by reason
of the growth of trade and commerce, the introduction of the
wage system, and a rapid influx of gold and silver from
America. Not without reason was national strength measured by the proportion of bullion in a country's wealth.
For one thing, money had a relative importance not enjoyed previously and which it does not normally possess at the

present time. Credit agencies were virtually undeveloped and industrial securities were in their infancy. Money, too, was the most readily exchangeable form of wealth, as is still the case, and its ready circulation of tremendous significance in stimulating economic activity. The mercantilists did not go to the extreme length, however, of confusing money with all wealth, as has sometimes been charged by incautious critics, notably by Adam Smith in his memorable indictment in *The Wealth of Nations* of what he termed the mercantile system.

On the contrary the mercantilists assigned preponderating importance to the precious metals merely because they seemed to be, and in fact were, the most acceptable forms of wealth then in existence. In a period when specie was flowing into Europe in vast quantities and when Spain, the recipient of a large part of this flow, occupied a dominating position in world affairs, reason appeared to favor the argument that national greatness was synonymous with extensive control over treasure and bullion.

For most of the countries of Europe, devoid of gold and silver mines, the only economic salvation possible was to accumulate specie through a proper ordering of their foreign trade. In the late medieval period, feudal lords had endeavored to bring the precious metals into their jurisdictions by manipulating the exchanges in such a way as to control each particular transaction. Advocates of the balance of bargain theory came in time to be known as bullionists. The futility of these measures had long since become apparent to many thinkers. Each country accordingly tried to sell to foreigners a total quantity of goods of greater monetary value than those purchased. On the assumption that exports represented money coming into, and imports, money going out, of the country, a "favorable" balance of trade through an excess of exports over imports was feverishly sought for. The balance due the exporting country, it was thought, would be paid in coin. The term mercantilism, in fact, is derived from this interpretation of the supposed advantages resulting from exchanges of merchandise.

Tampering with foreign trade.— To procure this favorable balance of trade, sovereigns resorted to a variety of expedients. Imports of goods, with the exception of raw ma-

terials needed for home industries, were restricted by prohibitive import duties. The exportation of raw materials of
manufacture was discouraged by export duties. Export trade
in general was stimulated by the granting of bounties to certain industries which produced commodities for export, by the
adoption of favorable treaties of trade, by exemption from
taxation, by breaking down barriers to the free movement of
internal trade through the abolition or mitigation of tolls,
octrois and the like, by patents of monopoly to owners of
new processes of manufacture, by promoting immigration of
skilled foreign workers, by subsidizing shipping and building
up the navies, by creating trading companies accorded exclusive privileges and encouraging colonization, by fixing prices,
wages, and conditions of labor, by fostering population growth
— in short, by an almost illimitable number of devices and
practices. The whole machinery of the nation was marshalled
in support of a program that seemed admirably logical. The
state became not only the natural political unit, but also the
natural economic unit. Never before had statesmanship as
the mainspring of economic prosperity been so glorified.

New business ideals.— Nor had trade and commerce ever
previously been elevated to such lofty eminence in the hier-
archy of occupations. Not all trade, to be sure, but rather
that part of it which brought in wealth to a country from
abroad. The immemorial ascendancy of the agricultural interests was for the time being at an end, and the merchant
class, to its amazement, perhaps, found itself exalted above all
others in popular and royal esteem. Next below the merchant
ranked the manufacturer of those commodities of which the
exportation exceeded the imports. Toward the foot of the
scale came the farmer, of importance chiefly because he fed
the population and under certain circumstances, as by intensive tillage, made the importation of some kinds of food unnecessary. Denied any sort of productivity, finally, were the
shopkeepers, domestics, scholars, professional men, gentry,
and others who simply transferred wealth at home, so it was
maintained, from one to another.

Colbert.— The restrictive policies of mercantilism appear
to have been carried farthest in practice under Jean Colbert

(1619-1683) in France, whence the term Colbertism. Ablest of the finance ministers of Louis XIV, it is to the great credit of Colbert that he proclaimed his measures to be only provisional. The entire roll of mercantile practitioners includes virtually all the monarchs of western Europe from approximately 1500 down to the end of the eighteenth century. In certain countries, the list includes rulers of the fourteenth and nineteenth centuries. To these sovereigns must be added that veritable army of administrators, many of whom have been dignified by history with the rank of statesman, who were often the chief executors of mercantilistic policy. Among these rulers and statesmen, in addition to Colbert, mention must more or less arbitrarily be made of Charles V and Philip II of Spain; Henry IV and the Duc de Sully of France; Henry VIII, Queen Elizabeth, Cromwell and Walpole of England; Frederick William, the Great Elector, and Frederick the Great of Prussia; Gustavus Adolphus of Sweden; and Peter the Great and Catherine the Great of Russia.

Business men as theorists.—The literature of mercantilism, so voluminous in extent that it has never been exhaustively studied and appraised,[1] possesses one characteristic of the utmost importance for the inquiring student of the development of economics. If economic speculation since the dawn of history to the beginning of the mercantile era be regarded as the contribution, in the main, of philosophers, lawgivers and members of the clergy, a novel current of thought may be traced to the writings of those who sought to defend or explain the mercantilistic policy. More specifically, this new current of thought was primarily the product of men of affairs. The crystallization of the idea of national economy was effected not by philosophers, priests, nor even administrators so much as by the business man. We cannot deny that among the thinkers of this period are names of many eminent philosophers, legislators, and scientists. But the bulk of the publications stemmed from the observations and thinking of a species of writer almost entirely foreign to all previous theorizing on economic phenomena. Merchants, men of affairs, practical business men—however they may be described—poured

---

[1] *See Predecessors of Adam Smith,* by E. A. J. Johnson, Chap. I.

forth a torrent of economic literature, usually fragmentary and unsystematic, that endeavored to interpret clearly the actualities of contemporary life, and displayed a marked belief in the efficacy of government to achieve any and all desired ends by means of legislation.

No exposition of economics as a whole appeared, it should be noted, except possibly in the volumes of several later writers, and countless examples of special pleading may be cited. All too often, for instance, the capitalistic enterpriser sought to cover up his goal of business profits by a public recital of the national benefits that would accrue from a grant of mercantile privileges, or a raising of the tariff on certain imports, or a continuance of low wage scales, and the like. In the main, however, new intellectual guiding reins appeared; men came to grips with particular problems; realistic thinking was dominant. Modern economics, though not yet a distinct and independent discipline, may truly be said to date from the sixteenth and seventeenth centuries.

Of indirect and yet far-reaching importance are the writings of two men not commonly regarded as mercantilists. Machiavelli (1469-1527), that penetrating political observer, stressed in his *Prince* the practical methods to be followed by a monarch in creating a' strong state. Jean Bodin (1520-1596), in his *Six Books of the Republic,* proclaimed the doctrine that an absolute government is necessarily best adapted to bring security and wellbeing to its people.

A detailed survey of mercantilistic literature would reveal many thousands of publications, called forth, for the most part, by special exigencies conforming in no manner whatever to any set type, and reflecting but imperfectly the myriad theoretical aspects of the subject. No one writer has the distinction of being the complete mercantilist. Rather should these works be regarded, broadly speaking, as counsel to rulers and administrators of the time,— counsel which at times embodied ideas quite out of harmony with the general tenets of mercantilism.

Foremost pamphleteers.— Probably the first approach to a systematic formulation of mercantilistic philosophy was by Antonio Serra, the most noteworthy of Italian writers on mercantilism, in a tract published in 1613 entitled *A Brief Trea-*

tise on the Causes which can make Gold and Silver plentiful in Kingdoms where there are no Mines. Other Italian mercantilists of more or less note were Davanzati, Scaruffi, Montanari, Belloni, and especially Antonio Genovesi, 1765, reputed to have been the first European holder of a university chair in economics.

In France three writers worthy of mention were Bodin, already referred to in another connection, and author of solid works on money and public finance ; Antoine de Montchrétien, whose *Treatise on Political Economy* (1615) is supposed to have embodied the earliest modern use of the phrase "political economy," and François de Forbonnais (*Economic Principles and Observations,* 1767).

Pre-eminent among English mercantilists was Thomas Mun, (1571-1641), successful merchant and a director for many years of the East India Company. A minor work, *A Discourse of Trade from England into the East Indies,* 1621, was followed much later by the posthumous publication in 1664 of *England's Treasure by Forraign Trade,* or *The Ballance of our Forraign Trade is the Rule of our Treasure,* most notable of all expositions of mercantile principles. Prior to Mun, and in several instances of a character more bullionist than mercantilistic, polemical discussions were engaged in by John Hales, Thomas Miller, Gerard De Malynes, Edward Misselden, John Wheeler, Sir Walter Raleigh, and Sir Dudley Digges. Contemporary with, or following closely upon Mun, came Sir Ralph Maddison, Thomas Manley, John Parker (*Of a Free Trade,* 1648), Samuel Fortrey (*England's Interest and Improvement,* 1663), Lewis Roberts, Gregory King, Sir Thomas Culpeper, Sir William Temple, Roger Coke (*A Discourse on Trade,* 1670), John Pollexfen, Hugh Chamberlain, Charles Davenant (*Essay on the probable Means of making a People Gainers in the Balance of Trade,* 1699), Nehemiah Grew, Charles King, and Joshua Gee (*Trade and Navigation of Great Britain,* 1729). Petty, Child, North, Barbon, and Asgill, sometimes classed as mercantilists, appear on the contrary to have been more anti- than pro-mercantilistic in their views. Several outstanding English philosophers of this period as, for example, Thomas Hobbes (1588-1679), may be regarded as at least semi-mercantilists, and John Locke (1632-

1704) must perhaps be looked upon as a supporter of the main tenets of the mercantile point of view.

Of all the English mercantilist writers of the eighteenth century, the ablest was Sir James Steuart, now known to fame principally as "the last of the mercantilists" and as the first Englishman, probably, to make use of the term "political economy." His pretentious work in two stout volumes, *An Inquiry into the Principles of Political Economy*, 1767, represented the most systematic survey of this subject in Great Britain down to the publication of Adam Smith's *Wealth of Nations* in 1776. Book I is entitled "Population"; Book II, "Trade and Industry"; Book III, "Money and Coin"; Book IV, "Credits and Debts"; and Book V, "Taxes." Unfortunately its unattractive style, labored reasonings, and lack of scientific soundness give this work nowadays merely an historical interest, in view of his comment on the economic conditions immediately preceding the appearance of Adam Smith's masterpiece.

Kameralism.— In the German states and in Austria, peculiar circumstances gave rise to a species of mercantilism known as kameralism (or cameralism). Chiefly due to geographical peculiarities, the attention of this part of Europe was directed more toward domestic economic and political problems and less toward those connected with foreign trade than was the case elsewhere. Not physical factors, solely, but the training and education of the people had to be taken into especial account; these states, invaded by foreigners and subject to almost continuous internal dissension and warfare prior to the peace of Westphalia in 1648, had a hard struggle to preserve their national existence.

✳Kameralism thus comprised the systematic efforts made by the prince to subordinate everything within his control to the life and death struggle to maintain and consolidate his security, plus the ideas pertaining to economic policy set forth by government administrators and councillors, professors of law, and others.✳ Unlike Italian, French, and English writers, of whom the vast majority were pamphleteers, the kameralists produced good-sized volumes in which topics such as internal industry, agriculture, population, and fiscal devices were dealt with on a scale befitting their more than ordinary importance. Typical kameralist writers were Obrecht, Bornitz, Seckendorf, Becher, Hornig (Hornick), Schroeder, Conring, Daries, and Johann Heinrich Justi, author of *A Systematic Treatise on all Economic and Cameral Sciences*, (1755), the first systematic German work on political economy.

Ancient and medieval theorizing.—As already noted, the economic thought of any age may usually be explained in terms of its economic life. Thus in antiquity the comparative scarcity of economic phenomena accounts in some degree for the tardy development and relative paucity of economic speculation during countless centuries. No theories of consumption were propounded, for instance, although the significance of this category was stressed from time to time. In the realm of production, attention was directed almost exclusively to the two factors of natural resources and labor, since capital had not yet been differentiated from wealth, and the enterpriser was generally the landowner. The topic of exchange was even more neglected because of the contempt attaching to trade.

With the appearance in the due course of time of a money economy some thought was devoted to the theory and functions of money, and from very early ages the distinction between value in exchange and value in use (utility) was pointed out on occasion. No theories of distribution emerged aside from the notion that interest was an unjustifiable exaction for the use of money. The concepts of rent, wages, and profits were conspicuous by their absence, inasmuch as the landowner controlled production and no wage earning class existed. Socialistic and communistic schemes abounded, however, and a favorite theme with many writers, accordingly, was that of economic and social reform. Public finance was discussed somewhat in connection with revenues from governmentally owned properties. To government expenditures, public credit, and taxation little consideration was paid.

Medieval economic thought confined itself likewise to comparatively narrow channels, deviating from that which had gone before chiefly in centering around the problems, not of production, but of exchange. Economic theory concerned itself fundamentally with the question of justice in price relationships and in interest taking. In the latter part of the period, as the rapid growth of trade and commerce launched a new economy upon a somewhat unsuspecting world, and the rise of monarchies made imperative a large augmentation of the public revenues, attention was increasingly focussed upon the topics of money and public finance.

The layman as economic theorist.— By contrast the writings of the mercantilists inevitably represented a very considerable break with the past. Economists were no longer primarily philosophers, as in antiquity, or theologians, as during the Middle Ages, but lay specialists. Economics became secularized; artificial took precedence over natural wealth; the maximizing of the material welfare of nations was stressed to the virtual exclusion of other matters; the emergence of new economic phenomena enlarged the horizon of economic speculation. The problems of greatest interest still remained those of production and exchange, now treated from the standpoint of the relation of private wealth to public welfare. The term "political economy" came into growing use as descriptive of that art whereby a people might be made wealthy and powerful through national development.

Broadening fields of theory.—Land as an agent of production was discussed primarily from the point of view of the conservation and best possible utilization of natural resources. Labor came into its own at last as thinkers propounded ways and means of adding to the sum total of a nation's labor power. Indeed, the programs of many of the mercantilists culminated in the population problem. Elimination of idleness, reduction to a minimum of those employed in occupations detrimental, it was assumed, to the nation's progress, e.g., pawn-brokers, lawyers and alehouse-keepers, the attraction of skilled and industrious foreigners, preservation of life and health, and promotion of early marriages were among the remedies frequently suggested. Heavy taxes on bachelors and dowries for impoverished spinsters were at times advocated, then as now.

The unprecedented growth of capital enlisted the interest of writers in such miscellaneous matters as the building of canals and improved roads, the increase and improvement of livestock, the encouragement of the fishing industry, and the subsidizing of certain manufactures.

Nothing is of more significance during this period than the

dominance in the economic world of the merchant and business enterprises, and the decline in importance of the clergy and the landed nobility. Whether or not this was due to the deliberate policy of the monarch (and it often was), the increase in the numbers, power, and wealth of the capitalist proprietors was truly remarkable. The business man reached an ascendancy never before attained, and one which has ever since prevailed to a greater or less degree in capitalistic countries.

Very common was the injunction laid upon consumers to live thriftily and to avoid all waste, in order that the importation of foreign goods might thus be reduced and a larger surplus for export be provided.

Fomenting foreign trade.— To the topic of exchange the contributions of the mercantilists were so voluminous as to far exceed in breadth of treatment all previous discussions. Advocacy of commercial devices for the greatest possible facilitating of commerce ran the gamut from the stressing of the freer employment of bills of exchange, establishment of banks (including land-banks) of deposit and circulation, minting of coins, swelling of the monetary supply, limitations on export and import and granting bounties to the furtherance of a colonial policy such as would largely confine the industry of colonies to the production of raw materials, which in turn would be converted into finished products in the mother country for sale to the colonists. The important but abstruse topic of value appears to have been dealt with more by the philosophers and jurists than by the general run of writers of this period. In the main, no novel ideas were set forth. Subjective theories were held by some, by others cost of production was emphasized, and normal value was distinguished from market value. Interestingly enough, the suggestions made by mercantilists formed the basis for the value theories enunciated later on by Adam Smith in *The Wealth of Nations*.

Undeveloped and naïve notions concerning rent and profits came to light at this time, and require no further comment. The growth of industrial capital did not apparently reach a point during this period sufficient to bring the problems of distribution into clear relief. Low wages, however, seemed to mean low costs. The predominant theory of wages, reinforced by the frequent assumption that the working classes were naturally shiftless, accordingly stressed the desirability of a condition approaching poverty for the mass of laborers. High wages, it was urged, would not alone fail to stimulate industry but would, on the contrary, greatly increase the costs of employees, breed dissolute habits among them, and render successful competition with other countries impossible. As for interest, the legitimacy of interest taking in general went unquestioned; the underlying relation between interest and the productivity of capital was but faintly perceived. Hopes were expressed by many that interest rates might permanently be reduced and kept low by the action of government.

In public finance the subject dealt with at most length was that of taxation. Taxes levied according to expenditure or according to benefits received from the states were those most looked upon with favor, quite in contrast to the modern doctrine which leans toward the more enlightened ability-to-pay principle of taxation.

Recapitulation.—A fair appraisal of mercantilistic policy, more especially in terms of its historical background, inasmuch as mercantilism was a natural product of its time, leads to conclusions at variance, in some respects, with the traditional judgment that has held sway until comparatively recently. The favorable-balance-of-trade theory, for instance, is now known to have been but one aspect of a comprehensive policy of national regulation. A favorable balance, furthermore, was of much greater importance then than at present by reason of the relatively insignificant nature of the "invisible" balances of trade in the form of payments for freight, insurance, and the like which characterized the mercantile era. Nor can this theory be regarded as anything but a temporarily justifiable expedient, given the need of the monarch for hard money and the scarcity of gold and silver mines in most of Europe. Whatever there was of error lay in the approval of this national policy as one proper for all time; in other words, a surplus of exports over imports of goods was confused with a permanent surplus of production over consumption.

In addition, a program of restriction of foreign trade and

of national protection of internal trade and resources very probably resulted in a net increase of economic freedom. As tariff barriers between nations were built up internal barriers to trade were broken down. The wider the territorial organization of economic life became, the less the narrow exclusiveness of the towns was able to assert itself, and the larger the zones of unrestricted commerce established by rulers in territories under their jurisdiction. The ratio of domestic trade to foreign trade became larger, naturally, as the number of governmental units diminished with the growth of monarchy. Mercantilism, in liberating industry and internal trade from the regulations of local economy, despite succeeding burdens imposed upon employers, employees, and consumers in the endeavor to make the nation self-sufficient, at a time when war was the normal occurrence, may lay claim with some justice to having introduced into Europe a greater measure of industrial freedom than that part of the world had ever before experienced.

On the other hand, mercantilistic policy contained within itself the seeds of its own partial destruction. Mercantilism, in accentuating national economic expansion, marked a memorable advance over the local economy of the medieval system. But in due course the conditions that gave rise to this policy underwent considerable change, and government interference, for so long a spur to industry, degenerated into something of a deadweight around its neck. Mercantilism sooner or later disintegrated, because business men ultimately discovered that government regulations often prevented them from putting their capital and their time to the most profitable use. When pursuit of private profit ran counter to the well-meant efforts of legislators a change in practice was inevitable, and mercantilistic policy became an anachronism.

The mercantilists erred, furthermore, in failing to grasp the idea that trade may be mutually advantageous. As they viewed the situation, what one country gained in trade the other necessarily lost,—an idea long since consigned to the limbo of discredited economic theories. And, finally, their theory seemed to lead to the deduction that production is paramount to consumption, that man exists for wealth, not wealth for man. If this interpretation be correct let it be remembered that many men of today still subscribe to this notion without the same reasons to support them in their conclusion that existed in the heyday of mercantilism during the six-teenth, seventeenth, and eighteenth centuries.

CHAPTER IV

REACTIONS AGAINST MERCANTILISM

ACCOMPANYING the conditions in process of development that gave birth to the rise of the nationalist state and the growth of capitalism were achievements in the field of science and the realm of thought of the utmost significance in the history of mankind.

The soil of science.— In all ages, it may safely be assumed, great men have desired to learn for the sake of learning. Science flourishes most, however, at those times and in those places where political stability exists, where the forces of nature are looked upon as beneficent instead of evil, and when wealth gives leisure for scientific pursuits or subsidizes scientists and their societies and journals. Such were the conditions that increasingly prevailed in much of Europe from the seventeenth century onward, and that paved the way for experimentation and scientific exploration of a character more extraordinary than any that had gone before. In the very year, 1642, in which Galileo died was born Isaac Newton, author of the *Principia* (1686), and overshadowing genius of his time. Epoch-making advances occurred in the fields of geography, geology, mathematics and astronomy, while physics, chemistry and biology definitely emerged as sciences. As learned men turned their attention to the study of nature, natural science, or "natural philosophy," as it was termed, gradually replaced the older studies of theology, the classics, and metaphysics as the most important branch of learning.

Natural laws.— With the growing discovery of the presence of natural laws in the physical, plant, and animal worlds in no way dependent upon the human will, the question inevitably arose as to whether not alone the body but likewise the mind and moral nature of man were also subject to the control of universal laws of nature. Those who accepted the point of view that men are capable of indefinitely extending the province of knowledge through the exercise of their reason, that observation is the proper method of ascertaining truth, and that the purpose of study in the field of society is to discover possible natural laws in accordance with which human societies function, came to be called, in the eighteenth century, "the philosophers." They were by no means philosophers as ordinarily thought of, but rather novelists, historians, dramatists and writers of books upon politics, economics, education, religion and the like. Upon one point they agreed : that men must be free to think and to act in order that the natural laws, to which every social phenomenon was thought to be subject, might be discovered and allowed full sweep as guides for right social action.

Early French political philosophers.— In this philosophical criticism of existing society during the eighteenth century it was France which led the way and caused this century to become known as the "Age of Enlightenment" and the "Age of Reason." Forerunners, in a way, had been Michel de Montaigne (1533-1590), Francis Bacon (1561-1626), Hugo Grotius (1583-1645), René Descartes (1596-1650), John Locke (1632-1704) and others. But the movement came to fruition in the writings of a group of illustrious thinkers headed by Charles Louis Montesquieu (1689-1775). In his great work, *The Spirit of Laws* (1748), he sought to analyze the foundations of existing types of laws and political institutions, and advocated a government with a separation of powers into legislative, executive and judicial branches. François Voltaire (1694-1778), prolific writer and foremost intellectual figure of the eighteenth century, championed reason and tolerance with all the resources of a mind rarely equalled for brilliance and versatility. Denis Diderot (1713-1784), assisted by many others (The Encyclopedists), exercised his editorial genius in the publication of the *Encyclopedia* (1752-1772), a summing up of the contributions of the rationalistic thought of the age. Jean Jacques Rousseau (1712-1778), more influential than any other writer in making the natural rights theory popular in France, expounded the principles of liberty, equality and fraternity in *The Social Contract* (1762).

These new intellectual attitudes, directed at first to religious thought and to the policies of sovereigns and statesmen, were in time applied to the economic life of France. Mercantilism, that unsystematic body of doctrines and beliefs which supplanted localism by reason of the community of interest that developed between the merchant class and the absolute monarch, should theoretically have resulted in the promotion of the welfare of the mass of the French population.

In practice, under the inefficient and even senseless rule of such kings as Louis XIV and Louis XV, France was brought to the very brink of ruin. No other country in Europe, by virtue of favorable climate and fertility of the soil, was better adapted for agriculture, yet in no other country, generally speaking, did agriculture languish and stagnate under the mercantilist régime as in France. In England, for instance, a new landed aristocracy arose as land ownership came more and more into the hands of wealthy merchants who realized the importance of a sound agrarian policy and accordingly sponsored a series of changes in technique which as a whole increased agricultural efficiency and production. True, as a result of this agricultural revolution the great majority of English agricultural laborers were dispossessed of their personal landholdings. But, for the time being, at least, the new capitalist farming increased the productivity of English agriculture.

Taxation in France.— Across the Channel, on the contrary, the *ancien régime* witnessed an actual decrease in the numbers of the farm population and an appalling neglect and decline of agriculture. Innumerable taxes, levied in theory, with the exception of the *taille*, upon all classes of the French population, fell as a matter of fact upon the land only, and rendered profitable farming impossible. From this ruinous taxation the privileged classes (the nobles and the clergy), owners of nearly one-half the area of the country, were free by law ; from much of it the upper middle class could buy exemption. Added to these many taxes were such occasional exactions as the forced labor of peasants (the *corvée*), monopolies leased to contractors, militia requisitions, seigneurial dues, and dues and tithes levied by the Church. During the period previous to the French Revolution, furthermore, profligacy in expendi-

tures and recklessness in borrowing to cover deficits brought
the credit of the government to virtual extinction. At this
juncture the physiocrats entered the scene.

The Physiocrats.— It was wholly natural that physiocracy
should arise in France, since the one essential ingredient of
the physiocratic philosophy, stripped of much of the glamour
that has surrounded their thinking, consisted in the promotion
of French extractive industry, and, in particular, of agriculture. The physiocrats were very largely members of a new
landed class, men who bought up the estates of bankrupt
nobles, married, when they could, into the nobility, became the
backbone of a new bureaucracy, and set about to make farming
a paying proposition. In other words, physiocracy owed its
origin to the rise of capitalist agriculture in France. To these
new landowners a primary consideration in the attainment of
their objective was the removal of the innumerable taxes that
fell, in last instance, upon the land. Accordingly they proposed the substitution of a single tax for the multiplicity of
taxes then in existence,—a tax to be levied, not upon the land
but upon the net product (*produit net*) of extractive industry.

Nature, they firmly asserted, labors along with man in
the extractive industries (mining, fishing, agriculture, etc.),
yielding normally a surplus over and above the cost of production involved out of which the remaining classes of society
are supported. By cost of production they meant all expenses
incurred in connection with the wages of laborers and interest
on capital, together with a fair profit on the investment. Their
proposal, if carried into effect, would therefore have committed
the government to a single tax on that part, only, of the total
produce remaining after the computaton of certain deductions,
and would thus have guaranteed to the landowners the recovery not alone of their ordinary costs of production but of a
fair profit.[1]

The single direct tax (*impôt unique*) upon surplus products
of extractive industry was both the major economic doctrine
upon which the physiocrats rested their case, and the basic
economic reform which they advocated. In addition, they
argued quite logically that extractive industry is the sole ulti-

[1] *See* "The Physiocrats," by Norman J. Ware in the *American Economic
Review* for December, 1931.

mate source of the wealth of a country, and that since all taxes must in the long run be paid from the surplus which land yields, it were better that the proprietor of land bear them directly, instead of waiting to pay them after they had passed through various hands, and their total amount had been correspondingly increased in the process of collection. Useful, indeed, they admitted, were manufacturers and merchants, as well as members of the liberal professions and all those engaged in personal service. But these classes they regarded, more fundamentally, as "sterile," on the ground that they produced no new goods but merely transferred to other people goods already in existence.

To landed proprietors and cultivators of land, only, did they grant the attribute of productivity. Production, to the physiocrats, meant creation of a material surplus above the cost of production. It meant the harvesting of wheat, or the catching of fish, or the mining of coal rather than the baking of bread or the marketing of commodities. Not labor but nature was regarded as the producer.

A further insistence was upon freedom of movement of the products of extractive industry within and out of France. The majority of the physiocrats were by no means ardent champions of free trade as such. What they desired was such freedom of trade as would lead to an increase in consumption of home products, and a corresponding augmentation of output in extractive industry. The greater the productivity, they averred, the larger the surplus and the richer the kingdom.

Systematization of economic phenomena.— In its beginnings, accordingly, physiocracy may be regarded as the practical proposals of a certain class interest designed both to improve the financial status of French land-owners and to promote the prosperity of France as a whole. Ultimately the economic doctrines of the necessity of a single tax, the desirability of a certain amount of free trade, and the sole productivity of extractive industry became mere corollaries to something much larger. In due time, under the influence of the teachings of the "philosophers" noted in preceding paragraphs, the physiocrats sought to reduce all social and economic phenomena to principle, and developed such an organized and systematic body of doctrine, that in the esti-

mation of many scholars they must be credited with the signal
honor of having founded economics as a science.

Non-intervention by government.— Probably the foundation of their philosophical structure was their view of natural
law (*droit naturel*).   There is a natural, or ideal, order of
affairs, they asserted, ordained by God and susceptible to discovery by man.   The object of all scientific study, moreover,
is to discover the laws to which all the phenomena of the
universe are subject.

This supernatural order, when once ascertained by intelligent
human beings, will spontaneously be followed by them, since
all members of society are led by nature to follow their own
self-interests.   Opposed to the natural order (*ordre naturel*)
is the positive, or existing, order (*ordre positif*), and it is the
primary function of positive laws to interpret natural law.   In
the economic sphere the chief natural right of man is to enjoy
the fruits of his own labor, provided that such enjoyment be
not inconsistent with the rights of others.   Governments, accordingly, should never extend their interference in economic
affairs beyond the minimum absolutely essential to protection
of life and private property and the maintenance of freedom
of contract.   Domestic, and, to a great extent, international
commerce should be free of all restrictions so that the most
advantageous price for all parties might be established.   In
picturesque phrasing the famous maxim, *laissez faire et laissez
passer, le monde va de lui-même* ("let do and let alone, the
world goes on of itself") formulated for all time the principle
of non-intervention.   Private property ; freedom of contract ;
free competition : these were the industrial rights of man that
flowed inevitably from the operation of natural law, and to
whose guarantee the state must consecrate itself.

Industrial, but not political, liberty, most peculiarly, since
in their opinion the task of introducing the policies which they
advocated could be entrusted to an hereditary monarchy alone,
— a form of government, they thought, far removed in vision
and selflessness from the party strife of constitutional assem-
blies.

Previous French theorists.— Prior to the physiocratic system not a few writings on economic subjects were published
in France of such note as to lay the physiocratic writers under

considerable, although indefinable, debt to them. Pierre de Boisguillebert, government official, contemporary of Colbert, and first important economic theorist of France, directed an earnest protest against the fiscal, economic and political abuses of the old régime in various statistical works and pamphlets written by him late in the seventeenth and early in the eighteenth century. At about the same time, and in similar vein, Marshal Vaubon proposed a radical reformation in existing taxes (1707). Of much greater significance was the publication in French in 1755 of a treatise originally written in English nearly twenty-five years earlier by Richard Cantillon, British merchant of Irish descent. Cantillon's *Essay upon the Nature of Commerce in General*, his sole surviving work, because of its highly abstract character made no wide appeal to the general public, but was much admired by several physiocrats, many of whose doctrines it foreshadowed.

Quesnay.— Founder and chief representative of the school of physiocrats, most compact of all schools of economists, was indubitably François Quesnay (1694-1774). By profession a medical practitioner it was only after he had passed the age of sixty, while court physician and possibly in consequence of extensive land holdings, that he became interested in economic matters. Very little of his economic writings was published under his own name. In his first two articles, on *Farmers* (1756) and on *Grains* (1757) appear the germs of his system as expounded more at length in the famous *Tableau Économique*, published in 1758 with the motto "poor peasants, poor kingdom ; poor kingdom, poor king." In later years appeared publications of minor significance such as his *Natural Law* (1768). The *Tableau*, known in history as the bible of physiocracy, and the subject of extravagant praise by his followers, endeavored to make an exact science of economics by trying to explain how wealth flowed among the different classes of society. This tract also set forth eight reasons for the decadence of nations.

Successors of Quesnay.— Oldest of Quesnay's disciples, and likewise his first outstanding convert, was the Marquis Victor de Mirabeau (not to be confused with his illustrious son, the Comte de Mirabeau of the French Revolution), who published in 1763, with the co-operation of his master, a volume entitled *Rural Philosophy*, designed as a complete treatise on the subject of economics. Other adherents of prominence were Mercier de la Rivière (*The Natural Order*, 1767); Dupont de Nemours (famous as the founder of the Dupont family in the United States and for his coinage of the term *Physiocracy* in a work bearing the same title, 1767 : most of the Physiocrats preferred to call themselves "The Economists") ; the Abbé Baudeau, author of a dozen volumes, of which the best remembered is his *Economic Philosophy* (1771), and perhaps the keenest thinker in the group, although his works have never been adequately studied, and Le Trosne (The Social Order, 1777). Vincent de Gournay, to whom, whether correctly or not, the maxim "laissez faire, laissez passer" is commonly attributed, was never formally a member of the sect.

Turgot.— Most eminent of the group in many ways, and yet standing somewhat apart from it, was Anne Robert Jacques Turgot (1721-1781), administrator, Controller General of Finance for two years (1774-1776), and author of treatises and memoirs remarkable in their range of subject and mode of presentation. In method, content and profundity of analysis his work marks a very decided forward step in the history of economic speculation. Of greatest import is his contribution in the field of distribution as evidenced in his book of a hundred short paragraphs, *Reflections upon the Formation and Distribution of Wealth* (1766).

He propounded a theory of capital (surplus utilized in production), accepted Quesnay's theory of rent (surplus above costs of production) and his theory of wages (wages tend to be at the level of subsistence), and laid down a theory of interest, holding that interest is paid not for the use of money, but for the use of capital. More clearly than any predecessor he seems to have recognized the growing separation of the ownership of the instruments of production from the use of those instruments by labor and capital, and thus to have hit upon the central theme of the economic order that was developing about him. Crude though his theories may appear, they nevertheless present very probably the first well-rounded treatment of distribution to appear in history, and by many scholars Turgot is accordingly acclaimed as the earliest of scientific economists.

The end of physiocracy.—Physiocracy enjoyed but a short span of life—fifty years or less. Although the school did not formally disband until toward the close of the eighteenth century, a veritable deathblow to its influence appeared in the publication in 1776 of *The Wealth of Nations,* a work of such breadth and balance as to include all that was best in Adam Smith's contemporaries and one of infinitely more popular appeal. Mercantilism, it will be remembered, was both a policy and a set of doctrines. Physiocracy, on the contrary, had in the main only a doctrinal aspect. In France its program was put into effect to a limited extent by Turgot while he served as *intendant* of Limoges (1761-1774) and later as French minister of finance. Elsewhere, sporadic attempts to carry out its principles, as in Baden, Austria and Sweden, ended in early failure.

In a direct way, therefore, the work of the physiocrats has but little value. But indirectly their influence on the subsequent course of economic thought has been considerable. Mercantilism had divorced economics from ethics; physiocracy further separated it from jurisprudence. The physiocrats dealt a severe blow at mercantilistic policy, brought into bold relief the notions of economic freedom and of cosmopolitanism, contributed much to the clarification of theories of distribution and taxation, and emphasized the presumable existence of certain social laws. Above all, they approached economic questions more from the standpoint of the whole people than from that of monarchs and the ruling classes. Interested in diminishing the suffering and injustice caused by extreme poverty, they aided tremendously in establishing the broad and philanthropic tone which is part and parcel of present day economics.

The reaction in Great Britain.—The decline of mercantilism began earlier in Great Britain, probably, than in any other part of Europe, and gathered momentum from the sixteenth century onward as capitalist farming and large-scale industry there struck their deepest roots, and regulative measures became more and more dead letters. Anti-mercantilistic ideas were voiced with increasing force and frequency until the culmination was reached in the epoch-making interpretation set forth in *The Wealth of Nations* of Adam Smith.

Among the pioneers of the new thought was Sir William Petty (1623-1687), distinguished physician and administrator, a man of wide philosophical interests, and one of the founders, with Sir Isaac Newton, of the British Royal Society, incorporated in 1662 for the advancement of scientific research (The French Academy of Sciences was chartered four years later, and in 1700, the Berlin Academy). In his two chief economic writings, *A Treatise of Taxes and Contributions* (1679) and *Essays in Political Arithmetick* (1691), he took vigorous exception to many of the mercantilist views. "Labour," he declared, for example, "is the father and active principle of Wealth, as Lands are the mother." Most noteworthy was his endeavor to apply quantitative methods to the discussion of economic and political problems, by what was known in his day as "political arithmetick" and is now termed statistics.

One of the meritorious services of many of the writers of this period, in fact, was their utilization and development of the statistical method. Following Petty, Sir Dudley North (1644-1691), in his only book, *Discourses upon Trade* (1691), and, of lesser importance, Sir Josiah Child, in *A New Discourse on Trade* (1690), and Nicholas Barbon in *A Discourse of Trade* (1690), stated unqualified opposition to numerous measures of state regulation, while endorsing, on the other hand, certain aspects of mercantilism.

Precursors of Adam Smith.—At this juncture, it should once more be borne in mind that no acknowledged definition of "mercantilism" exists. The ambiguity of the term is in truth so distressing as to warrant the assertion that in time the discontinuance of its use may result in more good than harm. Arbitrarily to label as "mercantilist" or otherwise any of the many thousands of writers who, to a greater or less degree, prepared the way for the composition of *The Wealth of Nations* is a hazardous and perhaps futile procedure. There seems, however, to have been a definite reaction against mercantilistic doctrines in the writings of those British writers who may be called the immediate precursors of Adam Smith.

With respect to these men convention has long assigned most significance to certain British philosophers. This is not to discount the importance of such men as Bernard de Mandeville (1670?-1731), Dutch immigrant to England, in whose interesting poem, *Fable of the Bees* (1714), occur pointed suggestions regarding self-interest and division of labor ; of Jacob Vanderlint, who advocated low prices and an increase in consumption in his *Money Answers All Things* (1734) ; of George Berkeley, Bishop of Ireland, who exposed many a popular fallacy in *The Querist* (1735) ; and of Josiah Tucker (1712-1799), dean of Gloucester, author of many essays on questions of contemporary interest and an ardent champion of free trade.

Outstanding in this group, nevertheless, were the philosophers Francis Hutcheson (1694-1746) and David Hume (1711-1776). Hutcheson was professor of moral philosophy at Glasgow College from 1730 to 1746, and was accounted by Adam Smith as his most inspiring and influential teacher. His *System of Moral Philosophy* (1755) set forth numerous ideas later incorporated in *The Wealth of Nations*, characteristic of which were the philosophy of utilitarianism, the psychology of hedonism, and the notion of God as a benevolent being.

Hume was alluded to by Adam Smith in *The Wealth of Nations* as "by far the most illustrious philosopher and historian of the present age." Youngest son of a Scotch lord and a gifted scholar in several fields of learning, he was preeminently the philosopher and essay writer.

His economic views are to be found chiefly in his essays *Of Money, Of Commerce, Of Interest, Of the Balance of Trade* and in his *Political Discourses* (1752). He wrote no systematic treatise on economics, and the opinion has long prevailed that if he had, his name would now be included in the ranks of the truly profound students of the science. Of late, however, evidence has appeared that his liberalism toward the prevailing economic ideas of his time was perhaps more apparent than real. His chief service, despite a certain measure of originality in his work, as in the field of money, seems to have been the endeavor to restate and reconcile the doctrines of his British predecessors. The contradiction in which he seemingly involved himself made necessary a fresh approach to the problem and the formulation of new doctrines, a task assumed by Adam Smith, his lifelong friend and admirer.[2]

---

[2] See *Predecessors of Adam Smith*, by E. A. J. Johnson, Chapter IX, "Hume, the Synthesist."

CHAPTER V

ADAM SMITH

ADAM SMITH, the most illustrious name in the history of economic thought, was born in the small town of Kirkcaldy, Scotland, near Edinburgh, on June 5, 1723, the posthumous and only child of a minor customs official. He never married, and during most of his life lived with his mother. A born student, he entered Glasgow College at fourteen, coming there under the influence particularly of Francis Hutcheson, the philosopher. Three years later he was awarded what would now be termed a fellowship or scholarship for six years of study at Balliol College, Oxford, an institution at that time sunk in intellectual lethargy. In 1746 he left Oxford, having steeped himself meanwhile in philosophy, classical literature and in the French and Italian authors, and after two years of semi-idleness was appointed to a lectureship on English literature at Edinburgh University. His lectures were sufficiently well received to lead to his appointment in 1751, at the early age of twenty-eight, to the professorship of logic at Glasgow College, and the next year to the more important chair of moral philosophy.

His earlier career.—In those days moral philosophy comprised a range of subjects much wider than is the case at present. The course which he gave consisted of four parts, the first dealing with natural theology, the second with ethics, the third with justice, and the fourth with expediency, under which head he discussed such political regulations as were calculated to increase the wealth, power and prosperity of the state. In the second part of this course were developed principles which presently took form (1759) in his first publication, a treatise on ethics entitled the *Theory of Moral Sentiments*, a book which went through six editions within his lifetime and enhanced very considerably his reputation in

56

Great Britain and on the continent. A full set of students'
notes on the third and fourth parts of the course as given in
1763 has most fortunately been preserved for posterity and
published (1896) under the title of *Lectures on Justice, Police,
Revenue, and Arms*. The main concepts of *The Wealth of
Nations* are accordingly now known to have been an elaboration in great measure of his lectures on expediency.

During his thirteen years of residence in Glasgow Adam
Smith entered rather fully into association with his fellow-
townsmen of that thriving commercial and manufacturing me-
tropolis. There can be little doubt, for example, that his
attendance at a weekly discussion club composed of representative business men and his intimate friendship with one of the
city's leading merchant-bankers did much to deepen his interest in economic problems, provide him with a wealth of economic data, and assist him enormously in formulating his
views concerning the nature and principles of trade as it was
actually being carried on in one of the most important business centers. Significant, also, was his fruitful acquaintance
with David Hume, then living in Edinburgh, and most forward-
looking of English writers of the day on economic matters.

Foreign experience.—In 1764, somewhat regretfully, he
resigned his professorship in order to accept a much more lucrative position as tutor for three years of the young Duke of
Buccleuch, ward of Charles Townsend, then Chancellor of the
Exchequer. For this service he was to receive a generous
yearly stipend of 300 pounds for the length of the tutorship
plus travelling expenses, and in addition, an annual pension
of the same amount for the ensuing twenty-four years. Setting out with his companion for the continent, he passed a
year and a half in the south of France where he began at Tou-
louse the writing of the book that in time was to grow into
The Wealth of Nations. Then followed a sojourn of a few
months in Switzerland and a year's residence in Paris. There
he came to know well various members of the physiocratic
group, including Quesnay and Turgot, men who were actively
thinking about the same problems with which he had concerned
himself for years. He also formed more or less intimate
friendships with many of the outstanding literary men of the
day.

His masterwork.— Returning to England he devoted himself for nearly ten years in an unhurried fashion to the completion of his manuscript, living mostly in seclusion until 1773 at his old home in Kirkcaldy and then repairing to London for further investigation and the application of certain finishing touches.   Finally, in the spring of 1776, his treatise was published in two volumes under the title of *An Inquiry into the Nature and Causes of the Wealth of Nations.*   Its success was instantaneous.   Before his death it had run through five editions and had been translated into numerous foreign languages.   Secure in his fame, he accepted in 1778 the post of commissioner of customs in Scotland, removed to Edinburgh, and there resided until his death on July 17, 1790.   His declining years were spent in almost princely affluence, although he left but a modest estate, so large were his contributions to charity during his lifetime.   Shortly before he died he caused to be burned, in the presence of friends, and without explanation, sixteen volumes of incompleted manuscript, an act of mystery which has ever since that time given rise to the supposition that he may have been at work on the preparation of a treatise on jurisprudence developing out of the third part of his Glasgow course on moral philosophy, much as *The Theory of Moral Sentiments* and *The Wealth of Nations* were outgrowths of the second and fourth parts of that course.

The *Wealth of Nations* was thus the product of years, even decades, of meditation by a man at once college professor of moral philosophy and keen observer of current events, a man of wide interests and varied associations, grounded in the classics and yet acutely aware of everyday goings-on in the business world.   Adam Smith's great work, in brief, was much more than its title would lead one to believe.   It was not only a treatise on economics, dealing in a many-sided fashion with the wealth of nations, but a comprehensive philosophical work, treating in a broad way of problems of human welfare.   Economic principles, ethical principles, principles of jurisprudence, principles of theology,— all these pass in review before the reader in this book of nearly nine hundred pages.   Here, indeed, is a history and a criticism of European civilization from the fall of the Roman Empire down to his own time. With entire fitness might *The Wealth of Nations* have been entitled "A History and a Critique of the Civilization of Western Europe."

Deductive method.—To be sure, there may be found in Adam Smith an exposition of an enormous amount of factual material, of which more in detail in succeeding pages. But of utmost importance in connection with this work is the circumstance that he was concerned not so much in summarizing the more or less common stock of knowledge of that day, or of adducing new facts, as he was in the inter-relation and interpretation of facts and the portrayal of a new perspective.

The Wealth of Nations, broadly speaking, is a series of reflections and conclusions much more than an addition to the accumulated total of human knowledge. It was the result not so much of investigation as of reflection and of the organization of material already in existence. In view of the very imperfect development of statistics at that time, Adam Smith had no choice but to proceed in the discussion of his general theme by the one method available that seemingly promised any large measure of success. With "little faith in political arithmetic," as he himself remarked, and with existing data of a fragmentary sort and most inferior in quality, he rendered the greatest service that could then be performed when, by means of deduction, he gave to the world the most carefully thought-out and sweeping conclusions on economic phenomena and the most closely organized body of economic learning, from the standpoint of organic unity, that had appeared in history down to 1776.[1] The book, indeed, is the outpouring of a truly great mind.

This is not to imply, it goes without saying, that, although he endeavored to check his deductions by means of personal observation and historical research, he is not full of contradictions and susceptible to error. Inconsistency has frequently been a leading characteristic of great minds, and Adam Smith can in no wise be regarded as the standard bearer *par excellence* of consistency or of accuracy of viewpoint. Nor should his powers of originality be overstressed. Over one hundred authors are quoted in his book. for instance, sometimes without acknowledgment, and certain it is that he built largely upon the work of his predecessors. No man can claim

[1] W. C. Mitchell, Unpublished Manuscript.

to be completely original. Yet no previous writer possessed his striking balance of thought or breadth of outlook, or so skillfully fused into a coherent whole the finest products of other minds. Making use only of materials freely accessible to all and seldom a pioneer, he nevertheless looked at economic phenomena in a manner more comprehensive than anyone before him and laid the groundwork for the speculations of those thinkers who were to follow. When to this is added the decided literary charm of *The Wealth of Nations* and the clearness and the fluency, for the most part, with which opinions are expressed and facts intermixed with reasoning, there can be little reason for denying him the attribute of genius.

Few indeed are the many economic truths now current of which he did not obtain at least a glimpse. Of no other economic work produced during this period can it be affirmed, furthermore, that it still continues to be widely read. Despite all its obvious shortcomings, it ranks, by nearly unanimous consent, as the most influential treatise on economics ever written and as one of the classics of all time.

Analysis of his masterpiece.— *An Inquiry into the Nature and Causes of the Wealth of Nations* consists of an Introduction of three pages, in which an outline is given of the "plan of the work," of five Books, and of a short Appendix. The first two books comprise what has come to be known in comparatively recent decades as "economic theory." The third book is historical in tenor and traces the progress of European civilization. Book four is devoted to a critical examination of mercantilism and physiocracy. In the fifth and concluding book consideration is given to the subject of government finance in many of its ramifications. The title of each chapter begins with the word "Of." Should this arrangement of topics seem somewhat peculiar, resort must be had to the apparently plausible explanation that the author, like many other college professors, simply expanded his lectures when he came to set them down in book form.

In the memorable opening sentence of the Introduction, Adam Smith expressed himself as firmly of the belief that "The annual labour of every nation is the fund which originally supplies it with all the necessaries and conveniences of life which it annually consumes, and which consist always either in the immediate produce of that labour, or in what is purchased with that produce from other nations." This celebrated passage, the cause of so many later misunderstandings, was in no way intended to minimize the part played in production by either capital or natural resources, but rather at the very outset to set off his own point of view (by no means an original one) from that which the mercantilists and physiocrats had promulgated. The physiocrats had erected their system upon the proposition that all wealth comes from the extractive industries alone, while the mercantilists had tended to exalt the precious metals in importance above all other kinds of wealth. Adam Smith clearly saw, on the contrary, assuming that the natural resources of all nations are more or less arbitrarily fixed in amount, that the true source of wealth is to be found in human activity, and that wealth is much more a flow of goods than a supply of goods on hand.

Labor the source of wealth.—Thus he was led in Book I, entitled "Of the Causes of Improvement in the Productive Powers of Labour, and of the Order according to which its Produce is Naturally Distributed among the Different Ranks of the People" to consider at further length labor as the source of the wealth of nations. This book of eleven chapters is concerned with the three topics of production, exchange, and distribution. In the first chapter—the most famous of all the thirty-two chapters of the treatise—he laid it down as the cardinal fact of economic life that the production of wealth can best be brought about by the proper organization of labor, explaining the advantages of division of labor in terms of the greater dexterity acquired by each laborer, the time saved in constant change of occupation, and the stimulus to invention inevitably resulting, and illustrating the consequent increase in the productive power of labor by his well known reference to the pin manufacturing industry. In succeeding chapters he sought none too successfully to find the origin of division of labor in the propensity of human nature "to truck, barter, or exchange one thing for another." But with his inimitable common sense he went on to state that division of labor is fundamentally grounded in man's need for the "co-operation and assistance of great multitudes." Men specialize in their work, he declared, because of the appeal to their self-interest.

The chief point of all this lies once more not in his various accounts of the principle and effects of the division of labor, but in the major role which he assigned to labor and its specialized processes and in the way in which he viewed production as a whole. To Adam Smith a nation lived in comfort only when there existed an abundance of goods available for equitable distribution among the different classes of society, —an abundance conditioned upon an increasing division of labor and in turn upon an ever widening extent of the market.

Money, prices and value.— Inasmuch as the extent of divison of labor rests upon the exchange of goods, Adam Smith next proceeded in Chapter four to a short and conventional consideration of the origin and the use of money as an instrument for the facilitation of exchange. And since money is nothing more than a means of expressing value, a discussion of the much mooted subject of value followed as a matter of course. Distinguishing between value in use (in general, the utility or power of satisfying wants possessed by goods) and value in exchange, much as the physiocrats and many others before him had done, he went on to develop the concept, in the next three chapters, of exchange value alone. What determines, he inquired in the first place, the amount of one thing which will be given for another. "Labour," he answered, must be regarded as "the real measure of the exchangeable value of all commodities." "The value of any commodity . . . to the person who possesses it, and who means not to use or consume it himself, but to exchange it for other commodities, is equal to the quantity of labor which it enables him to purchase or command." In actual practice, he commented, however, money (as today) and not labor is the measure of value. As to the *cause* of value he remarked that "the real price of everything, what everything really costs to the man who wants to acquire it, is the toil and trouble of acquiring it."

In early society, he added, exchange value was fixed solely by the amount of labor employed in production, whereas in the more advanced stages of civilization prices become more complex, due to the accumulation of capital and the increasing scarcity of desirable land, and consist in most instances of the three elements of wages, rent and profit. There is, furthermore, a natural price and a market price for goods, the former referring to that price which just covers the ordinary rate of wages, rent and profit necessary to the marketing of a commodity, while the market price is the actual price at which the commodity is sold, depending for its exact location upon the relation between the supply of a particular good and the effectual demand for it. Under the influence of competition the natural price is the price toward which market prices tend to gravitate, and value, apart from exceptional cases such as monopoly, thus constantly tends toward the cost of production. Such, all too briefly, were his views, elusive and vacillating at times, on the perplexing topic of value theory.

Distribution.— On the assumption that price (the money expression of value) is made up of wages, rent and profit, Adam Smith turned in the last four chapters of the first book to an analysis of distribution, since wages, rent and profit are as much the constituents of income as they are the elements of price. Now the curious thing about his discussion of both value and distribution is that neither of these two topics throws much, if any, light upon the main subject under consideration in this first book, that is, upon labor and division of labor.

The nearly universal conjecture, ever since the publication of *The Wealth of Nations,* has been that the interjection at this point of a theory of distribution was an afterthought, suggested most likely by his association with the physiocrats. There is some ground for the belief, however, that the commercial crisis of 1772 in Great Britain, involving the failure of a bank in the winding up of whose affairs Adam Smith seems to have taken some part, plus the appearance of monographs by William Temple and Dean Tucker, may have aroused in him a belated interest in the subject of capital and distribution and a realization of their significance. Whether or not his ideas on these topics were taken bodily from the physiocrats, his distribution theory seems like patchwork and is even less satisfying than his theorizing on value.

Channels of distribution.— Adam Smith declared there are three great "orders," or classes of income receivers, in every civilized society, all other individuals deriving their income from these three, namely, the laborers, who receive wages ; the landlords, who receive rent ; and the capitalists, who receive profits. Wages, he thought, depended on the relative bargaining strength of employers and employees, although tending in the long run, perhaps, toward a minimum-of-subsistence level fixed by the "ordinary or average price of provisions." Rent arose as land was appropriated ; it is a payment to the landowner for the use of land, varying with the fertility and the location of the land. The landowner he looked upon as a monopolist (contrary to the modern point of view), and rent as a form of extortion, although there would be no rent were it not for the bounty and generosity of nature. Profits were thought to be the total return made by the use of capital ; interest was that part of profits which had to be paid by a borrower to the capitalist for the use of capital.

These classes, moreover, did not tend to have uniform interests. That of the landlords, for example, would always coincide with the general interest of society, as likewise that of the laborers. But the interest of the capitalists, on the contrary, was held to be at variance with that of society, for capitalists are selfish and are constantly endeavoring to confine the workings of competition within ever narrowing limits.

Capital.— The subject of Book II — the second shortest of the five books — is "The Nature, Accumulation, and Employment of Stock." By "stock" Adam Smith had in mind what is nowadays very roughly thought of as capital. It is one of the many incongruities observable in *The Wealth of Nations* that the topic of production is introduced to the reader in the first few chapters of Book I, that the discussion is then broken into by a lengthy digression into the field of distribution (nearly four-fifths of the first Book is concerned with an analysis of distribution), and that the account of production is then resumed in Book II. More than offsetting this incongruity, however, is the circumstance that Adam Smith broke new ground and made original contributions in the subjects of production and distribution to an extent incomparably greater than in the remainder of his work. His is the glory of being the first to propound in developed form certain fundamental propositions which have exerted the utmost influence upon the vast mass of subsequent economic literature, as in the instance of the division of incomes into wages, rent, and profits. Again he was the first to give extended treatment to many important

1776

subjects but cursorily touched upon hitherto ; for example, see his chapter on the wages of labor. Much may, and should be, overlooked in the novel investigations of one whose writings, no matter how confusedly worded, have started economic thought in new fields, and whose theories have subsequently received substantial confirmation.

Book II is primarily a rather detailed examination of one of the three elements, stock, which Adam Smith had declared in the first book to be one of the three factors in production, the other two being labor and land. In the first book, likewise, he had stated that the degree to which division of labor may be carried was limited by the extent of the market and the nature of the monetary system. Carrying the argument a step farther in Book II, he held that division of labor was also limited by the amount of stock accumulated, and was, indeed, proportioned to that amount, because such accumulation, "must, in the nature of things, be previous to the division of labour," and thus "labour can be more and more subdivided in proportion only as stock is previously more and more accumulated."

Not only the amount of business, but even the efficiency of each business enterprise was deemed to be proportioned to the accumulation of stock. Briefly, the point which he endeavored to drive home in this book was that in division of labor the functions of the capitalist and of the employer (the business enterprizer) were of the utmost importance. Wealth came from labor, and the better labor was organized the greater the amount of wealth created. Capital, made possible through saving and directed by the employer, was the force, he affirmed, which set the productive machinery of society in motion by furnishing laborers with the necessary food, tools, machinery, buildings, etc., and determined its efficiency. These notions, regardless of their truth or falsity, were revolutionary contributions in his day.

After asserting, in the first chapter, that stock, whether individual or social, was of two kinds — that reserved for immediate consumption and that, secondly, which was so employed as to yield a revenue, and which he termed capital, he turned to a rather detailed scrutiny of capital under the two heads of "fixed" and "circulating." Then, in a notable and lengthy chapter on money, "the great wheel of circulation," in which occurs an able discussion of banking, paper money, and foreign exchange, he maintained that money, unlike other forms of capital, was an item of actual expense to society. Thus the gain arising to society from the substitution of paper money for the precious metals was explained in a happy metaphor, comparing the use of gold and silver to a highway on the ground and that of paper money to a wagon-way through the air.

Proceeding next to a study of the accumulation of capital, he was moved to draw a somewhat unfortunate distinction between productive and unproductive labor. Productive labor he termed that which resulted in the creation of "vendible" commodities or of a higher vendibility; unproductive, that which, however useful, did no more than render services. Under the latter head he classed "menial servants," "the sovereign," and "all the officers, both of justice and of war, who serve under him, and the whole army and navy," and also "churchmen, lawyers, physicians, men of letters of all kinds, players, buffoons, musicians, opera singers, opera dancers, etc. . . Like the declamation of the actor, the harangue of the orator, or the tune of the musicians, the work of all of them perishes in the very instant of its production."

Of much greater significance, in the same third chapter, were his remarks upon the influences which determine the magnitude of the capital fund of society. Capital was the result of saving. "Capitals are increased by parsimony, and diminished by prodigality and misconduct." Every frugal man was a public benefactor, and every prodigal a public enemy. What was annually saved was as regularly consumed as what was spent, but by productive instead of unproductive laborers, so that the value of their consumption was reproduced with a profit. Novel and constructive were these propositions, especially in that day and age!

Interest.— In the fourth chapter, he discussed interest and interest rates, censuring, as many others had done before him, the popular connection of the rate of interest with the amount of money in circulation (instead of with the demand for and supply of capital), and arguing, somewhat mistakenly, for the fixation of a legal rate by law.

Was Smith a physiocrat?— In the fifth and concluding chapter on "The Different Employments of Capitals" he tried to ascertain the amount of productive labor which a fixed amount of capital would set in motion in the various branches of production. Observing that in agriculture little or no capital in the form of raw materials was required, since the soil took the place of these, and that the amount of capital in the form of tools and machinery was less than in any other employment, proportionately to the number of laborers employed, he concluded that "no equal capital puts into motion a greater quantity of productive labour than that of the farmer." "In agriculture," he stated (and in agriculture he included all extractive industry), "nature labours along with man," and accordingly a surplus arises which makes possible the payment of rent. In agriculture alone, moreover, did nature actively co-operate with man,— an idea previously expressed in the final chapter of Book I on the rent of land. Next in order of productiveness came manufacturing, then wholesale trade, and lastly retail trade. Thus was revealed in his argument a large part of that marked infiltration of physiocratic doctrine which has ever since led not a few commentators to the opinion that at heart he was a physiocrat.

Having formulated in the first two books the general economic doctrine around which endless discussion was to revolve in succeeding decades, Adam Smith turned in Book III — the shortest by far of all the five books — to a brief consideration of "The Different Progress of Opulence in Different Nations." Here occurs the longest of the many historical studies in which *The Wealth of Nations* abounds,— studies for which his predilection and training had well prepared him. In four short chapters he sketched the history of European industry and agriculture, dealing with the factors which, in his opinion, had stimulated or retarded the growth of national wealth. He protested throughout, however, that social policy had in many respects been an entire inversion of "the natural course of things," according to which course "the greater part of the capital of every growing society is, first, directed to agriculture, afterwards to manufactures, and last of all to foreign commerce."

Government and business.— With Book IV, "Of Systems of Political Economy," Adam Smith addressed himself to the third and final phase of his task. With discussion of the relation of economic progress, first of all to labor, and secondly to capital, completed as to its main outlines in the first three books, he began in the fourth book that lengthy and penetrating analysis of the relation of government to economic progress which served to bring his argument to what he deemed a logical conclusion. Book V, "Of the Revenue of the Sovereign or Common Wealth" may thus be looked upon as the proper continuation of Book IV. Not alone an extension of division of labor and the right employment of capital on land, but also the helpful co-operation of the government with the activities of business men was essential, in his judgment, if an advance in economic progress and an increase in the wealth of nations were happily to take place. While the fifth book was constructive in tenor the fourth book was primarily a work of destruction. In it he delivered the most devastating polemic unleashed up to that time against mercantilism (or the commercial system, as he sometimes phrased it). Mercantilism was, to be sure, a dying institution in Great Britain when he attacked it, but his indictment aided mightily in undermining there its last vestiges of authority, and has ever since exercised a potent influence, for weal or woe, on subsequent economic legislation in many parts of the world.

In brief, he raised his voice in favor of economic liberty. He proposed the maximizing of wealth through a minimizing rather than a maximizing of governmental interference with business. In place of government-planned economy he called for the removal of legal obstacles to the exercise of private initiative,— for a policy which has since then often been dubbed the "be quiet" or "sit down" program. In stating this viewpoint he was, to be sure, in no sense original. Many previous thinkers had pleaded for the abolition of tariff walls and of all forms of monopoly, and for the production of those commodities, only, within a country for which that country was best adapted. At that very time, in fact, the physiocrats in France were ardently championing a policy of laissez-faire. Ideas of industrial liberty were in the air, so to speak, on the continent, in Great Britain, and elsewhere.

Hostility to mercantilism.—Adam Smith's belief in the superiority of individual initiative over governmentally supervised enterprise as the proper method of promoting national prosperity was based in no manner upon the results of statistical investigations, since that method of procedure was not open to him. In his day every important country in the world was pursuing, at least theoretically, a policy of mercantilism, and such statistical data as were available were both scanty and none too reliable. He came by his opinion, on the contrary, by contemplation of what he saw about him.

He observed, as time passed, the increasing disintegration of the mercantilist régime, as ever growing numbers of his countrymen disregarded economic legislation which ran counter to their own private interests. He observed, for instance, craftsmen successfully pursuing this or that trade without having served a prescribed apprenticeship, or engaging in trades forbidden to them by law, or evading regulations laid down by the government with regard to the scale of wages paid to and the number of hours worked by employees. He observed merchants and, indeed, virtually all classes of people involved in a system of smuggling goods duty free into Great Britain to an extent that now hardly seems believable. He observed, furthermore, a tacit acquiescence on the part of many legislators in the breakdown of a policy to which theoretical allegiance was still the rule throughout the country. In promulgating his belief, accordingly, he found the minds of energetic enterprisers already prepared for his formula, because it assured them that in reality what they were doing was not at all wrong but rather wholly desirable from their own standpoint and that of the nation as a whole.[2]

Assumptions about human nature.—The basis for his conclusions lay in his assumptions concerning the character of human nature, assumptions by no means novel nor wholly discarded even today. He took it for granted, in the first place, that "the uniform, constant, and uninterrupted effort of every man is to better his condition." In other words, every man is a Scotchman at heart. "Every individual," he stated, "is continually exerting himself to find out the most advantageous employment for whatever capital he can command. It is his own advantage, indeed, and not that of society, which he has in view. But the study of his own advantage," he added, "naturally, or rather necessarily, leads him to prefer that em-

[2] W. C. Mitchell, Unpublished Manuscript.

ployment which is most advantageous to the society. . . He is in this, as in many other cases, led by an invisible hand to promote an end which was no part of his intention. . . By pursuing his own interest, he frequently promotes that of the society more effectually than when he really intends to promote it."

He assumed, in the second place, that every man is his own best judge in the employment of his time and labor. "Every individual, it is evident, can in his local situation judge much better than any statesman or lawgiver can do for him. The statesman, who should attempt to direct private people in what manner they ought to employ their capital, would not only load himself with a most unnecessary attention, but assume an authority which could safely be trusted, not only to no single person, but to no council or senate whatever." The logical conclusion to these two premises followed soon after in one of the most celebrated passages in the entire book : "All systems, either of preference or restraint, therefore, being thus completely taken away, the obvious and simple system of natural liberty establishes itself of its own accord. Every man, as soon as he does not violate the laws of justice, is left perfectly free to pursue his own interest in his own way, and to bring both his industry and his capital into competition with those of any other man or order of men. The sovereign is completely discharged from a duty, in the attempt to perform which he must always be exposed to innumerable delusions, and for the proper performance of which, no human knowledge or wisdom could ever be sufficient ; the duty of superintending the industry of private people, and of directing it towards the employment most suitable to the interests of society."

The rôle of competition.—Such was the "invisible hand" made famous by Adam Smith, that divine and miraculous agency which automatically would reconcile the self-interest of the individual with the prosperity of the community were but natural tendencies permitted a free rein. On one score, however, he had no illusions. Believing in the innate selfishness of business men, he saw no way of protecting the public against their extortionate practices but by the widest possible application of business competition. Automatic control of industry through competitive prices, he believed, would compel enterprisers to produce and trade in those commodities which the people wanted and would thus actually turn the control of production and commerce over to consumers. The offering of goods at lower prices or of goods of better quality at the current price by some producers would effectively nullify, in his opinion, the efforts of the more unscrupulous producers to profiteer at the expense of society through the exaction of higher prices.

As to the welfare of employees in a régime of economic liberty he was by no means so hopeful. Mindful of the fact that the single-handed wage earner labors under a great disadvantage in bargaining with his employer, and yet convinced of the social desirability of high wages (in striking contrast to the low wage doctrines of mercantilist thinking), he put his trust somewhat haltingly in the throwing open of occupations to the free choice of all.

Economic liberalism.—Adam Smith is without doubt the most noted exponent in history of that great body of economic theory which has come to be known as economic liberalism. The three major principles of economic liberalism are : personal liberty ; private property (defended on the ground that it secures the most desirable utilization of wealth) ; and individual initiative and control of enterprise. The maintenance of liberty requires a laissez-faire policy of government, the activities of which should be reduced to a minimum, in order that a nation may be supplied with the greatest possible amount of goods and services. Adam Smith was no mere doctrinaire in this matter, however. Laissez faire to him did not connote, as many have assumed, the entire absence of governmental restrictions on business.

He recognized the duties of the sovereign as the following : "first, the duty of protecting society from the violence and invasion of other independent societies ; secondly, the duty of protecting, as far as possible, every member of the society from the injustice or oppression of every other member of it, or the duty of establishing an exact administration of justice ; and, thirdly, the duty of erecting and maintaining certain public works, and certain public institutions, which it can never be for the interest of any individual, or small number of individuals, to erect and maintain ; because the profit could never pay the expense to any individual, or small number of individuals, though it may frequently do much more than repay it to a great society." In this latter category he had in mind such undertakings as the building of roads and canals, the improvement of harbors, and the furnishing of free education to those unable to pay for it.

Other measures of governmental interference likewise met with his approval, since he was very definitely a patriot, aware that economic interests must on occasion be sacrificed to those essential to the defense of a country. Defense, he asserted, was of more importance than opulence, and thus he favored the protection of English shipping afforded by the Navigation Acts and stood for taxes on the importation of such a commodity as saltpeter in order that a nation might be self-sufficient in time of war. In addition, if taxes were placed on goods produced at home, corresponding taxes should be levied on imports of these goods, thus removing the burden that would otherwise fall upon home producers. In line with this argument was his justification of the granting of temporary monopoly privileges to companies undergoing great risks in enterprises which promised in the long run to redound to the prosperity of a nation.

It would not be fair to take leave of Adam Smith without mention of his matured conviction on two matters of utmost significance. With rare good sense he held that the sudden and universal promulgation of economic freedom would prove both harmful and impossible; looking far into the future, he contemplated the probable rise of a civilization in which considerations of public health or of public morals might call for limitations of the principle of laissez-faire far greater than those which he deemed proper for the European countries of his day.

His views on physiocracy.— Two more topics considered in Book IV remain for the briefest of discussion. In the last chapter (chapter nine) of this book, curiously entitled "Of the Agricultural Systems, or of those Systems of Political Economy which represent the Produce of Land as either the sole or the principal Source of the Revenue and Wealth of every Country" he proceeded to a criticism of the doctrines of physiocracy much more concise and much less damaging than that which he had hurled in the previous eight chapters against the tenets of mercantilism. Agreeing with the physiocrats in his denunciation of such measures of the mercantilists as elaborate regulation of industry, monopolies, fixation of wages and prices, commercial treaties, drawbacks, bounties, embargoes, and high tariffs, he likewise agreed with the physiocrats in stressing the greater productivity of the extractive industries over all others. Whether or not, in accepting the essence of physiocracy, he ranked himself with the physiocratic line of thought will doubtless long be a matter of controversy.

The consumer.— Tucked away toward the end of chapter eight, finally, is a short reference to a field of economics, consumption, which has only begun to come into its own in present-day literature. For an untold number of centuries the pressing economic problem of mankind has been that of an increase in production, by reason of chronic shortages in the necessities of life, so that ample justification exists for the failure of thinkers until comparatively recent times to pay extended attention to the subject of consumption. To the great credit of Adam Smith, although the idea was borrowed from the physiocrats, he recognized the great importance of the part played in society by the consumer. "Consumption is the sole end and purpose of all production ; and the interest of the producer ought to be attended to only so far as it may be necessary for promoting that of the consumer. The maxim is so perfectly self-evident that it would be absurd to attempt to prove it." This dictum is today no less valid than when stated in *The Wealth of Nations*. In truth, consumption stands at the head of the whole economic system, and there can be no more fundamental need of business than a fuller understanding of the principles of this particular branch of economics. To anyone who looks beneath the surface, it should be perfectly obvious that those businesses thrive best in the long run which adapt their products and their services most successfully to the known wants of consumers.

Taxation.— In the fifth and concluding book, "Of the Revenue of the Sovereign or Commonwealth," Adam Smith examined the economic functions of the state and inquired into the effects on the wealth of a nation of the expenditures made by governments and the methods by which its revenues were raised. Book V is in reality the concluding portion of a thesis begun in the fourth book that economic progress depends in last analysis upon proper co-ordination of the activities of gov-

ernment with those of business men. There is little original
in the three lengthy chapters of this final book, yet much that
is suggestive and constructive. Opposing the long accepted
view that the Crown land should be drawn upon as a principal
source of public revenue, he centered his attention upon the
use of taxes alone. His famous four rules (or canons) of
taxation,— to be found, by the way, almost word-for-word in
some of his French predecessors, are probably the best known
feature of this book. In language deservedly admired, he
prescribed the essentials of a just system as consisting of taxes
(a) levied according to the ability of those called upon to
pay them, (b) characterized by certainty in amount, (c) levied
at the time or in the manner most convenient for the contributors, and (d) so contrived as to be as economical in collection as possible. Specifically, he held that the most desirable basis of taxation was rent, rather than wages or profits,
thus inclining to the position upheld by the physiocrats.

Business men and landowners were to be reached by means
of taxes on luxuries. He strongly urged the replacement of
the then prevailing system of innumerable taxes on production
and importation by the levy of a few taxes, only, on such commodities as wines, alcohol, sugar and tobacco. That England
followed these words of advice during the course of the nineteenth century is a tribute to his reasoning such as has seldom
been granted to any thinker. The last chapter closed the case
on a lofty plane with a brilliant presentation of the disastrous
effects of an abuse of public credit.

Summary.— Such, all too briefly stated, are the leading
points in the great work of Adam Smith — the most influential
treatise ever written in that province of knowledge now designated as economics — influential not alone in the development
of thought, but in the shaping of public policy in many parts
of the world. Rather curiously, however, those portions of
The Wealth of Nations which nowadays are most assiduously
perused (often, unfortunately, under the whiplash of the college instructor), were not the parts to which his contemporary
readers tended to turn. Their interest was not so much in his
discussion of certain technical doctrines like value, wages, rent
and profits, as in what he had to say about practical problems
of more or less immediate moment. Economics, it must be

remembered, has concerned itself throughout most of history with the discussion of problems closely allied to everyday life, such as poor relief, labor policy, just price, lending at interest, and the like.

Thus *The Wealth of Nations* was written for the ordinary man, not for the specialist in theory. Although the principal task of the author was to hasten the overthrow of the economic system then prevalent, the chief merit, perhaps, of the work is that it envisaged the economic world of ordinary men to a degree not reached up to that time, and gave a considerable measure of unity and system to a veritable host of miscellaneous ideas. His writing was but an attempt to rationalize what he saw and felt about him. It was, further, an "inquiry" into the nature and causes of the wealth of nations, a modest endeavor to contribute to a fuller understanding of the numerous problems with which his generation was confronted.

That the industrial world of his day was in many respects vastly different from that of our times has frequently been commented upon. Adam Smith, writing on the eve of the industrial revolution, lived in the midst of that stage of capitalist enterprise which has come to be known as the "domestic system." On the continent the gild system still continued in the towns and cities, and agriculture retained by a wide margin its supremacy over all other occupations. In Great Britain, however, industrial and commercial development had progressed to a considerable extent. The noteworthy circumstance in industry was that the craftsman had rather generally ceased to be a merchant and had become a maker of goods only. The worker, speaking generally, was no longer an independent manufacturer working directly with the consumer, but merely a laborer executing orders for a newly arisen merchant class that supplied the materials on which he worked and at times the workplace and machines as well. Craftsmen had degenerated into mere wage earners, and the direction and control of industry had definitely passed into the hands of capitalist employers differentiated both from employees and landowners.

It was of this domestic system that Adam Smith wrote, and it is of this system that he is by far the leading theorist as he is the most outstanding of the earliest interpreters and defenders of capitalistic enterprise. We have no right to seek in his pages for an explanation of the vexing problems forced upon the world of today by the onrush of the factory system. Enough that he is the central figure in the development of economic thought, and that withal *The Wealth of Nations*, designedly limited to a consideration of only the material side of life, remains an imperishable landmark in the history of human thought.

CHAPTER VI

FROM ADAM SMITH TO DAVID RICARDO

THE Europe of Adam Smith's day, despite many remarkable advances in civilization occasioned by the passage of human society from the medieval age to modern times, was a Europe, very broadly speaking, in which life went on much as it had for countless previous generations. Notwithstanding daring explorations and colonization in distant regions of the globe, a tremendous growth in commerce, the emergence of capitalism, the rise of a middle class, and the renaissance of science, the material culture and spiritual outlook of the average person had undergone but little transformation. Existence continued to be narrowly hemmed in by custom and tradition. The vast majority of the population lived on the land in abysmal ignorance of developments going on beyond the horizon of their provincial isolation. Education was of a most rudimentary sort and confined to the upper classes ; newspapers were few ; travel of any sort was the exception.

Industrial Revolution.— From this placid existence to the rush and roar of contemporary civilization is the story of changes in the manner of living brought about by changes in the making of a living of a truly stupendous character. To an almost unbelievable degree improvements in methods of production and communication and new types of industrial organization have so revolutionized ways and means of living that the marvels of today would appear miraculous to men who lived two short centuries ago could they now view the spectacle. In recent decades the term "Industrial Revolution" has been applied by Arnold Toynbee, English economist, and others to these revolutionary changes as they affected England during the three or four decades before and after 1800. Still other scholars have so broadened the conception of this term as to call this "revolution" a continuation, merely, of trends in technique and organization in Europe visible as early as the seventeenth century, embracing all the economic changes since then which have created the material culture of the present.

Hence in this latter sense, every new technical discovery and every new factory furnishes evidence that the Industrial Revolution still flows on in an ever deepening stream. Viewed very broadly, therefore, the Industrial Revolution may be looked upon as comprising three phases : (1) changes in the technique of manufacturing, transportation, and communication, involving the growing substitution of power-driven machinery for hand tools ; (2) the rise of the factory system and the consequent shift from small-scale production in the home to large-scale production in the factory ; and (3) reactions of the new technology and factory system upon the entire civilized world.

Technology and society.— These reactions have been most diverse and startling. An enormous increase in production, commerce, and wealth has occurred ; vastly improved transportation has tapped raw products and markets hitherto inaccessible ; new and larger banking and credit institutions have appeared ; novel forms of large-scale industrial organization with monopolistic tendencies have emerged ; mass consumption has strikingly developed ; agriculture has abolished the open fields and commons of the Middle Ages and has become increasingly scientific ; machines and factories have hastened the triumph of capitalism ; the distinction between labor and capital has grown apace. On the social side, the population of the world, growing at a rate unknown in any earlier period, has about doubled since 1800 ; urban communities have shown a phenomenal growth ; internal and international migrations from backward regions have occurred on an unparalleled scale.

In a cultural way, the average person has gained immeasurably through the widespread development of free public education, of newspapers, books and magazines, lectures and concerts, and the radio. Politically, the middle class has risen to power in the great majority of industrialized nations, its ascendancy threatened in recent years, however, by dictators on the one hand, and socialistic states, on the other. It is indeed a world such as Adam Smith could never have dreamed of.

English pre-eminence.— Nor in 1776 would a reasoning person have ventured to predict for England the unexampled development which she was about to experience. The smallness of the country precluded any extensive growth in agriculture. Manufacturing still implied making things by hand, and England was no more favorably situated than France or Belgium, her leading competitors, to develop manufactures by hand processes. Her iron and coal mining industries were in a state of depression. France, by far the strongest power on the continent, was much larger in area and three times as populous. Yet it was in England, in the seventeenth and eighteenth centuries, that the pioneer work in industrial transformation began.

Not until the close of the Napoleonic wars (1815) did the Industrial Revolution leap across the English Channel to France, and not until the middle of the nineteenth century did that country, together with Belgium and Holland, definitely industrialize. Several decades later, the Industrial Revolution was systematically introduced into Germany (1871) and Scandinavia. In other parts of Europe, such as Spain, Italy, Austria, the Balkans and Russia, the new forces were not felt to any great extent until 1900. In remaining portions of the globe, outside of those countries not yet touched by its mighty advance, the revolution did not make its appearance until comparatively recently, except that in the United States a real foothold was secured as early as 1815. Throughout most of the nineteenth century, therefore, England led the world in economic matters. The position of the United States as the industrial leader of the world, due largely to iron and coal deposits larger than those of all Europe combined, and to an abundance of other raw materials, is a phenomenon of the twentieth century. Hence it is but appropriate that the earliest theorists of the new industrial system should, and did, appear in England where the Industrial Revolution began.

Reasons for England's advance.—Conditions in England, contrary to what might have been expected, made her particularly ripe for the impending change. In the first place, the results of the Commercial Revolution were more deeply felt there than on the continent. Serfdom and the gild system, with its application of the "closed-shop" to labor, gave way to the domestic system sooner in England than elsewhere. The spirit of freedom was likewise manifest in the early abolition of customs barriers between towns, and in a state of religious security which made her a veritable haven of refuge for skilled workers from other countries. Geographical isolation, plus supremacy on the seas, rendered her free from foreign aggression. Her markets abroad were large and constantly expanding. Large reserves of coal and of iron ore existed. A damp climate was favorable to textile processes. Her scientific activity had a practical bent. Her surplus capital far surpassed that of other countries, for England had become the leading commercial nation.

In the second place, the Political Revolution of the late seventeenth century (1688) marked the end of absolutism and the beginning of parliamentary government at least a century prior to the evolution of representative government on the continent. England's business men and investors thus could free themselves of capricious royal interference with their activities long before their rivals abroad were able to do so. And lastly, the Agricultural Revolution, a movement that started in England and that still persists in advanced countries, so augmented the productivity of agriculture as to make possible both a vastly increased urban population and the huge supplies of raw materials required by innumerable factories.

British agriculture.— Down to the eighteenth century, agriculture remained throughout Europe backward, primitive and medieval. But few crops were grown; the yield per acre was small; the "three-field" system kept one-third or more of the land idle each year; crude wooden plows, sickles and flails were the chief tools employed; the infrequent farm animals were small in size. Beginning early in the eighteenth century a series of improvements by gentlemen farmers in England was destined to raise agriculture to the level of a science. New farm implements were invented by Jethro Tull, more especially the seed drill and the horse-drawn cultivator. Somewhat later, Lord Townshend introduced crop-rotation; he had discovered that planting of turnips and clover made possible the use of land every year. Judicious changing of crops in successive years has been found to be as effective in maintaining the fertility of the soil as allowing the acreage to remain fallow, and naturally makes for much larger yields.

Later on, Robert Bakewell introduced revolutionary improvements in stock-breeding. By selecting only the best animals for breeding he speedily increased the weight of horses, cattle and sheep. Drainage of waste land, mixing of soils, and improvements in fertilization all aided in the transformation of agriculture, knowledge of which was spread through the agricultural press and by such widely travelled men as Arthur Young. The rise of large estates intensified the trend toward capitalistic farming. By 1800, there were three agricultural classes in England ; (a) the landed aristocracy, comprised mostly of those who had become rich in commerce ; (b) the renters ; and (c) the agricultural laborers. Ownership of land had already passed to comparatively few men.

British inventions.— The outburst of inventions in England, from shortly after 1750 onward, is chiefly attributable to the Commercial, Political and Agricultural Revolutions which had in a sense prepared the way for the Industrial Revolution. English economic society needed only a slight push or shock to crystallize in a new form, a push supplied by inventions in the textile industry in response to a rapidly increasing foreign demand. The inventive genius of Hargreaves (1764), Arkwright (1769) and Crompton (1779) in the development, respectively, of the spinning jenny, the water frame, the spinning mule, and of Kay (1738) and Cartwright (1784) in the perfection of power weaving, introduced mechanical inventions first in the cotton manufacturing industry, and much later, after the new machinery had proved itself, in the woolen industries.

The improvement of the steam engine by James Watt in 1785 furnished factory owners with power that gradually supplanted that supplied by animals or water. This improvement made possible great advances in the iron industry, and in the fabrication of iron machines and of machine tools. Advances in one line naturally caused advances in another. The need for cheaper and more rapid methods of transportation was met first by improvement of roads, by building a network of canals, and by the development of steam locomotion. With the demonstration by Stephenson, as early as 1814, of the practicability of the steam locomotive, the Industrial Revolution was launched on its irresistible course.

Classical economics.— This digression emphasizes the fact that, in the generation or so subsequent to the publication of *The Wealth of Nations,* economic conditions in England underwent decided change, thus creating new and pressing problems which called for fresh attempts at analysis. Moreover the repercussions of the French Revolution and the Napoleonic Wars, with all the enormous ensuing social, political, and economic changes, made evident the need of a thorough revision of economic theory. Just as mercantilism was engendered, in part, by the Commercial Revolution (the rise of modern trade) and physiocracy, in part, by the Agricultural Revolution (the rise of capitalistic farming), so the English classical economics was born from the combined effect of the Industrial Revolution in England and the gigantic upheaval in France.[1] Changing phenomena naturally stimulate economic thought.

Jeremy Bentham.— But some attention must first be given to the potent influence of one who, although not regarded primarily as an economist, must yet be classed as one of the most important and earliest members of that school of economic thought which is now variously designated as classical, Ricardian, English, or orthodox. Most influential of the immediate successors of Adam Smith, Jeremy Bentham (1748-1832), contemporary of both Adam Smith and Ricardo, and intellectual leader of the English school of utilitarian philosophy, was the outstanding representative of a group of reformers called the philosophical radicals. Possessed of great natural abilities, he attended Oxford University, receiving the B.A. and M.A. degrees before he was twenty. Trained for the law, he soon found its practice most distasteful, and turned to a life-long examination of the fundamentals of social philosophy.

Inherited wealth allowed him to occupy himself exclusively during the remainder of his eighty-four years with the problem of the welfare of mankind. His literary production, including unpublished material, was prodigious. His earliest writings were terse, but as he grew older, he tended toward over-elaboration. Some technical terms which he coined, such as "utilitarianism," "minimize," and "codification" have considerably enriched our language. Curiously enough, he appears but rarely to have written on a basis of study or presentation of fact. His works specifically in the field of Economics were *Defense of Usury* (1787) (in which he took Adam Smith to task for favoring the enactment of a maximum legal rate of

---

[1] Peck, *Economic Thought and its Institutional Background*, p. 50.

interest) ; *Protest against Law Taxes* (1795) ; *Observations on the Poor Bill of Mr. Pitt* (1797) ; and *A Manual of Political Economy* (1798).   His most significant contributions, however, were in government and law.   A *Fragment on Government* (1776), published anonymously, was followed by *An Introduction to the Principles of Morals and Legislation* (1789), a book which today is frequently assigned reading in college courses dealing with philosophy or sociology ; this book contains the most systematic formulation of his general principles.   Other volumes are *Theory of Pains and Recompense* (1811), *Treatise on Judicial Evidence* (1823), and *Judicial Organization and Codification* (1823).

Bentham and the social sciences.— Deeply impressed by the methods which scientists like Sir Isaac Newton had worked out in the physical sciences, Bentham set for himself an astonishing goal in those subjects now called the social sciences.   He dreamed of developing a science of human behavior applicable to jurisprudence, politics, economics, education and even religion.   This science could be erected, he thought, by measuring the forces which control society, much as the physical sciences rest upon accurate measurement.   These controlling social forces, in his opinion, were pleasure and pain.

The first paragraph of *Introduction to the Principles of Morals and Legislation* reads in part as follows : "Nature has placed mankind under the governance of two sovereign masters, pain and pleasure.   It is for them alone to point out what we ought to do, as well as determine what we shall do. . . They govern us in all we do, in all we say, in all we think ; every effort that we can make to throw off our subjection will serve but to demonstrate and confirm it. . . The principle of utility recognizes this subjection and assumes it for the foundation of that system, the object of which is to rear the fabric of felicity by the hands of reason and law.   Systems which attempt to question it, deal in sounds instead of sense, in caprice instead of reason, in darkness instead of light."

Hedonism.— This was his celebrated "principle of utility," or, in other words, hedonism.   Desire for pleasure and dislike of pain, he said, are the two sole motive forces of human conduct ; individuals are governed by a calculated balancing of pleasures and pains.   Ideas of pleasure or of pain were supposed to present themselves to the human will; the will, in case of indecision, handed on the problem to the understanding. The understanding thereupon calculated the amount of pleasure in prospect and decided accordingly in favor of action or inaction. If action was decided upon, and the proper means selected, the will became dominant and translated thought into deeds.

In measuring pleasures and pains, he had resort to his famed "felicific calculus," by which he hoped to turn the moral disciplines of his day into real sciences. Pleasures and pain were believed to possess seven different dimensions or qualities, differing with respect to intensity, duration, certainty, propinquity (by comparison with remoteness), fecundity (from the standpoint of increasing the capacity for future enjoyment), purity (the degree to which the pleasure is mixed with pain), and extent (the number of individuals participating, no one person being counted as any more important than any one else).

This calculation of pleasures and pains was most complicated, since each of the seven dimensions had to be reckoned in units peculiar to itself. As to whether the feelings of different people are really comparable — a most debatable issue — Bentham decided in the affirmative. And, finally, in seeking a common denominator whereby to compare all sorts of pleasures and pains, he concluded that the only common measure was money. Many decades later, the great Alfred Marshall likewise declared that in terms of money alone can people measure the force of motives. Later on, economists in various parts of Europe added to the "felicific calculus" the idea of marginal increments for purposes of comparison, and thus introduced refinements but not fundamental alterations in the classical political economy.

Hedonism and laissez-faire.— This conception of human nature was adopted wholeheartedly by his contemporaries, to the exclusion of any other psychological theory; it has ever since been widely prevalent. He further maintained that happiness consists of the presence of pleasure and the absence of pain,— a principle previously enunciated by Hutcheson, Beccaria and Priestley among others. Social institutions should accordingly be contrived so that the greatest happiness for the greatest number should result. This was his famous statement of the utilitarian ethics. His chief efforts were devoted to the formulation and propagandizing of this doctrine. He argued that all government has been established by force and is perpetuated by habit. Urging that to increase the national happiness "nothing ought to be done or attempted by government" he voiced his oft-quoted rule of government : "Be Quiet." He averred that, "without some special reason," government action in economic matters was both needless and pernicious, because every law was an infraction of liberty, involving restraints upon individuals, and "pain is the general concomitant of the sense of restraint." Like the economic liberals, therefore, he favored unrestricted competition and the enlightened self-interest of the individual as the chief channels through which the utilitarian program might be attained.

Reforms.— Yet to "Benthamism" can be traced, at least in part, most of the reforms accomplished during the early part of the nineteenth century in Great Britain. Although advocating the abolition of restrictive legislation, he and his followers nevertheless urged positive reforms, more especially the education of the masses (in order to improve their calculation of pleasures and pain), safe-guarding of public health, a new poor law, and prison reforms. He became indeed an ardent reformer, hostile to every artificial social distinction. Believing that the happiness of any one person, no matter how humble his status, was fully as important as that of any other person, he favored a more equal distribution of wealth ; other things being equal, he said, such a redistribution would increase the sum total of happiness throughout the world. Yet his views changed with time. Horrified by the devastation wrought by the French Revolution, he became, in his closing years, a staunch believer in the sanctity of private property.

Bentham will ever be remembered for his phrasing of the "greatest happiness" principle : "the greatest happiness of the greatest number, that is the measure of right and wrong." He held that the social sciences are useful only as they contribute to an understanding of how pleasure may be obtained and pain avoided. Unfortunately, and tragically, he failed to observe what people were actually doing. Only recently have cautious inquirers adopted the procedure — now looked upon as wholly obvious — of carefully observing how individuals act under all sorts of circumstances, before attempting to generalize about human conduct.

Immediate successors of Adam Smith.— For several decades after the publication of *The Wealth of Nations* in 1776, no economist of first rank appeared in Great Britain or elsewhere. Adam Smith's contemporaries and close successors tended, in the main, to acknowledge the doctrinal supremacy of that mighty work, busying themselves merely with criticism of certain of his theories or with descriptive or historical writings. Rarely has an economic treatise gone unchallenged by theorists in the degree accorded *The Wealth of Nations* in the long period from 1776 to the presentation in 1817 by David Ricardo of a markedly new type of economic theory. All too readily might one infer that these forty-one years were so dominated by the genius of Adam Smith as to be comparatively barren of worthwhile economic writings, always excluding the contributions of Bentham and the investigations of Malthus, in the domain of population. Patient research has effectively demonstrated, however, that this was a period of immense activity; not a few original scholars aided considerably in paving the way for later theorists.

In pure economic theory, Lord (James) Lauderdale (1759-1830), Scotch nobleman, author of several monographs and of a short book entitled *An Inquiry into the Nature and Origin of Public Wealth and into the Means and Causes of its Increase* (1804) was probably the most independent thinker in Great Britain during this period, except for Bentham and Malthus. In a spirit thought by some commentators to be somewhat carping, he charged Adam Smith with faulty reasoning on several fundamental issues. He criticized the "eminent philosopher" for his broad generalization that the wealth of a nation is the sum total of the wealth of the individuals in that nation, by pointing out that it can never be to the interest of society as a whole to promote a scarcity of a commodity, though the individual may increase his wealth by so doing. This distinction rests upon the difference between economic value and economic welfare, and suggests a lamentable antagonism, rather than an affinity, between public and private interest. Further, he challenged the notion that social wealth is best increased by parsimony (saving); parsimony, he said, might result in overproduction of capital and underproduction of consumable commodities. His observations upon value, capital, distribution, and the nature and importance of consumption displayed unusual acumen.

Lauderdale's teacher was Dugald Stewart, successor of Adam Smith and Adam Ferguson in the chair of moral philosophy at Glasgow College, and the first man in Great Britain to deliver a separate course of lectures on political economy (1800). Many of Stewart's students, including Francis Horner, Sydney Smith, and Thomas Chalmers, became figures of importance in the early formulation of classical political economy. Other theoretical writers aided in this task, among them James Anderson, Colonel Robert Torrens, Sir Edward West, and John Rooke.

Beginnings of Socialism.— The momentous changes under way at this time were responsible for a great deal of descriptive, historical, and controversial literature. Much of this was stimulating to constructive thought. Marshall, Sinclair, and Arthur Young dealt with practical problems of agriculture; Lord Sheffield wrote voluminously on trade and commerce; Pinto published a brilliant *Essay on Credit,* and hundreds of tracts discussing government finance poured from the presses when the Napoleonic Wars laid a crushing burden of taxation and public debt on the population of Great Britain. Suspension of specie payments by the Bank of England and abandonment of the gold standard by England toward the end of the eighteenth century, as the war against Napoleon presaged a long and indecisive struggle, were followed by a steep rise in prices and an outburst of pamphlets on the vexing question of the relation between credit and prices.

The increasing misery of the laboring classes called forth analyses of the social conditions of the day, including the impressive treatise by Eden on *The State of the Poor.* Thomas Paine, noted author of *The Rights of Man* (1791-1792), and whose works are still popular, endeavored to create a working-class movement for democratic reform. Finally, a group arose, known as "The Radicals," composed of men who today would be classed as socialists and anarchists. Inspired by the French Revolution, from which modern socialism may be said to date, they devoted their speculations to the nature and feasibility of a future ideal society. The leaders of this movement laid stress on the increasing poverty and misery of the masses, and asserted that defective human institutions were responsible for the desperate plight of the laboring class ; they vigorously pleaded for a more equitable distribution of wealth. Representative of this point of view were Condorcet in France and Godwin in England.

William Godwin, chiefly a political theorist, yet by some classed as an anarchist, and by others as the first scientific socialist of modern times, published in 1793 *An Enquiry concerning Political Justice* — a work in two volumes which soon attained wide circulation. Four years later, he restated many of his views in a volume entitled *The Inquirer.* Declaring that even the best of governments is an evil, he traced the evils of society to the viciousness of existing human institutions. Were all wealth equally divided, the institution of marriage discarded, and man freed from all restrictions save the moral censure of his fellows, the advancement of science, in Godwin's opinion, plus the influence of reason upon human actions, would in time so increase productivity as to enable each person to live at the cost of but half an hour's labor a day and likewise keep the population within available means of subsistence.

No new important concept can be discovered in this vision of a future state of society, based on the supposed perfectibility of man, yet Godwin's influence on the stream of economic theorizing has been pronounced. Many English socialists, such as Owen and Thompson, subsequently adopted several of his criticisms and theories. Yet one of the most epoch-making pamphlets in all economic literature appeared in 1798 and attempted to refute Godwin's picture of an age of human perfection. This pamphlet was anonymous. It was penned by a young parish clergyman named Malthus, and bore the voluminous title, *An Essay on the Principle of Population as it affects the Future of Society, with Remarks on the Speculations of Mr. Godwin, M. Condorcet and other Writers.*

Malthusianism.—Thomas Robert Malthus (1766-1834), most outstanding of economists in the period from Adam Smith to David Ricardo, came of an old distinguished English family. Soon after graduation from Cambridge University, he took orders in the established church and in 1797 became a parish

priest.   A year later the *Essay* appeared, the result of a series
of arguments with his father concerning the perfectibility of
man.   Overnight the pamphlet attained amazing prominence,
a prominence due not alone to its anonymity and the dismaying
tenor of its contents but to its compact size and timeliness.
Malthus vigorously denied that there were no limits to the
progress of mankind in happiness and wealth.   On the contrary an instinct implanted in man by nature was a well nigh
insurmountable obstacle to such progress.   The sexual instinct,
he averred, was scarcely susceptible of control either by reason
or by self-interest.   Thus even in the utopia envisioned by
Godwin, scarcity of means of subsistence (foodstuffs) would
sooner or later follow in the wake of increased numbers, the
age-long struggle for self-preservation would recommence, and
inequality in wealth would once more prevail.

This alleged tendency of population to increase faster than
the food supply was illustrated in a memorable formula.
Geometrical progression in the natural rate of increase of population was contrasted with an arithmetical progression in the
possible increase in the food supply.   He conceded that
population is necessarily limited by the means of subsistence ;
and that it invariably increases wherever the means of subsistence increase, unless the growth in population is prevented
by powerful checks.   There would seem to be only two such
checks.   These two checks he classified as *positive* (acting
through an increase in the death rate), including famine, war,
plagues, common diseases, intemperance, infanticide, cannibal-
ism, and the like, and as *preventive* (acting through a decrease
in the birthrate), chiefly the various vices which result in in-
capacity for parenthood.   Since these two checks on population
comprised the unavoidable misery imposed by nature and by
human nature, he concluded that the very characteristics of
population forever made impossible a state of perfection.

The *Essay*, as it appeared in 1798, was in no sense a scientific
treatise on population.   Nor was there any great originality
in this dashing polemic.   As Malthus himself observed, he had
merely worked out in detail and built into a principle dominating all human life the incidental remarks on this subject previously made by such writers as Wallace, Price, Hume, and
Adam Smith.   In any event, the pamphlet gave rise to an

almost unprecedented amount of discussion and precipitated a controversy the echoes of which have not yet died away. No doctrine has ever been more reviled or misinterpreted. Its most immediate and enthusiastic adherents were the employers of low-paid labor, since the theory seemed to imply, at least on the surface, that the poverty of the poor was of their own, or their parents', making. Low wages seemed to have their origin in the intensity of "the passion between the sexes" and the consequent superabundance of the population, thus absolving the propertied classes from all responsibility, and even ennobling them as benefactors of the human race.

Malthus, a man of kindly instincts, was prompted by the bitter attacks against his opinions to make extended researches, in the course of which he journeyed through France, Switzerland, Russia, and Scandinavia. A second edition of the *Essay* appeared in 1803 under his own name, enlarged to four times its former size, and devoted mainly to the marshalling of historical and statistical evidence in support of his theory. The book passed through four more editions in his lifetime, in all of which he endeavored to answer the leading objections raised by his opponents. In the second edition, published under the impressive title of *An Essay on the Principle of Population,* or *A View of Its Past and Present Effects on Human Happiness with an Inquiry into Our Prospects Respecting the Future Removal or Mitigation of the Evils Which It Occasions,* he modified his argument to the extent of adding a third check to the two checks of misery and vice adduced in his first edition.

Having noted the existence of many old bachelors and spinsters, obviously neither vicious nor in a condition of misery, he introduced the new element of "moral restraint" (that is, virtuous celibacy and postponement of marriage) as a method of controlling the birthrate through man's reasoning faculty. By this qualification he abandoned his previous denial of the perfectibility of man, in favor of an appeal to the intelligence of human beings to abstain from marriage as long as the necessary provision for a family of average size was lacking or could not reasonably be anticipated. To the end of his days, however, he continued to think of population as tending constantly to press ahead of the food supply and to view the future gloomily. His melancholy conclusions unfortunately were regarded by leading economists of his own and a later era as unanswerable. Belief in Malthusianism thus has led many a generous and high-minded person to refrain from advocating governmental intervention to improve the social and economic conditions of the laboring classes.

Malthus, although reasoning from imperfect observation, did economics the great service of raising population to the major place in economic speculation which it has ever since maintained. He opposed the mercantilist doctrine that the prosperity of a nation depends partly upon the population. He held, on the contrary, that population depends upon prosperity. Modern methods of production and agriculture, which he could hardly have foreseen, enabled the world's population to increase at a phenomenal rate during the nineteenth century. Yet in many parts of the world, as in Europe today, the food supply kept but little ahead of the added population. The general truths of the Malthusian theory seem to be irrefutable as a statement of broad tendencies.

In 1804 when nearly forty Malthus married (thus practising what he had preached), and the next year became professor of modern history and political economy at a new college at Haileybury, near London, created by the East India Company as a training school for employees. This chair of political economy was the first established in England. He retained his position until his death in 1834, thoroughly enjoying the life of a scholar and teacher. To his students he was affectionately known as "Pop."

Other works of Malthus.— In 1800 he had published anonymously a pamphlet entitled *An Investigation of the Cause of the Present High Price of Provisions,* a pamphlet foreshadowing the approach to economic problems which he was to develop in later years. In 1807 appeared a pamphlet on the Poor Laws, and in 1814 and 1815 *Observations on the Corn Laws.* In 1815, likewise, he published his trenchant *Inquiry into the Nature and Progress of Rent and the Principles by which it is Regulated and Ground of an Opinion on the Policy of Restricting the Importation of Foreign Corn.* In 1817 appeared *The Poor Law* and in 1820 his second book, *The Principles of Political Economy considered with a View to their*

Practical Application, a treatise which contained his matured opinions on economic theory.   His final publications were *Measure of Value* in 1823 and *Definitions in Political Economy* in 1827, neither of any great importance.

His intimate friendship with Ricardo, that began in 1811 and flowered in the most precious literary correspondence in the history of economic thought, is another significant phase of his life.   For ten years they were regular correspondents, stimulating each other's development by vigorous criticisms, all the more valuable since the two men were intellectual opposites.   These letters set forth the divergent lines along which economic reasoning might proceed in future.

To explain the new and extraordinary orientation in economic theory for which Ricardo was responsible, some attention now must be devoted to the background in terms of which Ricardo and Malthus and their contemporaries thought and wrote.   Economics set itself up as an independent science early in the nineteenth century.   It is highly important to note the problems that were put into the foreground by the writers of that time,—problems greatly different from those which confronted Adam Smith, and for which, naturally, there was no solution in *The Wealth of Nations.*   These new problems resulted primarily from far-reaching changes in British economic life ; the Napoleonic wars brought a revolution in production, exchange and distribution.

The French Revolution began in 1789.   Ten years later its force was spent and Napoleon Bonaparte rose to power with incredible rapidity.   For fifteen years he kept Europe in nearly continuous warfare.   During these long wars the perilous character of international commerce in grain, and government purchases of foodstuffs for soldiers and sailors greatly stimulated the demand for home grown grain.

In Great Britain, as in some other countries, much pasture land was converted into arable land, poorer and poorer soils were cultivated, and land already under cultivation was tilled more intensively.   In 1700 fully three-quarters of the inhabitants of the British Isles had been occupied with agriculture ; a surplus of food for export was produced.   A century later, the Industrial Revolution found the population engaged in agriculture reduced to about two-fifths of the total ; Great

Britain now depended upon foreigners for a not inconsiderable part of her food supply. Heavy taxation, mainly upon the newly-rich manufacturers and merchants, plus huge borrowings from the Bank of England, had to be resorted to by the government to prosecute successfully the war against Napoleon.

Effects of Napoleonic wars.— Because of the stimulus to domestic agriculture, and because of bad harvests at home, and of a large increase of money in circulation, there ensued a very marked rise in prices during this period. Increased prices, however, brought prosperity only to landowners, to the manufacturing and merchant classes, and to fortunate speculators. The working classes in no way shared in these new gains. If anything, workers wholly dependent upon money wages fell into ever deeper poverty. Agricultural wages, still determined by local justices of the peace, were rarely raised to meet the increased costs of living. The wages of the increasing army of factory and mine workers were kept down to a pitifully low level by severe competition for jobs and by growing employment of women and children. Scanty earnings were likewise the portion of those unfortunates who continued like their countless ancestors to work at home. Landowners and, to a much lesser degree, business men rode on the crest of the wave.

Chapter VII

DAVID RICARDO

Out of these practical issues developed a new political economy, the central figure of which was David Ricardo (1772-1823), destined to exert an influence upon the current of economic thought second only to that wielded by Adam Smith.

Biographical summary.— Born in London, the third child of a Hebrew immigrant from Holland who had prospered as a merchant and broker, he received but the rudiments of an elementary and commercial education before entering his father's business at the age of fourteen. His father was a member of the London stock exchange, and in this business the son soon exhibited exceptional ability and secured a type of training requiring the continual use of discriminating good judgment. A growing breach with his father in regard to parental discipline became absolute when he renounced Judaism, embraced Christianity, and at the age of twenty-one married a Quakeress.

His bold course justified itself within five years. Before he was twenty-six, aided in part by the backing of leading members of the exchange, he had made himself financially independent. From stockbroker he soon became a financier. A combination of business genius and opportunity made him within a few years one of the wealthiest men in all Europe. In 1816 he closed out his business, invested the bulk of his fortune in land, and settled down to the life of a country gentleman in the southwest of England. Eager to enter Parliament he bought his way in 1819 into the House of Commons through the purchase of a "rotten" Irish borough, becoming in a short time one of its most highly regarded members.

An independent in politics, he consistently championed programs at that time looked upon as radical. He was zealous for parliamentary reform, greater freedom of the press, Catholic emancipation, and a steep levy upon capital in order to reduce the greatly swollen war debt. With Malthus he was one of the original members of the Political Economy Club of London. His untimely death in 1823, at the comparatively early age of fifty-one, cut short one of the most talented careers in English history, distinguished by exceptional success in nearly everything to which he turned his attention.

Views regarding banknotes.—Ricardo was self-educated. In his middle twenties, once he had assured himself a competence, he resumed his study of mathematics and began to work somewhat systematically at chemistry, geology and mineralogy. In 1799, by the merest accident, he came across a copy of *The Wealth of Nations*. With awakened interest, he turned more and more to the economic inquiries which were increasingly to claim his leisure time. Instinctively an observer, he began to follow closely the rapidly increasing pamphlet literature on the economic questions of the day.

His first venture into print, in 1809, was in connection with a violent public controversy regarding the Bank of England banknotes, then by far the most important form of money in circulation in Great Britain. His tract, *The High Price of Bullion a Proof of the Depreciation of Bank Notes,* grew out of certain letters which he wrote to a London newspaper, in which he convincingly showed that it was not gold which had appreciated in value but paper money which had depreciated in value, and that the measure of this depreciation was the premium charged for gold.

This pamphlet on monetary theory attracted attention by its unusual method of argumentation. He might naturally have been expected to set forth in great detail all pertinent facts bearing on the situation, inasmuch as he was fully acquainted with the factual side of the controversy, and then to have drawn conclusions based on a summarization of these facts. But no! He began with a broad generalization concerning the distribution of the precious metals the world over, and throughout his pamphlet such facts as were cited were brought in merely by way of illustration. His natural bent for abstract reasoning, due possibly to his Semitic origin, was given full sway in his subsequent writings. This pamphlet met with popular favor. Its principles were incorporated in the report of the parliamentary Bullion Committee. Still greater publicity resulted from a second pamphlet on monetary theory, published in 1811, under the title of a *Reply to Mr. Bosanquet's Practical Observations on the Report of the Bullion Committee*. At about this time began the exchange of letters with Malthus, then recognized as the outstanding economist of all Europe, and friendships with Jeremy Bentham, James Mill, and others.

Upheaval resulting from Napoleonic wars.— Ricardo's next entrance into the economic arena was occasioned by heated public discussion regarding the reconstruction program to be adopted in Great Britain as the war against Napoleon neared its end. Her people faced problems such as are very likely to present themselves in any modern country after prolonged warfare. The public debt had reached unprecedented heights, suspension of specie payments still prevailed, taxation was heavy, the cost of living had risen out of all proportion to wage increases, landowners were fearful of a vast influx of foreign grain, and powerful manufacturing and shipping interests were clamoring for concessions. The corn laws aroused the most violent controversy of all.

For centuries, these "laws," consisting normally of duties on imports, and at times of government bounties on exports of grain, had existed in England. In England "corn" means any edible grain (wheat, oats, rye, barley, etc.). During the Napoleonic conflict the price of corn rose enormously ; war thus imposed an artificial barrier of protection against importations. With the surrender of Napoleon in 1813, agriculturists anticipated with alarm a threatened flood of cheap continental grain upon the domestic market, and took vigorous steps to safeguard their position of vantage. Somewhat plausibly they argued that their cause was indeed that of the general public. They emphasized the cost of improvements on both old and new land to which they had been put in order that the war requirements for grain might be met. For England to be dependent upon outside supplies, they argued, was most unwise. Artificial stimulation of agriculture would furthermore in time so increase the output that competition between farmers would ultimately result in lower prices. They therefore proposed an increase in the import duty on corn to a nearly prohibitive level.

Protest against tariff on grain.— Upon the introduction of a bill to this effect in both houses of Parliament, committees of inquiry were appointed to take evidence and report. A storm of protest from the business interests greeted these committees. Contending that high prices for corn meant high wages for wage-earners, and that high wages meant high production costs, business men asserted that a high tariff on corn would prevent them from successfully selling their manufactured products abroad in competition with the goods of continental employers not subject to equally high wage scales. Furthermore, various foreign countries had levied duties against the entry of British goods. Thus the corn law question divided Great Britain into two great hostile camps. An intense class struggle began between the agricultural landowners and the business men. Never before had the distribution of income been so sharply debated in theoretical discussion.

The maximizing of the wealth of nations was again in the forefront of discussion, as with Adam Smith and the mercantilists, but now somewhat more from the standpoint of the distribution of wealth than heretofore. Yet the social point of view did not loom large in this acrimonious dispute. Thinkers were still concerned primarily with ways and means of increasing either the wealth of the nation or the wealth of a particular group within the nation. It has remained for a later generation to analyze the various categories of the total social income with a view to their social justification or non-justification.[1]

In this burning question of the day, however, economists throughout Great Britain naturally took a very lively interest. Almost simultaneously, important publications from five men appeared; each wished to put his thoughts before the public, prior to a decision by the parliamentary committees.

First in the field were John Rooke with a series of articles in the *Farmer's Journal* during 1814 (continued in 1815), and Malthus with a pamphlet entitled *Observations on the Effects of the Corn Laws*. In 1815 appeared two other pamphlets by Malthus, entitled respectively, *The Grounds of an Opinion on the Policy of Restricting the Importation of Foreign Corn* and *An Inquiry into the Nature and Progress of Rent and the Principles by Which It Is Regulated;* an *Essay on the External Corn Trade* by Colonel Robert Torrens; an anonymous *Essay*

---

[1] W. C. Mitchell, Unpublished Manuscript.

on the Application of Capital to Land by Edward West; and, last in time, an *Essay on the Influence of a Low Price of Corn on the Profits of Stock* by Ricardo.

It matters little that a Tory (or Conservative) Parliament, still under the thumb of the landed interests, passed the Corn Law of 1815, providing for the exclusion of all foreign corn whenever the price at home was less than the prohibitively high price of eighty shillings the quarter (a quarter is eight bushels). Of much greater importance is the fact that the ideas which were to dominate orthodox economic thought throughout the world for the next half century were present in the little pamphlet of twenty pages submitted by Ricardo. His keen interest in current events led him to take a decided stand in regard to the momentous issue as to whether the landowners or the business men of Great Britain should receive favorable state action.

Diminishing returns in agriculture.—The five writers above noted agreed remarkably on two major points, although each one seems to have formed his opinion independently. Aware of the progressive resort to poorer and poorer soils, and of the increasingly intensive utilization of land already under tillage, which had characterized British agriculture during the preceding quarter century, they all emphasized the diminishing returns of agriculture. In other words, at any given time there is a point in the investment of labor and capital upon any fixed amount of land beyond which any further investment of labor and capital, even though yielding a greater total income, will yield a less than proportionate return to the units of labor and capital utilized. This was a doctrine by no means new. Indeed it was one of the fundamentals upon which Malthus based his principle of population, and is to be found in embryo in earlier English writings, in Turgot, the distinguished French physiocrat ("It can never be imagined that a doubling of expenditure would result in the doubling of product"), and in probably other authors.

Now for the first time this economic law was clearly stated. Economists have since learned that diminishing returns apply not alone to a fixed amount of land, but also to a constant number of laborers, a constant amount of capital, and an unchanging number of managers (enterprisers). As at present stated, the law of diminishing returns may be summed up as follows : at any given time there is a point in the investment of any three of the agents of production upon any fixed amount of the fourth agent, beyond which any further investment, although increasing the total return, will yield a less than proportionate return to the three agents which are applied to the fourth fixed agent.

Economic rent.—These five writers moreover expressed the belief that differences in productivity of soil explained the differences in the yield of land ; the term "rent," they held, might be applied to all the income from land over and above the income from the use of labor and capital on land. By "land" was meant all the resources of nature supplied by man's physical environment, including, for example, minerals, water power, and the fisheries. Economists nowadays are inclined to substitute the term "economic rent" for "rent" as employed by Ricardo and his contemporaries ; in common usage "rent" denotes the payment for the use of durable goods of any kind owned by another.

Be that as it may, Rooke, Malthus, Torrens, West, and Ricardo all maintained that much of the land in Great Britain was yielding a surplus to the landowner equal to the excess of the price of the produce of the land over the cost of production on that land. That surplus obviously was yielded by the better grades of land only, and tended to increase as the price of produce rose. This doctrine, likewise, was not original with any one of these five writers, since as early as 1777 a Scotch farmer named James Anderson had proclaimed in his *Observations on the National Industry of Scotland* a differential theory of rent, demonstrating that rent was a premium for the cultivation of the better soils (although it is true that he failed to grasp all the phases of the rent theory).

Malthus' ideas regarding rent.—Where Malthus and Ricardo parted company, however, was in the conclusions drawn from this concept of rent. Malthus, like Adam Smith, looked upon society as primarily an agricultural community. A true successor to Adam Smith, he viewed rent as the chief form of whatever surplus society was creating, and the rate of increase in this surplus as the true index of national progress. Agricultural produce, he averred, unlike any other commodity, generated its own demand. Other commodities were not necessarily in demand after production, and thus, if produced in abundance, tended to sell at a low price per unit. But food, in his opinion, was a demand for population, and hence the reason for the high price of food lay in its abundance and not in its scarcity, as would have been the case with all other goods. Rent should therefore be regarded as an increase in the sum total of the wealth of society. It was a spontaneous gift of nature to the owners of the best land, diffused in time, furthermore, among other classes of the population.

"The grand object of all inquiries in Political Economy," he stated, was "the causes of the wealth and poverty of nations." High rents were the best possible evidence that a country's land was fertile, that its agricultural products were abundant and that the nation was in truth wealthy. Consequently he favored a high tariff on the importation of corn into Great Britain in order that the British Isles might continue to enjoy the prosperity which was then their portion. If it seem strange that Malthus looked with disfavor on grain imports, and yet regarded death by famine as the inevitable fate of a considerable part of the human race, it must be borne in mind that in his opinion famine conditions within a country could be much better averted by government protection to agriculture than by exposing that country to the vagaries of unregulated competition. Adam Smith himself might have come to this very same conclusion, in spite of being a strong believer in free trade, had he lived to view the changing environment of the early nineteenth century.

Ricardo's ideas on rent.— To Ricardo, on the contrary, society presented itself in a much different light. Whether or not he was the genius that many have pictured him, he correctly predicted that England's future prosperity was to rest, not on agriculture, but on the proper development of capital. Like Malthus he worked from the concrete and actual economic facts, but unlike Malthus he broke with Adam Smith and the physiocrats in regard to the relation of nature to the wealth of nations. He denied emphatically that nature co-operates with man in the process of production. Rent, he stated, far from being a free gift of nature to mankind, was much rather striking evidence of her lack of generosity, since it came into existence only "when the progress of population calls into cultivation land of an inferior quality or less advantageously situated."

In other words, rent arose within a country not by reason of the liberality of nature, but of her niggardliness. Rent was not creation of new wealth, to be retained by landowners without detriment to other classes of society, but simply a deduction from the wealth of others. What the landed interests gained others lost. These others must be either the business men of Great Britain or their employees.

Views regarding wages and profits.—It could not be the employees, because their wages were a fixed quantity, determined by their customary standard of living. Wage-earners, he thought, tended to receive in wages just enough to enable them, "one with another, to subsist and perpetuate their race, without either increase or diminution." If the market rate of wages were temporarily to rise above this "natural" price of labor, a stimulus to the growth of population would ensue and increasing competition of employees for jobs would in time cause the rate of wages to fall. The poverty of the masses was of their own making. Their wages tended to correspond closely to the cost of the commodities which they consumed. The main cost of their maintenance was the price of food, more especially since the progressive application of division of labor constantly tended to reduce the price of such manufactured goods as they required (clothes, for example).

Granted, then, that the chief burden of the employer was the cost of the food supplied to his employees, a rise in the price of food, thus necessitating the payment of higher wages, would inevitably cut down the profits of the employer. Profits were thus the "leavings of wages." What the landed interests gained through high rents was lost by the employer class and by no other. Food was high in price because of the increasing cost of providing food for Great Britain's growing population ; high prices for food meant high wages for wage earners ; high wages for wage-earners meant decreased profits for employers. He concluded that wages and profits varied inversely to each other. Profits fell as wages rose, and could not rise unless wages fell.

Industry advocated rather than agriculture.—It were far better, concluded Ricardo in this brief analysis of industrial society, that national prosperity be thought of in terms of industrial rather than agricultural prosperity. The progress of the Industrial Revolution in Great Britain, he reasoned, made it possible for Britishers to manufacture goods at a lower cost per unit than was possible on the continent. It was accordingly wise for England to devote her energies more and more to industry, and to export her manufactured goods in exchange for grain grown more cheaply abroad, in countries more adapted to efficient agriculture than the British Isles.

The chief, and perhaps the only, obstacle to the fulfilment of this program was the high cost of food in Great Britain, result. ing in high costs to business men. If the duty on the importa. tion of corn were abolished, the necessity of resort to poorer and poorer soils would be obviated, the price of food would drop considerably, business men would no longer face impoverishment, profits would rise to their former high level, and England would prosper. In effect, although the conclusion must be implicitly drawn, he argued for a redistribution of wealth in order that an augmentation of Great Britain's wealth might take place. To his credit let it be added that, even after the transfer of the bulk of his fortune from securities to land, he remained as implacable an opponent of the corn laws as previously. It is one of the delightful anomalies of economic literature that Ricardo, landed proprietor, fought the battle of the capitalists against Malthus, defender of agricultural protectionism in an institution of higher learning maintained by a trading corporation. The intellectual integrity of both men is beyond question.

Ricardo's first book.— Chagrined by the disappointing reception accorded his *Essay on the Influence of a Low Price of Corn on the Profits of Stock,* Ricardo set about working up this tract in more extended form, hoping in a much larger manuscript to make himself more intelligible to his circle of friends. This labor of composition was interrupted somewhat by the preparation and publication early in 1816 of a pamphlet opposing the monopoly powers of the Bank of England in the issue of paper money, under the title of *Proposals for an Economical and Secure Currency, with Observation on the Profits of the Bank of England.*

Early in 1817 (or possibly late in 1816) this task was completed. He had re-read Adam Smith, Malthus and several contemporary writers, not bothering, however, to examine the writings of the physiocrats or mercantilists. Ricardo was in no sense a scholar like Adam Smith or Malthus. Of history, for example, he knew little and cared perhaps less. It was hardly to be expected of him, any more than of present-day industrial leaders, that business genius should unite with meticulous scholarship. Nor did he concern himself with statistics or the gathering of materials of any sort. Feeling that he already had his subject well in hand, he was convinced of the validity of his premises, and proceeded on the basis of that assumption.

Very reluctantly he consented to the publication of his manuscript. He had in no way intended to write a book. Furthermore, he clearly recognized his deficiencies as a writer, and feared that the awkwardness of his style and his abstract reasoning would repel readers and endanger his reputation as an economist. But the insistent pressure of friends and of James Mill in particular finally wore down his resistance, and in 1817 his assemblage of notes and memoranda appeared in print as *The Principles of Political Economy and Taxation*.

Much to his surprise, a second edition was called for in 1819, and a third was published in 1821, by which time he stood unquestionably at the head of economic science in Great Britain. The book has since become an economic classic. His remaining important publications were an article on *The Funding System*, contributed in 1820 to the Encyclopaedia Britannica; a pamphlet published in 1822 on *Protection to Agriculture*; and a pamphlet, issued shortly after his death in 1823, called a *Plan for the Establishment of a National Bank*. His lengthy and illuminating correspondence with Malthus has recently been published under the editorship of Professor Hollander of Johns Hopkins University.

Poor literary quality.—Although all of Ricardo's writings are significant, his chief title to fame rests upon the *Principles of Political Economy and Taxation*, a volume now perused chiefly, it may be assumed, by college and university professors and the hard-pressed students under their jurisdiction, to whom it is prescribed reading. This book, if indeed it can be called such, cannot honestly be described otherwise than as bad or indifferent writing. The befogged reader looks in vain for an integrated plan, or for a single instance of the beautiful passages with which *The Wealth of Nations* abounds. Not one illustration graces the fewer than three hundred pages of this formless treatise, and "ifs" and "supposes" are sprinkled liberally throughout.

It is in truth one of the amazing paradoxes of economics that Adam Smith and Malthus, with academic backgrounds, wrote in a practical and sprightly fashion, while Ricardo, the man of affairs, wrote as if living in a world of abstractions. Various explanations have been offered. Mention has been made of his connection with the London stock exchange, in which post he found it necessary to resort frequently to the nicest of calculations. The topic of money in its relation to foreign trade, upon which he wrote his first pamphlet, lent itself peculiarly, furthermore, to the subtleties of the abstract method. The unusual capacity of the Jewish race for deduction has likewise been cited. And finally he wrote, not for the ordinary man, as Smith had done, but for a small group of special friends already conversant with masses of business facts.

Outline of his Principles.—The *Principles of Political Economy and Taxation* comprises a preface and thirty-two chapters. About one-third of the chapters deal with problems of taxation. Others treat of the various aspects of trade, both domestic and foreign, of bounties, currency and banks, and machinery. The remaining chapters, fewer than ten in number, discuss value and distribution. Thus Ricardo covered a much narrower range of topics than Adam Smith. There is no discussion of production as such, no reference to the underlying significance of consumption, no sketch of the history of economic institutions, and but little evaluation of the contributions of other economists. His particular attention was naturally devoted to the redistribution of wealth and income, inasmuch as he believed this to be the gravest economic problem confronting the people of Great Britain.

As he himself declared in the original preface : "To determine the laws which regulate this distribution is the principal problem in Political Economy." An inquiry into the nature and causes of the wealth of nations, he thought, was useless, because such an investigation would cover the quantity rather than the proportions of wealth. Whatever be the truth of this assumption, he declared that there were three factors in the production of wealth — land, labor and capital, corresponding to the three great social classes of the time, namely, landowners, wage earners and capitalist-employers. The share in the products of industry going to landowners was rent ; to wage earners, wages ; and to business men, profits.

Before analyzing these three shares, he devoted his first chapter (the longest in the book) to a discussion of value, a topic concerning which he never succeeded in putting on paper a statement entirely to his satisfaction. He considered that value was in no way related to distribution. Modern economists, on the contrary, tend to regard value and price as the central theme in their economic analysis of society, and to regard rent, wages and profits as prices ; prices of any kind belong in the general category of value problems.

Ricardo, like Adam Smith, began by distinguishing between value in use (the modern "utility") and value in exchange. Value in use, he asserted, was absolutely essential. (Obviously, if a thing is not wanted by some one, it will have no power in exchange.) But Ricardo added that he saw no way of measuring or determining value in exchange from the standpoint of whatever power a good might have to satisfy human wants. With Adam Smith, therefore, he approached the problem of value in exchange from the side of the seller, rather than the buyer, of goods, and his analysis is one of sellers' costs. Values in exchange, he continued, were of two sorts : market value and natural value. The former was determined at any instant by the temporary conditions of the demand for and supply of goods in the market. Natural value was that which would exist with no disturbances in market conditions. It was to natural value alone that he turned his attention.

The exchange value of commodities he declared to be due either to scarcity or to the quantity of labor or capital required to obtain them. Scarcity was caused by the fact that certain commodities were no longer reproducible (for instance, "scarce books and coins"). The exchange value of goods in this comparatively unimportant group was determined solely by demand and supply. The second class of commodities comprised goods which might be multiplied "without any assignable limit."

These freely reproducible commodities, he said, exchanged for each other in no certain ascertainable fashion.

Note Ricardo's language : "Besides the alteration in the relative value of commodities, occasioned by more or less labour being required to produce them, they are also subject to fluctuations from a rise of wages, and consequent fall of profits, if the fixed capitals employed be either of unequal value, or of unequal duration." [2] Here is no labor theory or labor quantity theory of value, as many readers of his *Principles* have erroneously surmised. He expressly stated that commodities will have relative values different from their relative labor costs, if labor and capital are employed in different proportions in the production of these commodities. Value depends on changes in the rates of wages paid and the rates of profits received, assuming no change in relative labor costs. This is a cost-of-production theory, with rent expressly excluded.

As to the disturbing circumstance that labor is not of the same quality (compare the labor of the ditchdigger with that of the symphony conductor) he argued that "the estimation in which different qualities of labour are held soon comes to be adjusted in the market with sufficient precision for all practical purposes," and that in the case of the same commodity, over a period of time, variations in quality of labor might be disregarded. He was never satisfied, however, with his explanation of the perhaps unsolvable problem of value ; shortly before his death he acknowledged most creditably his failure adequately to deal with this fundamental question.

Views regarding distribution.— With relief Ricardo must have turned to the much more congenial task of analysing distribution. The chief problem then facing the economist, he believed, was the determination of the proportions in which the national income was shared among landowners, laborers and capitalists. This problem he attacked by propounding a law of rent, a law of wages, and a law of profits applicable at a given time and, in addition, three more laws of distribution governing the long-run trends of rent, wages and profits, not to speak of collateral propositions designed to explain differences in rent, wages and profits in different branches of employment. His doctrine of rent is the one most inseparably

[2] Ricardo, *Principles of Political Economy and Taxation*, first ed., p. 23.

connected with his name. Rent, he argued, determines the proportions which labor and capital receive. Accordingly, after disposing of value in his first chapter, he turned to rent in chapters two and three, reserving for the fifth chapter a discussion of wages and for the sixth his treatment of profits. To his great honor, by the way, he laid no claim to having originated the doctrine of rent, hailing Malthus, although erroneously, as its discoverer.

Rent theory.— Rent is "that portion of the produce of the earth which is paid to the landlord for the use of the original and indestructible powers of the soil." A very restricted definition! The ordinary person thinks of rent, in connection with land, as a payment not alone for the use of land but also for the buildings and other improvements upon it. Next, at great length, Ricardo considered how rent, as he defined it, arises. There are three causes of rent: First, the differences of natural fertility between different soils; secondly, differences of situation with relation to the market (a point which he made but incidentally); and finally, differences in the yield of labor and capital, not on different land, but on the same soil over the course of time, by reason of the law of diminishing returns. The *quality* of land was stressed rather than its location, and only farm land was taken into account.

Two major premises were laid down: (a) desirable farm land exists in strictly limited quantities, and (b) population normally presses upon the food supply (the Malthusian principle). Thus rent is simply the differential return exacted by landowner from tenant because of the superior fertility or more advantageous location of his land. In technical language, rent is the value of the produce yielded by a piece of land over and above what a similar area of the poorest land in cultivation would yield with a like outlay of labor and capital. The unfortunate would-be tenant had no choice. His was the option of working on poor (no-rent) land and of eking out a living, if that, or of paying rent for the use of better land and still only making a bare living, since competing tenants, speaking generally, stood ready to pay the landowner the rent demanded. All gain went to the parasitic landowners, who rendered absolutely no services in return for that part of the produce which they avariciously seized. Worse still (and this was his long-run law of rent), rent tended to rise inexorably as increasing wealth and population necessitated resort to ever inferior land and the more intensive tillage of land already utilized.

Wage theory.—Ricardo next turned to the explanation of wages. At any given time, the price paid by employers for the services of wage earners was held to depend on the proportion between the demand for and supply of labor, or, more exactly, between the accumulated fund of capital and the number of wage earners. This market price of labor tended constantly toward its natural price, due to the Malthusian principle of population; the natural price was simply that fixed by the minimum cost of production of laborers. Over long periods *real* wages (that is, the purchasing power of the money earned by laborers) tended to remain constant, fixed by a rather inflexible standard of living,—a doctrine reminiscent of Turgot's bare minimum of subsistence standard.

Inadequate as Ricardo's laws of rent and wages may appear to the twentieth century reader, his law of profits seems even less satisfactory. Modern economists endeavor to explain profits on independent grounds. Not Ricardo, however. To him it seemed perfectly obvious that with the annual income divided into three parts, and with rent and wages already explained, whatever was left over constituted the profits of the capitalist. The rate of profits thus depended on the rate of wages, since landowners tended inexorably to take to themselves an ever larger proportion of the total annual produce. There was no possible way for profits to grow except at the expense of wages. As he expressed it : "profits depend on high or low wages, wages on the price of necessaries, and the price of necessaries chiefly on the price of food." Money wages tended constantly higher because of the rising cost of food, although real wages remained fairly constant, and hence inevitably the rate of profits tended to fall. Improvements and discoveries in machinery and in agricultural science, it is true, checked this tendency at repeated intervals, but could never eliminate it.

Other doctrines of Ricardo.—Such is the merest outline of those doctrines of Ricardo with which his contemporaries most concerned themselves and regarding which violent controversy has ever since raged. In other economic fields he made contributions equally illuminating and more enduring.

Yet because these other contributions have, in the main, gone unquestioned by later theorists and have become part of the large body of generally accepted economic truths, his claim to deathless fame must be said to rest principally upon his views regarding value and distribution. In the present brief volume we cannot discuss Ricardo's notions regarding the incidence of taxation, nor his masterly analysis of international trade, in which he improved upon Hume and others in formulating both the "law of comparative advantage" and the laws that normally govern the international distribution of the precious metals. Regretfully, too, we refrain from discussing his exposition of the quantity theory of money or his championship of a banking system operating only through a government owned bank. Never did his eminently practical genius display itself more brilliantly than in his treatment of these pressing problems of the day.

Environment significantly influenced Ricardo in the formulation of his theories. His work rested on certain assumptions, most, if not all, of them borrowed. For instance, he accepted Turgot's law of diminishing returns and the principle of population as expressed by Malthus. Again, he regarded the social organization of his time as fully mature and stabilized. True, he looked forward to the remote day when "the progressive state," as he termed his era, would degenerate into "the stationary state,"—one in which population would no longer increase and capital would no longer accumulate. But even in that stationary state he visioned no substantial change; in his opinion any substantial departure from the capitalistic order would be for the worse. He deplored the existence of irreconcilable class conflicts, and yet firmly believed that the substitution of communism or socialism for capitalism would so diminish the amount of employment as to leave the mass of the people worse off than ever.

The chief trait of human nature was the calculating pursuit of self-interest; Ricardo thus held the same notion of human nature which Bentham had done so much to popularize. His conception was not so inflexible as Bentham's, yet he was convinced that to depart from the capitalistic order would be to leap from the frying pan into the fire. Certain acquired habits and ingrained instincts in landowners, wage earners and capitalists effectively barred the way to that increase in general welfare which he so earnestly desired.

Pecuniary basis of modern society.— At the core of Ricardo's economics, is the connection which he stressed between the cost of food and the rate of profits. The overshadowing problem of the relation of production to distribution he handled in a scholarly manner far surpassing any previous attempts. Whatever be his defects in analysis, he at least had the vision to recognize, beyond all others of his age, that the business man had become the center of the economic system. Nowadays the pecuniary character of modern life is rather self-evident. Such was not the case in the early decades of the nineteenth century. He is justly famed for pointing out that the modern system centers around the exchange of goods and services for money prices. He indicated the terms, in other words, in which the business man thinks, stressing the vast importance of the subject of price in all economic life. Whether a merchant or manufacturer is to survive in the competitive struggle depends upon the relation between his costs (wages paid to employees, outlays for materials and so on) and the prices which he is able to get for his products.

Ricardo saw this issue, perceived that prices are no mere playthings of chance, and strove manfully to delve beneath the surface confusion. That most of the edifice which he erected has long since crumbled before the onslaughts of later criticism is not to be denied. What must be emphasized is that Ricardo pioneered in the analysis of the price arrangements which the factory system had engendered, and that all serious study subsequently of the economic theory of that system goes back to the Ricardian doctrines.

Summary.— Indictment of Ricardo is easy. His theory of value was no real improvement over that of Adam Smith ; he failed to see that there are differentials (now commonly called "quasi-rents") as well in wage payments and the earnings of capitalists as in land rents ; his treatment of profits was most rudimentary ; he made but a faint distinction between interest (the return to the capitalist) and profits (the income of the employer above all costs) ; he did not comprehend the true relation of wages to profits ; he overrated the functions of the capitalist and the business man. His theory of distribution replaced the harmony of interest of Adam Smith's scheme with a natural diversity of interest between wage earners and their employers, on the one hand, and between landowners and all other classes of society, on the other. His conception of human nature was faulty; his view of the future markedly pessimistic. His writings constituted a veritable arsenal from which Marx and others gratefully pillaged their siege guns of socialist argument.

Yet despite shortcomings in exposition, Ricardo's contributions to the evolution of English economic thought make him seem like a giant among pigmies. An immortal pioneer, who dissected economic phenomena in the light of his own experience, he started a new train of speculative thought, extraordinary for its persistent survival long afterwards.

CHAPTER VIII

FROM RICARDO TO JOHN STUART MILL

IN HIS later years Ricardo associated himself with that remarkable group of reformers known as the philosophical radicals. Notable in this group, in addition to Jeremy Bentham, its central figure, were James Mill and George Grote, the historians ; Joseph Hume and Sir Samuel Romilly, members of Parliament ; Lord Chancellor Henry Brougham ; John Austin, leading authority in jurisprudence ; and prominent journalists, literary figures and others. Somewhat previously there had arisen an even more radical group sometimes referred to as the early philosophical radicals, which had included such eminent authors as Wordsworth, Shelley and Byron. Toward the middle of the century the work of these loosely knit organizations was continued by the later philsophical radicals, most renowned of whom was John Stuart Mill, son of James Mill.

The economic theory of that day was by no means the conservative body of doctrine which it now seems. Ricardo and contemporary economists were regarded as radicals, and very dangerous radicals at that, by the vast majority of intelligent Englishmen. With fellow philosophical radicals they made use of all agencies, aside from affiliation with either of the two great political parties, the Tories and Whigs, in their effort to effect sweeping reforms in the social life and government of Great Britain. The influence of the philosophical radicals cannot be said to have been a dominant one, except occasionally, in the passage of reform legislation ; but the assertion is warranted that the economists of that age were men who were much more than economists, men, indeed, who may justly be characterized as practical reformers.[1]

Economic reforms.— Reform legislation may be said to have been initiated with the factory acts of the early part of

[1] W. C. Mitchell, Unpublished Manuscript.

the nineteenth century. The Tory (Conservative) party, composed primarily of landed proprietors, joined forces somewhat with the reformers on this issue, in the belief that the profits of manufacturers would be reduced if the hours of factory work were shortened and better working conditions introduced. Workers' organizations, frowned upon for centuries and actually outlawed by the so-called Combination Laws of 1799 and 1800, received tacit recognition in the repeal of these Laws in 1824 and 1825, although fifty more years were to elapse before these organizations became legal entities.

Repeal of the Corn Laws was finally accomplished in 1846 under the leadership of Sir Robert Peel, after a stirring campaign of seven years carried on by the Anti-Corn Law League, of which Richard Cobden was the dominating spirit and manufacturers were the financial supporters. This campaign convinced a reluctant Tory Parliament of the necessity of cheaper food for Great Britain's rapidly growing industrial population. By 1869 protection was completely abandoned, and free trade held sway until 1931, when England returned to a protective system.

In the extension of democracy lay the most far reaching British reform of the nineteenth century. In 1800, England could by no stretch of the imagination be called a democratic country. Only property-holders could vote ; certain religious qualifications were in effect ; no reapportionment of seats in the House of Commons had been made since 1664, with the result that many "rotten boroughs" existed and several new and large industrial cities were unrepresented ; the House of Lords dominated the House of Commons. England was ruled by the nobility and the landed interests.

Agitation for reform gained its first victory in 1828 and 1829 when religious qualifications were removed. The Reform Bill of 1832 extended suffrage to the middle classes, and redistributed seats in the House of Commons. The Reform Bill of 1867 further reduced property qualifications, thus enfranchising most of the factory workers. In 1872 the secret ballot was adopted. Another Reform Bill in 1884 extended the suffrage to the majority of agricultural laborers. A new reapportionment of seats followed in 1885. The veto power of the House of Lords was emasculated in 1911, all property qualifications for men were removed, limited suffrage was granted to women in 1917, and women were finally placed on the same suffrage footing as men in 1928.

Many other illustrations of reform could be mentioned, all of them a series of changes in the direction favored by the philosophical radicals. Penny postage for letters was introduced in the eighteen forties ; the Bank of England was reorganized in 1844 ; special taxes on newspapers were discontinued in 1861; and the establishment of elementary schools was begun in 1870.

Heyday of economics.— The prestige of economics during the fifty odd years following the publication of Ricardo's *Principles* was immensely enhanced by the adoption of many reform measures advocated during that period, more especially by the repeal of the Corn Laws in 1846. Seldom has the economist won such popular favor or wielded such authority as in those particular years. Professorships in political economy were established at Oxford University in 1825, at Cambridge University in 1828, and shortly afterwards in Dublin and Edinburgh. Economists were consulted by the government on the drafting of new statutes, were appointed to royal commissions, and occasionally took government posts,— forerunners, in a mild fashion, of latter day "brain trusts." Orthodox economic doctrines were preached from the pulpit. Popularizing was carried on through lectures, newspapers, pamphlets, and innumerable small textbooks, not to speak of works of fiction, such as those of Harriet Martineau, which endeavored, in their telling, to point some economic moral.

The acme of the ridiculous was reached in assertions by overenthusiastic devotees that the principles of political economy were simple enough to be understood by children still in the nursery. The writings of Adam Smith, Malthus and Ricardo were republished in other English-speaking countries, and translated into numerous foreign languages. Finally, the other social sciences, such as jurisprudence, psychology, anthropology and history, leaned upon economic doctrine to an extent never before or since experienced for authoritative stimulus and guidance. The situation was truly unprecedented. Economics was in its heyday.

Unorthodox murmurs.— Despite the immense popular success of the Ricardian propositions, economics as a science made but relatively little progress in Great Britain in well nigh half a century following the publication of Ricardo's *Principles of Political Economy and Taxation*. This is not to imply that this period was sterile. On the contrary, theoretical issues and contemporary problems of the day called forth a flood of pamphlets, monographs and books whose treasures were hardly suspected prior to the opening of the twentieth century; further study of these is still bringing rich rewards to the painstaking student of the history of economic thought. Particularly has the period from 1820 to 1848, long spoken of as the Dark Ages of English political economy, been found to be one of the most fruitful periods in all economic literature.

During these years many a writer appeared whose views anticipated much that has had to be rediscovered and redeveloped in more recent generations. A few examples at random will suffice. John Craig objected strenuously to the Ricardian doctrine of the opposition between wages and profits. Samuel Bailey held that business men would reap larger gains if high rather than low wages were paid to employees. Percy Ravenstone was the first to propound the surplus value theory immortalized by Karl Marx. Samuel Read stressed the fact that employers have obligations to society as well as rights. Mountifort Longfield clearly expressed the marginal idea as applied both to utility and cost. Above all, the Oxford professor, W. F. Lloyd, in a pamphlet entitled *A Lecture on the Notion of Value* (1834) put forward for the first time what is nowadays termed the "marginal utility theory of value," one of the most significant and firmly established doctrines in the economic thought of the civilized world.

But views such as these were not in accord with those of the dominant school and they fell on deaf ears. Rarely indeed were any of the unorthodox publications vouchsafed even the favor of a reading, and their authors soon sank into an ill-deserved obscurity. Thus did Great Britain, home not only of classical political economy but of most of the unorthodox theories now incorporated in it, reward those of its sons who ventured to blaze new trails in the forest of economic science.[2]

Popularity of orthodox school.—Explanation of the long continued dominance of orthodox economics must be sought on several grounds. As a program of economic reform the doctrine of free trade made a powerful appeal to an ever growing number of the thinking population of the British Isles. Not only economic but political factors entered into this point of view. Then, as now, there existed people who believed that nations should specialize in and exchange those commodities in the production of which they are best fitted, and that the resulting dependence of country upon country would lessen the danger of war. Of more importance was the taking over of the classical theories by the merchant and manufacturing classes in their rise to dominance by the middle of the century.

These two classes made a practical political issue out of the social theorizing of Adam Smith and Ricardo ; once in politics, orthodox doctrines gradually ceased to be looked upon as hypotheses applicable to a given set of circumstances, and more and more hardened into an inelastic finality. The history of the protective tariff in the United States since the Civil War affords an admirable illustration of the tendency of certain business interests to call upon economic law for the justification of a position once defensible upon the "infant industry" basis of reasoning.

Absence of skepticism.—Of even greater influence, probably, was the absence of a critical attitude toward the conclusions of Adam Smith, Malthus and Ricardo on the part of the vast majority of the people who interested themselves in economics during this period. Whenever confronted with facts contradictory to these conclusions, they answered usually that economics dealt with tendencies or assumptions, that the logic which had built up these tendencies and assumptions was beyond reproach, and that if facts were at variance with the theory laid down by the masters, it simply meant that the facts were but temporary deviations from that theory. Ricardo had stated, for instance, that business profits were tending

[2] *See* "Some Neglected British Economists," by E. R. A. Seligman, *Economic Journal*, Vol. 13.

toward a minimum. When he made that statement, the available facts seemed to warrant it. Could he have seen the rapid development of steam railways after his death, a development that was in time to create huge profits more than offsetting the losses incurred in the building and operation of canals, very probably he would have restated his theory of profits.

But the economists who followed him did not, in the main, possess his humility and power of discernment. They worked in a rather unrealistic fashion, ignoring Malthus' example of reaching conclusions by means of personal observation and gathering of statistics, and preferred merely to restate in a rigid form the doctrine that had come down to them. Turning their backs on reality and the investigations of their unorthodox fellows, they failed to come to grips with the problems of their generation as Adam Smith, Malthus and Ricardo before them had endeavored to do.

With the death of Ricardo ended the first era of the classical period. The tradition was carried on in Great Britain by a large number of writers, to only a few of whom may attention be directed. James Mill (1773-1836), father of John Stuart Mill, intimate friend of Ricardo, and author of a *History of British India,* published in 1821 the *Elements of Political Economy* in which he dryly and sternly summed up the orthodox doctrines under the four significant heads of production, distribution, interchange and consumption. The Scotchman, John Ramsay McCulloch (1789-1864), prolific, but unoriginal author and noted biographer of Ricardo, represented, with James Mill, the quintessence of English classicism in his *Principles of Political Economy* (1825). Colonel Robert Torrens, Richard Whately, archbishop of Dublin, Ireland, and Thomas De Quincey reformulated the postulates of their predecessors.

N. W. Senior.— But of all the orthodox representatives who followed Ricardo and preceded John Stuart Mill, first place must be accorded Nassau William Senior (1790-1864). Educated for the legal profession, he became a famous lawyer. Professor of political economy at Oxford University from 1825 to 1831, and again from 1847 until his death in 1864, he served actively on several royal commissions. He traveled widely on the continent, meeting in the course of his travels most of the great men of Europe. To his contemporaries he was known more as a social reformer than as an economist. He gave freely of his strength and ability in championing a considerable increase in governmental interference in such matters as health, housing and education. Besides several volumes dealing with his travels, of particular interest because they relate his conversations with many eminent Europeans, he published many small works on economic subjects. The principal book which appeared during his lifetime was *An Outline of Political Economy* (1836), first published as an article in the Encyclopaedia Metropolitana.

In 1928, many economists thrilled to the publication in two volumes entitled *Industrial Efficiency and Social Economy* of original manuscripts by Senior, the existence of which had gone unsuspected until recent years. To the unflagging industry of Mr. S. Leon Levy, a graduate student at Columbia University under Professor E. R. A. Seligman, and to the generous co-operation of Mr. J. St. Loe Strachey of London and his wife, Senior's granddaughter, we are indebted for the unearthing of a large portion of these valuable documents, which reveal the matured thinking of the author on the general principles of economics. Volume I deals with the purpose, scope, and method of economic science; political economy and the art of government; classification, nomenclature, and definition; human wants and the pursuit of wealth; production of wealth; the nature, functions, origin, and growth of capital; and the pressure of population on the means of subsistence.

Volume II treats of value, cost, and price; money, credit, and exchange; domestic and foreign commerce; the distribution of social income; and government control and social progress. These volumes afford additional evidence of Senior's remarkable powers of critical analysis. Without question he was the most brilliant and original of all the many members of the classical school who came after Ricardo, not even excepting the much more celebrated John Stuart Mill.

Senior's four postulates.— Senior maintained that economics is an abstract and objective science and nothing more. The business of the economist, he stated, is not to show men how to be happy or virtuous, but merely how they may become rich. Economics should have nothing to do with morals or with legislation, but should confine itself to the study of the nature, production, and distribution of wealth.

In line with this idea that the sphere of economics should be strictly limited and that the economist should confine himself to deductions from a few propositions, he laid down four postulates as foundations on which economic science should be erected. In abridged form they were: (1) the desire of every person to accumulate wealth with as little sacrifice as possible (in other words, the principle of hedonism); (2) the Malthusian principle of population; (3) the principle of increasing returns in all business enterprise except agriculture; and (4) the principle of diminishing returns in agriculture. He thus sought to reduce economics to a small number of unchangeable principles in which observation of facts was to yield precedence to reasoning, and to remove from its subject matter all semblance of the study of human welfare. Fortunately, yet unaccountably, he did not adhere to this rigid program. Few indeed are the economists who have attempted thus to delimit the field, and still fewer those who have actually carried their determination into practice.

Abstinence theory.— His greatest contribution to the elucidation of economic principles is generally considered to be the concept of abstinence as a cost of production. This concept was not original with him. A minor writer, G. P. Scrope, had previously declared that owners of capital received a return as compensation for abstaining from present consumption. Moreover in the writings of Ricardo this idea had been definitely, though none too clearly, presented. Senior declared the primary instruments of production to be labor and natural agents, and abstinence to be the secondary instrument. He thus replaced the conventional term "capital" with the revolutionary word "abstinence," defining the latter as "the conduct of a person who either abstains from the unproductive use of what he can command, or designedly prefers the production of remote to that of immediate results."

Senior did not say that abstinence creates wealth but rather that it constitutes a title to, or claim on, wealth, inasmuch as abstinence, in his opinion, caused pain and sacrifice to the capitalist as labor did to the wage earner. In his own language: "To abstain from the enjoyment which is in our power, or to seek distant rather than immediate results, are among the most painful exertions of the human will."

To sum up, assuming that the two primary elements in production are labor and natural resources, a third element was necessary for the proper employment of labor on those resources and a consequent large volume of production. A farmer may conceivably cultivate his farm without tools, but how much easier his task and how much larger the return, when he uses a spade or a hoe! This third element was not capital (man-made material goods), according to Senior, but rather the abstinence from consumption which made possible the calling into existence of that capital. Costs of production were therefore to be thought of, not in terms of the money expenses to which employers are put, but in terms of the sacrifices undergone by the wage earner and the capitalist. In this connection, incidentally, he was probably the first to call attention to the so-called *disutility* of labor. Prices charged for commodities must be high enough to reward both the worker with wages and the capitalist with interest. Here, then, was a unique cost-of-production analysis of price, regarded from the subjective instead of the objective standpoint. Not past labor, he added, but only that amount of labor required at the time of the exchange of commodities, entered into the determination of price.

Summary.— Senior's abstinence theory of interest may have thrown much light upon the problem of the origin of capital, but it did not clarify the issue with regard to the origin of interest. Furthermore, any cost theory of value fails to explain fully the why of value. Employers pay wages, not necessarily because of sacrifice undergone by employees, but because the employers find that certain products are in demand, or at least hope that what is produced will be sold at a satisfactory price. Correspondingly, capitalists do not receive interest solely as compensation for any sacrifice in abstaining from consumption, but rather because the capital which they own is desired temporarily by borrowers. Senior was cognizant of this difficulty and evolved the rudiments of a marginal utility theory of value, as others like Craig, Longfield, and Lloyd were doing. Value, he stated, rested upon both demand and supply, and demand, in turn, somewhat upon the degree to which a commodity was desired.   Yet value was held to depend principally upon factors limiting the supply of goods; in short, upon the subjective costs of wage earners' sacrifices and the abstinence of capitalists.

Valuable, also, were his remarks on rent, on the relation between profits and wages, on the nature of monopolies and their classification, on the distribution of the precious metals between different countries and on the economic consequences of absentee ownership.   Less fortunate were his observations on wages.   Some scholars consider his chief contribution to economics to have been his enunciation of the famed wages-fund doctrine of wages, a doctrine in high favor at that time among economists and one that may be read into the writings of Adam Smith and Ricardo.   This belief led him to oppose vigorously the growing trade union movement ; he was honestly convinced that a reduction of hours of labor in factories would wipe out the profits of the factory owners.   As he put it, the whole net profit was "derived from the last hour" of operation.   As "Last Hour" Senior, accordingly, he has been known subsequently, an economist of high ability, yet one who trailed the procession instead of leading it.   He represents the final stage of economic liberalism.   Rare is the man whose vision is wide and deep enough to compass the drift of the age in which he lives !

CHAPTER IX

JOHN STUART MILL AND
JOHN ELLIOTT CAIRNES

NEXT to *The Wealth of Nations* the most widely read work by an orthodox economist is the *Principles of Political Economy* by John Stuart Mill (1806-1873). Mill is the dominating name in English economics in the seventy-year period from David Ricardo to Alfred Marshall. Few writers have exercised a more extensive influence on the thinking of Anglo-Saxons.

Extraordinary precocity.— From his father, James Mill, the historian and philosopher, he received an education so rigorous in its intellectual requirements that it still excites astonishment ; the elder Mill is known principally as the tutor of his incomparably more famous son. As described by the latter in his *Autobiography,* his formal education began with the study of Greek when he was but three years old and continued for approximately the next twelve years. In this extraordinary educational experiment, the precocious youth read voluminously in the classics and in standard historical works, mastered arithmetic, was introduced to logic and science, and at the tender age of thirteen applied himself to the masterpieces of Ricardo and Adam Smith. A year of residence in France was followed by several years' study of law. At seventeen, however, he entered the service of the East India Company and remained with this organization in varying capacities until its reorganization in 1858. In 1851 he married Mrs. Taylor, a widow. For ten years (1858-1868) he was a member of Parliament. (As an adult he is reported always to have dressed in black.) He died in France in 1873.

Invaluable contacts developed in his young manhood and continued throughout his life. His strait-jacket education was supplemented by acquaintance with Bentham, Ricardo, Carlyle and many other noted writers, and by membership in clubs and debating societies. He thus knew and appreciated the opinions of men whose views on a variety of matters differed widely from those implanted in him by his austere father. For many years he was a leading figure among the philosophical radicals. Fortunately, also, like Adam Smith and Ricardo, he often came into close association with men of affairs. To the end of his days he remained primarily the social philosopher, widely read in the most important branches of knowledge and deeply interested in the political and social movements of his time. A singular fair-mindedness pervades his writings, together with a total absence of self-conceit.

System of Logic.— Blessed with physical energy beyond the average, despite non-participation in athletic sports during his youth, Mill devoted most of his leisure, from the very outset of his career with the East India Company, to writing. He never shirked his work at the office and yet found time to accomplish an immense amount of intellectual labor. In his 'teens he wrote articles for newspapers and essays for magazines. In his middle thirties, because of the growing disintegration of the philosophical radicals as a party, and in consequence, also, of an earlier mental crisis, he withdrew from politics and ordinary social life. Turning to the production of treatises, he first gave to the world his *System of Logic* in 1843, a work that ran through eight editions in his lifetime. This book has perhaps influenced modern thought even more than his economic writings.

The immediate success of the *System of Logic* secured him a publisher in 1844 for a collection of *Essays on Some Unsettled Questions of Political Economy* written many years previously, and emboldened him to undertake a complete work on economics. In an almost incredibly short period of time (less than two years) he finished the manuscript and in 1848 it was published under the title of *Principles of Political Economy with Some of Their Applications to Social Philosophy.* Such a treatise, somewhat longer than *The Wealth of Nations,* could only have been written thus rapidly by one who had been turning over economic matters in his mind for a good many years. Six more editions followed before his death and translations were made in the most important foreign languages.

The *Principles*, together with the *Logic*, raised Mill to a pinnacle of fame throughout the English speaking world. Never before or since in any country has an economist won such acclaim from both the thinking and the unthinking portions of the population. As philosopher, economist and spiritual leader, he enjoyed a position among his contemporaries superior even to that attained by Adam Smith in the preceding century.

Remaining works.— Other works have likewise become classics, notably his *Liberty and Thoughts on Parliamentary Reform* (1859), *Considerations on Representative Government* (1861), and *Utilitarianism* (1863). *Comte and Positivism* appeared in 1864 ; *England and Ireland* in 1868 ; and *Subjection of Women*, a defense of the rights of women on grounds furnished by his wife, in 1869. After his death in 1873 three more books were published from materials which he left behind : the *Autobiography* in 1873 ; *Three Essays on Religion* in 1874 ; and *Chapters on Socialism* in 1879, in which may be found his matured opinions on economics. *Dissertations and Discussions*, a collection of some of his essays and magazine articles, has been issued in five large volumes. Were all of his essays and articles to appear in book form, at least another five volumes would be needed to contain them.

Widening field of economics.— In the *Principles of Political Economy*, Mill attempted, with no pretence at originality, as he himself admitted, to write a treatise designed to replace in popular use *The Wealth of Nations*, inasmuch as he viewed Adam Smith's work as "in many parts obsolete and in all imperfect." Like his renowned predecessor, he wrote for the ordinary man and not for the specialist. Like him, also, he endeavored to associate the principles of political economy with their applications, and thus to appeal to much larger considerations than are usually associated with the domain of pure economic theory. He aimed, in fact, as stated in the preface, to place before the public a volume "different from that of any treatise on Political Economy which has been produced in England since the work of Adam Smith."

Mill was an ardent social reformer. He considerably widened the scope of economic and political theory. One who looks for the true Mill must look for him, not in his economic theorizing, but in his ardent proposals for reconstruction of the social and economic life of Great Britain. He was the first orthodox economist to admit the cogency of the contentions of the socialists. He went so far on one occasion, indeed, as to declare that communism was preferable to the present state of affairs.

Analysis of "Principles."—In place of writing an up-to-date Adam Smith he produced an up-to-the-minute and richly embellished Ricardo, a book in which there are regrettably few traces of originality, and one in which the theoretical portions are mainly based on the ideas of Malthus, Ricardo, and his own father. The great esteem which Mill won rests on his comprehensive point of view, his high and steady moral tone, and on his unusually attractive style. There are many pages of magnificent writing in this hastily composed work of approximately one thousand pages, and here and there are statements of unforgettable formulae. Ironically enough, however, only one economic law attaches to the name of this man whose book has enjoyed such widespread use as a textbook.

He informed his readers that he purposed to discuss the phenomenon of wealth (defined as "all useful or agreeable things which possess exchangeable value"), but instead proceeded to survey human behavior in the getting, consuming, exchanging and distribution of wealth. In this respect, he followed in the steps of Adam Smith and Malthus and Ricardo.

In the first book, on Production, he devoted his attention to the three "requisites of production" (natural agents, labor and capital), briefly surveyed division of labor and large and small scale production, and concluded with a statement of certain laws of production (including the Malthusian law of population and the law of diminishing returns on land).

His second book, on Distribution, is of interest because in the first chapter of this book he revealed what he thought to be "the chief merit of his treatise," a merit that, in his eyes, marked off his book from all previous expositions of political economy, and placed himself in a category far removed from what he termed the "common run" of economists. The laws of production, he stated, were immutable, because based on unalterable natural facts, whereas the laws of distribution were by no means inexorable but were subject to the control of mankind. The laws of the production of wealth were held to "partake of the character of physical truths," and to have "nothing optional or arbitrary in them." The law of diminishing returns, for example, which he termed the "most important proposition in political economy," was incapable of modification. But, on the contrary, society might change the laws by which the distribution of wealth is effected. The laws of wages, rent, and profits were declared subject to human action, and amenable to whatever rules society sees fit to promulgate.

Optimism of Mill.—This distinction between the laws of production and distribution was a definite step forward. What Mill failed to understand was that the laws of production can likewise be altered in some measure by the action of the individual or of society. But to him it was an all important conclusion that man can so reduce existing inequality in the ownership of wealth, that eventually all worthy members of society, including laborers, would be assured of security and of a reasonable amount of comfort. He thus did not share the dreary views of Malthus and Ricardo in regard to the future of society, views which had caused economics to become known as the "dismal" science. The vast majority of earlier orthodox economists held that no matter how wrong an economic system might be, it operated according to fixed laws, and any attempt to interfere with them would only make matters worse.

Mill's optimism was due in part to the arguments of social reformers, in part to his own nature, in part to the persuasive reasoning of the woman who became his wife. In his chapter on "Remedies for Low Wages further considered" he stated a firm belief that men could reasonably be expected some day to develop into much more intelligent human beings. Sexual instincts would be repressed, and the birthrate would diminish. Restriction of population was the one sure method of abolishing poverty.

Original theories of Mill.—In the third book, on Exchange, he made his most enduring original contribution to economic theory. This book is in the main a rehash of Ricardo. But Mill is responsible for the theory of joint costs in production, for the application of the quantity theory of money to convertible paper money, for the best account up to that time of the nature and services of speculation, and for the doctrine that international trade rests upon the interaction of demand and supply (this is his celebrated law of the "equation of international demand." Ricardo had gone no farther than to consider differences in comparative costs), and for the clarifying declaration that value tends to oscillate about that point of equilibrium where the quantity of goods offered is equal to the quantity demanded. Yet in the first chapter of this book Mill voiced a most unfortunate statement. "Happily," he averred, "there is nothing in the laws of value which remains for the present or future writer to clear up; the theory of the subject is complete." Would that this were the case!

Dynamic approach.— With the fourth book, "Influence of the Progress of Society on Production and Distribution," Mill came to the second and final division of his *Principles*. As he stated in the first chapter, "The three preceding Parts include as detailed a view as our limits permit, of what, by a happy generalization of a mathematical phrase, has been called the Statics of the subject. We have surveyed the field of economical facts, and have examined how they stand related to one another as causes and effects; what circumstances determine the amount of production, of employment for labour, of capital and population; what laws regulate rent, profits and wages—under what conditions and in what proportions commodities are interchanged between individuals and between countries. We have thus obtained a collective view of the economical phenomena of society, considered as existing simultaneously. . . All this, however, has only put us in possession of the economical laws of a stationary and unchanging society. We still have to consider the economical condition of mankind as liable to change. . . We have to consider what these changes are, what are their laws, and what their ultimate tendencies; thereby adding a theory of motion to our theory of equilibrium —the Dynamics of political economy to the Statics."

He was by no means the first to raise this distinction between static and dynamic problems. In brief retrospect, Ricardo had done the same thing in the field of distribution, distinguishing between short run and long run tendencies. Mill, however, regarding economics as fundamentally a study of ways and means of furthering human welfare, was much more interested in dynamic than in static aspects of his study.

Industrial progress was resolved by him into three features — increase of capital, increase of population, and improvements in production. He came approximately to the same conclusion reached by Ricardo, namely, that in the long run rent would tend to rise, real wages to remain constant, and profits to reach a minimum. In due time, despite unlimited progress in the arts of production, a stationary state would be attained, where increase in material production and in population would be at a standstill.

Unlike Ricardo, he looked forward to that state with equanimity, nay, with considerable assurance. For, although capital and industry and population would indeed be stationary, men would probably have arrived at more just methods of distribution. "The future well-being of the labouring classes," he declared, was "principally dependent on their own mental cultivation."

Utopian hopes.— In his much debated chapter at the end of book IV on the "Probable Futurity of the Labouring Classes" he visioned a plan of producers' co-operation, initiated by scattered bodies of workingmen, that in the not too distant future might include a comparatively large proportion of all business enterprises. With workers as recipients not alone of wages but of interest and profits as well, it seemed to him probable that the competition of these worker-owned-and-managed businesses would more and more compel ordinary firms to adopt the producer-co-operation form. Co-operation of laborers in production connoted, in his opinion, a much greater incentive to efficiency, leading to lowered cost per unit of production, than the wage system afforded.

Thus he hoped that in future the payment of wages by employers to employees, with retention of profits by the employers, would gradually yield to a form of organization in which the employees would become their own managers, thus promoting that peaceful redistribution of wealth which he so ardently desired. "In this or some such mode" (profit-sharing, for example), "the existing accumulations of capital might honestly, and by a kind of spontaneous process, become in the end the joint property of all who participate in their productive employment : a transformation which, thus effected . . . would be the nearest approach to social justice, and the most beneficial ordering of industrial affairs for the universal good, which it is possible at present to foresee."

Fortunately or unfortunately, this dream has thus far failed of realization ; the wage system appears as firmly intrenched as ever. For various reasons, the record of producers' co-operation is one of almost continuous failure. Co-operative marketing and co-operative banking, on the contrary, have shown a remarkable growth ; in retail distribution (consumer co-operation) an even more impressive record of success has been achieved. In fact, so rapid has been the momentum of this movement and so enormous its scope that consumer co-operation must be ranked as among the economic marvels of recent decades. But profit sharing has apparently spent its force. Nor has the modification of the wage system under any form of co-operation been effected in any marked degree.

Economic rôle of government.— In the fifth and final book Mill considered at length, as Adam Smith had done, the "Influence of Government" on business and on society. Distinguishing between "necessary" and "optional" functions of government, meaning by the former those "which are inseparable from the idea of a government, or are exercised habitually and without objection by all governments" he passed to a consideration of the place of government in human economic affairs. Laissez-faire, he said, should be the general principle of political expediency. Private activity appeared to him, on the whole, preferable to government intervention, since it makes for greater cheapness of commodities and for more interest in one's work, tends toward the preservation of the institutions of democracy, and aids tremendously in building up character and individuality. The problem was mainly one of utilitarianism, that of the increase or decrease of the sum total of human happiness, taking both the present and the distant future into account. The government should step in only when the greatest good of the greatest number required such action.

This intervention was of a two-fold nature : "authoritative," in which the government ordered its citizens to do certain things or to refrain from doing other things ; and "unauthoritative," in which it merely gave advice, or promulgated information, or set up agencies parallel to existing private agencies.

Unhampered by Adam Smith's belief in natural law and keenly aware of the socialist criticism of the capitalistic system, Mill departed from the laissez-faire principle to a much greater extent than most of his orthodox predecessors. He stated, however, that a heavy burden of proof rested upon those who advocated "authoritative" intervention. He indorsed the fundamental importance of state aid to education, holding that people are born with an equal capacity for improvement and that economic inequalities result from differences in education and environment. This education should be practical, preparing men and women for their duties as intelligent consumers, trained producers and liberty-loving citizens. He advocated emigration of laborers to foreign colonies, sale of government land in small parcels in order to build up a class of sturdy landed proprietors, and lease of state land to farmers and to agricultural associations. He urged, also, that the government appropriate the future unearned increment of land (termed by him variously "increment of rent," "unearned appendage," and "unearned advantage"). This was, of course, a rather revolutionary proposal for a classical economist, and one which even today finds little or no favor with many who consider themselves orthodox.

Mill favored redistribution of property by regulation and taxation of inheritances. Even the legal establishment of a shortened work day seemed to him desirable, given certain conditions not then prevailing. As to a legal minimum of wages, however, he found himself unable to see eye to eye with certain social reformers ; such legislation he said, would weaken instead of strengthen the feeling of responsibility among parents in the procreation of children. Nowhere is the influence of the Malthusian law of population on his thinking more apparent than in this connection.

Summary.— Regarded in broad perspective Mill's Political Economy falls into two parts. There is, in the first place, the restatement and harmonizing of the doctrines of Adam Smith and Ricardo together with the addition of such theories as the Malthusian principle and Senior's abstinence theory. Here appear the time-honored beliefs in self-interest as the sole motive in economic activity, in private property, laissez-faire and free competition as the best arrangements for giving full expression to self-interest, and in the validity of such notions as the cost of production and wages-fund theories. For this abstract reasoning his unusual education had prepared him. But his lasting contributions as social idealist were concrete and humane.

Mill was a pioneer in the human element approach to economics. His influence is manifest on every hand in the numerous works uniting abstraction and ideals which ever since have poured from the press, even in those textbooks on economics which form the basis of the required study of many college students in this particular field of learning. For this service the world, though somewhat in debt to his wife and to Auguste Comte, must chiefly thank the very generous inclinations of Mill himself. What matters it, essentially, that his writings are full of inconsistencies, that in 1869 he made his famous recantation of the wages-fund doctrine, and that in his later years he flirted with socialism and very possibly became a convert, as some surmise, to its tenets. "Consistency is the refuge of small minds," said Simon Nelson Patten, an eminent American economist. Whether or not this be true, the ever-growing recognition of the importance of the human element as distinguished from the mechanical element in economics, is sufficient homage to this prolific scholar.

Cairnes.— The restatement in the grand manner of the doctrines of the English classical school was the work of Mill. In him most commentators are likewise inclined to find the culmination of that school. But the last stand of the classicists, omitting all mention of the writings of Henry Fawcett, was made by John Elliott Cairnes (1824-1875), ablest of Mill's disciples. Born in Ireland, educated at Trinity College in Dublin and later a member of the bar, he turned through natural inclination to the study of economic and social questions. In 1856 he was appointed to the chair of political economy at his alma mater, publishing his lectures the following year in book form under the title *The Character and Logical Method of Political Economy*. From 1861 to 1866, he held a similar professorship in Queen's College, Galway. The *Slave Power, its Character, Career, and probable Designs*, which he published in 1862, is a masterwork of deductive reasoning. In 1866 he became professor of political economy in University

College, London, resigning in 1872 by reason of ill health. Despite intense physical suffering, he carried to completion by 1874 his longest work entitled *Some Leading Principles of Political Economy Newly Expounded*. His unusual charm of manner in the face of hopeless disease, united to his keen interest in contemporary affairs and his strength of intellect, made him the most highly respected economist in Great Britain at the time of his death in 1875.

Stratification of labor.—Cairnes is now perhaps best remembered for his acute theory of "non-competing groups" of workers. An almost complete mobility of labor had been taken for granted by his predecessors in the classical group of economists. To this discussion he brought a discordant but realistic note, by showing that society had become stratified to such an extent that but little movement was actually taking place between different groups of employees. As he wrote : "What we find, in effect, is not a whole population competing indiscriminately for all occupations, but a series of industrial layers, superposed on one another, within each of which the various candidates for employment possess a real and effective power of selection, while those occupying the several strata are, for all purposes of effective competition, practically isolated from each other."

In brief, because of heredity and environment, members of one group find it difficult to pass into a higher one. The entire labor force of the world resembles, it is now recognized, a huge pyramid resting on an enormous base of unskilled workers and rising at the top to a tiny apex where congregate the comparatively few wage earners of extraordinary ability. Automobile mechanics do not compete for jobs with bank presidents, nor farm laborers with college professors.

Had he been as uniformly successful in strengthening the classical system as in the statement of the above principle Cairnes would probably now rank among the truly great economists of the nineteenth century. Unfortunately, like Senior, he looked backward instead of forward. His subtle mind, it is true, critically examined Mill's restatement of classical doctrines, and made valued corrections in the fields of value, labor and capital, and international trade.

But he failed to see the new approaches to economics made

by Mill, Jevons, Menger, the socialists and others of his contemporaries. He staunchly sought, for example, the resurrection of the wages-fund theory. Worse still, he looked upon economics as solely an abstract, formal study of wealth. "Economic Science," in his words, "has no more connection with our present industrial system than the science of mechanics has with our present system of railways." The solution of moral and social problems, he held, was no concern of the economist. "Time marches on," leaving behind in the race men, like Cairnes, who regarded the subject-matter of economics as wealth and wealth alone and who placed all their faith in deductive reasoning. Economics bestows its richest rewards, as a rule, upon those who open up a new line of thought.

CHAPTER X

THE CLASSICAL SCHOOL OF ECONOMICS IN CONTINENTAL EUROPE

BY FAR the largest contributions made to economics have been by writers in the classical group. That group traces its inception to *The Wealth of Nations,* and it is but fitting that its last important representative, Cairnes, should have been a native of the British Isles. The classical tradition is not confined, however, to the English classical school. Its interpretation, elaboration, and systematization was the work in some measure of thinkers who lived in France and that part of Europe now called Germany, and to a much lesser extent in other parts of the continent and elsewhere. In a sense, the erection of the classical edifice has been a world-wide undertaking.

J. B. Say.—The first translation of *The Wealth of Nations* appeared in French as early as 1779, and it was to France that the theories of Adam Smith first penetrated. Leading in the demolition of the decaying doctrines of the mercantilists and the physiocrats was Jean Baptiste Say (1767-1832), founder of the French classical school, and probably most eminent of the continental disciples of Adam Smith. Say's career was very interesting. In turn soldier, editor and politician, he turned to economics toward the end of the eighteenth century, publishing in 1803 his well known work *A Treatise on Political Economy.* Then followed ten odd years as owner of a cotton factory, after which he devoted himself to writing and delivering a course of lectures on economic matters. His last two years were passed as professor of political economy in the College of France at Paris. *A Catechism of Political Economy* appeared in 1817, and *A Complete Course in Practical Political Economy* in six volumes in 1828-29, a treatise in which he considerably enlarged the sphere of his previous discussions.

In his *Political Economy,* patterned essentially after *The Wealth of Nations,* Say made it his chief mission to reduce what he termed the "vast chaos" of Adam Smith's ideas to an orderly and popular statement of economic principles. Gifted with a peculiarly lucid and fascinating style, he produced a work that before long ran into numerous editions, was translated into numerous languages, and even served for several decades in the United States as the most popular textbook for the use of college students in economics.

He was more than a mere popularizer, however, for important original contributions are to be ascribed to him. First may be mentioned his grouping of the general principles of economics under the headings — production, consumption, and distribution — which have since become conventional. Influenced, perhaps, by business experience, he introduced the memorable term *entrepreneur* into economic terminology, wisely distinguishing between the loaner of funds (the capitalist) and the one who combines land, labor and capital in business enterprises (the entrepreneur — enterpriser in English). His definition of wealth was much more inclusive than that of Adam Smith ; he refused to limit it to material goods only, — a point of view now more and more accepted by economists. Nor did he share his master's predilection for agriculture, preferring rather to accord the primacy among occupations to manufacturing, and building his economic philosophy around the activities of industrial leaders.

His theory of markets (*débouchés*) was long considered his greatest achievement, inasmuch as he argued, in opposition to Malthus and others, that since goods fundamentally are bought with other goods, there can be no general overproduction. Of much greater significance were his views — advanced for that time — on value. His statements were confusing and at times inconsistent ; yet he appears to have looked toward human wants for an explanation of the origin of value to an extent far surpassing his contemporaries. In common with others, he never pushed his approach to a logical conclusion.

It was Say's ambition to be accounted the foremost economist of his age, but history has denied him this distinction. He ranks, however, as the most important French economist of the entire nineteenth century, — no inconsiderable honor. After his death, his influence was perpetuated and possibly deepened by successors at the College of France, including Michel

Chevalier (1806-1879), and by others, including Charles Dunoyer (1786-1862), Antoine Cherbuliez (1797-1869), and Joseph Garnier (1813-1881). The doctrines of the orthodox economics maintained their supremacy in France for several decades after being discredited in Great Britain. Mention should be made of the picturesque journalist and agitator, Claude Frederic Bastiat (1801-1850), commonly viewed as the most important representative, after Say, of the French classical group.

C. F. Bastiat.—Successively gentleman farmer, justice of the peace, legislator and man of affairs, Bastiat crowded into the last six years of his short life no small number of publications. Although he devoted himself early to the study of languages, history, philosophy, and economics, his literary career hardly began until he had passed forty. His most constructive work, *Economic Harmonies,* of which he was able to complete the first volume only, appeared posthumously (1850). Several years previously, many of his articles for current periodicals and essays were published under the title of *Economic Sophisms.* After his death, other articles and essays came out in book form with the title *Essays on Political Economy,* wherein his gift for satire held full sway.

Bastiat can scarcely be accounted a great scholar. Rather was he a publicist, somewhat out of his depth in the discussion of fundamental economic problems. Yet it is a pity that he is now so little read, for few writers possess such felicity of expression and illustration and such capacity for deftly satirizing opposing doctrines. Not to have glanced through his pages is to have missed one of the most delightful repasts in economic literature. His is seemingly effortless writing.

Bastiat is best known as the most confirmed optimist of modern economics. Man would experience no evil, he stated, if only he refrained from interfering with nature's harmonies. Let nature have her way, and the most perfect conceivable world would come into being. Accordingly he argued in vigorous fashion for complete liberty of business enterprise, launching his broadsides particularly at the upholders of socialism and of protective tariffs. Government, he declared in his best vein, was "the great fiction, by means of which everybody contrives to live at the expense of everybody else,"

— a statement that deserves to go down in history as expressing the earnest conviction of an innumerable army of hard-pressed taxpayers.   The state, in his opinion, had resolved itself in the course of centuries into an agency of spoliation and oppression, defrauding the many and enriching the few.   Liberty or spoliation ; mankind must choose between the two.

Refusing, further, to share the apparently pessimistic attitude toward the future taken by Malthus and Ricardo and others, he denied the existence of economic rent and the validity of the Malthusian theory of population.   On the contrary, he drew a rosy picture for wage earners.   Wages were rising and would continue to rise still faster with complete laissez-faire.   This gain, moreover, was both absolute and relative as compared with returns from the employment of capital and land, since the present services of man, expressed in labor, were thought of as progressively increasing in value by comparison with man's past services accumulated in the ownership of capital and land.

Unfortunately this manner of reasoning went counter to the facts of social life.   In particular, his analysis of the distribution of wealth was seriously at fault.   Hence Bastiat lives on, better known for his grievous errors than for whatever of his work is sound.   Yet would that more writers possessed his extraordinary aptitude for enlisting and holding the interest of the reader !

Influence of Adam Smith.— The English classical economics dominated British thinking on economic matters for approximately one hundred years, or until about 1875 or 1880. Its supremacy in France lasted throughout a similar period, beginning toward the end of the eighteenth century and running its course by no later than 1900.   In the United States, these doctrines likewise enjoyed a vogue of about a century in the teaching profession.   It is not possible to indicate the exact decade during which the orthodox economics secured a firm foothold or later slipped from its pre-eminence.   In other parts of the civilized world the influence of Adam Smith's ideas made itself manifest in varying degrees toward the close of the eighteenth or in the early part of the nineteenth century.   Thus the first Italian translation appeared in 1779 ; the first Spanish translation in 1794 ; the first Danish translation in 1780 ; the first Russian translation in 1806 ; and volume one of the first German translation in the very year, 1776, in which *The Wealth of Nations* was published.

The exact extent of this influence ; how far his views were accepted because of their believed merits ; how far his influence depended upon his charm of style, or upon the fact that his treatise presented opinions which were already in the air ; to what degree the doctrines of his British successors in the classical tradition gained credence outside Great Britain are matters which have never yet been cleared up, and very possibly never will be. Thus let us close this summary account with mention of certain German writers of distinction in whom the classical economics found important advocates.

German partizans of Smith.— The earliest German expositors of Adam Smith did little more than merely reproduce his theories. During the first half of the nineteenth century, these theories became decidedly influential from time to time with the German bureaucracy, although it is to be doubted whether they were ever accepted by public opinion. Karl Heinrich Rau (1792-1870), in an encyclopedic work, and Friedrich Nebenius (1784-1857) did more than any others to popularize *The Wealth of Nations*. The independent contributions of the two foremost German liberal economists of this period made an appeal, unfortunately, to only that limited number of readers technically equipped for abstract reasoning. These two writers were Johann Heinrich von Thünen (1783-1850) and Friedrich Benedikt Wilhelm von Hermann (1795-1868). It was only much later that these two men came into their own.

Von Hermann.— Von Hermann is commonly referred to as the German Ricardo. This widely read university professor and statistician ranks as one of the most acute theorists of the nineteenth century. His chief work, *Investigations in Political Economy* (1832), resembles Ricardo's *Principles ;* he discussed particular subjects only, more especially production, consumption, capital, value, price, rent, and interest. These he reviewed with great thoroughness, pointing out what he deemed the chief weaknesses of the science. He appears to have been the first economist to perceive the distinction between productive and consumption capital. He distinguished clearly between income and capital, laid it down that land is really a part of capital, developed a well-rounded theory of profits, expressed opposition to the wages-fund theory, analyzed price and value determination, and introduced numerous other refinements in theory.

Von Thünen.—Of quite a different stripe was von Thünen, noted as the author of a truly extraordinary economic work, *The Isolated State in Relation to Agricultural and Political Economy,* of which the first volume was published in 1826 and the third volume not until 1863. Son of a landed proprietor, he pursued university studies in agricultural economics for a short time, and then purchased an estate in 1810 at Tellow in north Germany, residing there until his death forty years later. The treatise is a formless compilation of notes, comments, and arithmetical and algebraic calculations jotted down over the course of many years, interspersed with suggestive remarks on the humanitarian aspects of the labor problem. This work, though a classic in its particular field, is of no great interest to the general and hurried reader.

Marginal productivity theory.— By the deductive method, of which, like Ricardo, he was a past master, he arrived independently at a law of rent virtually identical with the Ricardian law. Postulating a large city state, encircled by farming land of uniform fertility, devoid of rivers or navigable canals and isolated from the rest of the world, he studied in minute detail the effect of varying distances from the central market upon land rent. Ricardo had emphasized the element of soil fertility; von Thünen corrected this somewhat one-sided formulation by stressing the equally important factor of situation. He originated the idea of marginal productivity of labor and capital, now the most widely held theory among economists in respect to earnings received by wage earners and capitalists. Von Thünen stated, for instance, that beyond a certain point soon reached, additional workers yield an ever smaller increment to the total product, so that the final worker added to the work force yields an addition just equal to the wage which he receives, a wage, moreover, which sets the pace for all those employed, since it is hardly to be expected that the employer will pay unequal wages for the same sort of work.

Profoundly disturbed by the prevailing low rates of wages, which he ascribed to exploitation of employees by employers, he inquired into the nature of just wages. The result of his investigations was the promulgation of a curious and still appreciated formula for wages, namely $\sqrt{ap}$, the square root of a product composed of the value of the subsistence required for workers, (a), times the value of the productivity of the workers, (p). To this formula he was so devoted that he directed that it be engraved on his tombstone — a touching evidence of his fundamental belief that wages should vary with the amount of the product.

CHAPTER XI

THE HISTORICAL SCHOOL OF ECONOMICS

IT WAS inevitable that sooner or later the doctrines of the classical writers should, in some measure, become discredited. Writers belonging to the classical school employed deductive logic ; they tried to set forth how human beings tend to act under the guidance of certain "laws" derived from observation of human nature and the external physical world. Little or no claim was made that these laws embraced the totality of human nature or the physical universe. Ricardo, for example, declared that the political economy of his age was still in its infancy. In the main, therefore, the inadequacy of the classical doctrines is due either to shortcomings in exposition, or to the fact that these doctrines were but half true instead of wholly false. Nothing is more astonishing in the history of economic thought than the remarkable survival-power today of orthodox economics in the face of the enormous changes of all sorts during the past seventy-five or one hundred years. There is abundant ground to believe that comparatively recent theories may have merely supplemented rather than superseded the doctrines of the classical system to a large extent.

Points of attack.— Classical economic thinking was vulnerable on many a score. Its very simplicity, by which the production, exchange, and distribution of wealth seemed to be properly explained by fewer than a dozen definite propositions, was also perhaps its chief drawback. Increasing opposition, rising to a crescendo in the second half of the nineteenth century, was accordingly directed at such typical doctrines as the wages-fund theory, the cost theory of value, the Ricardian theory of rent, and at the concepts of wealth, production, capital, interest and profits ; at the method and scope of the science ; and at the philosophic assumptions of its adherents regarding the relation of the individual to his government.

This growing opposition arose from a number of sources. It came principally, and with entire justice, from the ranks of the economists themselves, as they subjected the classical theories to an ever more searching examination. It came, further, from students of biology and psychology, who recognized the importance of change in all forms of organic life, and who gained a deeper insight into human behavior. It stemmed, also, from the fruitful criticism of those who may be grouped together under the broad category of socialists, people who urged that the whole social and economic structure should be made over, and that, in particular, competition and private ownership and operation of at least the basic industries should be replaced by some sort of collective ownership and operation. Opposition developed, finally, from a variety of other critics difficult of classification among whom, possibly, primary consideration may be given to the moralists and social reformers.

Contemporary readers of the volumes of Malthus, Ricardo, Mill, Say, Senior, and others of the classical school were occasionally more influenced by the theoretical passages than by other sections. In some of these books and pamphlets, indeed, they would have looked in vain for anything except theoretical discussion, as in Ricardo's *Principles of Political Economy and Taxation*. In others, they encountered theories which ran counter to well-established facts, and yet which were put forth without qualification. Ricardo, for instance, is reported once to have replied to the reproach of a friend, that certain of his doctrines did not tally with the facts, that it was "so much the worse for the facts." He and his followers properly contended that they were writing not so much about actual happenings in any limited period of time as about long-run tendencies inherent in economic phenomena.

The classical economists were therefore open to legitimate attack on the score of the all-too-abstract character of their reasoning. True, Adam Smith, Malthus, and Mill paid a good deal of attention to historical developments ; many classicists, notably Malthus, were strongly interested in historical research and at times made elaborate use of historical materials. Yet it must be acknowledged that such facts as were introduced were ordinarily brought in to illustrate conclusions already formed and stated. For this failure adequately to study the problems of economics from the historical viewpoint, extenuating circumstances may with some fairness be pleaded.

At the time of the publication of *The Wealth of Nations* and for several decades thereafter, historical thinking was, so to speak, out of vogue. Historical materials were deficient in quantity, and the technique employed by modern statisticians had not been perfected. In other sciences, moreover, including even the natural sciences, deductive methods still held sway. But even so, the tendency to undue abstraction was carried all too far in the Ricardian school; inevitably critics eventually took issue with the conclusions of the classical writers. These critics showed, with increasing cogency, not only that the premises of the classical system were not always of universal validity, but also that generalizations deduced from these premises often failed to correspond to concrete conditions.

It goes without saying, by the way, that the historical method cannot be contrasted too sharply with the abstract and deductive method, inasmuch as the historical approach properly at times likewise uses deduction. An outstanding feature of the historical approach is probably the emphasis on the dynamic rather than static elements in economic society. Yet further difficulties here arise, because motionless equilibrium exists only in imagination. Much internal movement and fluctuation characterize even the most static human society of which economists have any knowledge.

Historical method.— Many commentators have bestowed the appellation, "historical school," upon those numerous writers and teachers who favored the historical approach to economics. Such commentators speak of a "world wide school, with representatives in all important countries," although, in fact, the economists so labeled were natives of either Great Britain or of Germany. If there ever was an historical school, it no longer exists. And if by the term "school" is meant a group of scholars who center their attention upon some common problem, pursue a common method, and work in virtual collaboration, it would seem fitting to confine the designation to certain Germans whose qualifications are more in line with this definition than the natives of any other country. It is entirely proper, therefore, to speak of the German historical school. Since the controversy with regard to method has happily long since evaporated, we need waste no words regarding the existence or non-existence of a British or an Italian or other historical school.

Among those who first endeavored to temper the rigor of the classical teachings, Jean Charles Leonard Simonde de Sismondi (1773-1842), Richard Jones (1790-1885), Auguste Comte (1798-1857), and Friedrich List (1789-1846) are important. Sismondi (to be discussed in another connection on page 193), keen observer of the new forces which were to rule the nineteenth century, pioneered shortly after 1800 in the application of historical research to economic analysis.   This versatile and vastly prolific Swiss writer, much more the historian than the economist, has attained a due meed of recognition only in recent decades.   We now see him as the first important thinker who set forth some of the good ideas which were incorporated in the New Deal in the United States.   Comte, patient French scholar and by some considered to be the founder of modern sociology, reinforced the arguments of Sismondi in holding that economics cannot be divorced from history, ethics and politics.   These fields, he insisted, must be cultivated in common and from the point of view of evolution and inductive methods.

Richard Jones.— In Great Britain, the historical movement was fathered by the Rev. Richard Jones, successor of Malthus at Haileybury College.   In his *Essay on the Distribution of Wealth and on the Sources of Taxation* (1831), a book which dealt chiefly with the conditions attaching to rent contracts on land not tilled by its owners, he assailed the abstract assumptions of the Ricardian doctrine ; he showed that they by no means described the actual rent system of the past and of his own age.   After extensive investigations into peasant rents as opposed to farmers' rents, he concluded that rents were incapable of explanation on any single principle.   "Look and see," he maintained in another work, was the only possible way of arriving at proper generalizations,— a phrase that since his death has been repeated by unnumbered economists, even though for many years the voice of Jones was like that of one crying in a wilderness.

Walter Bagehot.— Next is Walter Bagehot (1826-1877), distinguished British banker and scholar, and author of several books of which one, *Lombard Street* (1873), has become a classic in the field of finance. A staunch admirer of Ricardo, he nevertheless called for greater verification of economic theory, maintaining that the historical and abstract methods did not essentially conflict. Of the United States he sagely remarked that no other country at that time constituted such a laboratory for the testing out of self-evident truths.

T. E. C. Leslie.—Of more importance was the gifted Irish economist and teacher, Thomas Edward Cliffe Leslie (1825?-1882), in some of whose fragmentary writings is to be found the first systematic statement of the essence of the historical method by any native of the British Isles. "Facts," he insisted, "instead of being irrelevant to the economist's reasoning, are the phenomena from which he must infer general principles, and by which he ought constantly to verify his deductions."

J. K. Ingram.—Better known than Leslie was another Irishman, John Kells Ingram (1824-1907), likewise professor of economics at Trinity College, Dublin. He is best known for his brilliant *History of Political Economy*, originally published in 1885 as an essay in the ninth edition of the Encyclopaedia Britannica and the first serious study by any British writer of the development of economic thought. In its latest edition (1915), to which is appended a supplementary chapter by Professor William A. Scott, this work is eminently useful. An ardent disciple of Comte, he predicted the approaching overturn of the classical doctrines, consigned economics to a "single chapter" in the one great, all-inclusive science of sociology, and pleaded eloquently that no social fact be considered apart from its historical setting.

Toynbee.—Arnold Toynbee (1852-1883), originator of the term "The Industrial Revolution" and keen student of social and economic history, whose promising career was cut short at the age of thirty-one, was a pioneer in what has come to be called "settlement work." More level-headed than some of his predecessors, he did not condemn the deductive method as wholly false, but preferred to believe that "abstract propositions are seen in a new light when studied in relation to the facts which were before the writer at the time when he formulated them. . . Ricardo becomes painfully interesting when we read the history of his time." Seeking to supplement theory by patient historical and statistical investigation, he was able to prove, for instance, that the real wages of the average English workingman had risen in the generation preceding his own, thus challenging the Ricardian analysis of wages.

Other British writers.—With James E. Thorold Rogers (1823-1890), professor at Oxford and author of such models of patient research as *History of Agriculture and Prices in England* (1866-1882) and *Six Centuries of Work and Wages* (1884), British economists settled down to the serious business of enriching economic literature with much needed historical monographs. As he said in the preface to his *Economic Interpretation of History:* "Two things have discredited political economy—the one its traditional disregard for facts; the other, its strangling itself with definitions. . ." "Much which popular economists believe to be natural is highly artificial;—what they call laws are too often hasty, inconsiderate, and inaccurate deductions;—much which they consider to be demonstrably irrefutable is demonstrably false."

Shortly after 1875 courses in economic history began to appear in college and university curricula. William Cunningham began to teach economic history at Cambridge in 1878, and in 1892 Harvard University established probably the first chair in this field, and appointed as the occupant William J. Ashley, England's commanding exponent of the historical method. During the present generation has come a tremendous outpouring of works of research in Europe and the United States which have served to modify and at times to obliterate the views and interpretations of previous scholars.

The movement in Germany.—In Germany, however, the historical approach received the most thorough exploitation; with Germany alone may the phrase, "the historical school," safely be employed. The German historical school has the distinction of being first to react systematically against the methods of the British orthodox economics.

It is customary to trace the origins of this school to the stimulus of important developments from 1800 to 1850 in the world of thought outside of economics. The triumphant philosophy of George William Friedrich Hegel, lecturer at the University of Berlin from 1818 to 1831, was one of these stimuli. He believed the universe itself to be a process of thought, moving in an innately determined cycle from the abstract to the concrete. In staunchly extolling the State, he warred upon the doctrines of individualism and natural rights popularized by eighteenth century philosophers. Of interest, also, was the "historical school of jurisprudence" under the leadership of Savigny, Eichhorn, Goschen and Puchta ; a fundamental tenet of this school is that law is a result of the social conditions of the time and thus the ever expanding product of national culture. Finally, researches in philology and history by German scholars gave added proof of the merit of the comparative study of history in all its ramifications.

The opinion is now gaining ground that the rise of the German historical school of economics was not in imitation or emulation of developments occurring in other sciences. It would seem rather to have been a campaign of opposition by German economists against the transplanted classical theories of political economy. *The Wealth of Nations* was translated soon after its publication in 1776 in England and quickly the German version became popular. Yet the doctrines of Adam Smith and more especially of Ricardo naturally were engendered by distinctively British economic conditions ; it was hardly to be expected that they should apply with any great amount of accuracy to the German environment unless deliberately revamped for this purpose. This work of correction was first undertaken early in the nineteenth century by Friedrich List (1789-1846), long regarded merely as a forerunner of the German historical school, but now recognized as its earliest important representative ; many living scholars acclaim him as the foremost of all German economists.

Friedrich List.— List was born in the Kingdom of Württemberg in south Germany, received a rudimentary education, and at seventeen entered the civil service. By hard work and native ability he advanced rapidly ; in 1818 he was appointed to the newly established professorship of political science at the University of Tübingen. Dismissed the next year on account of his liberal opinions, he became a member of the Württemberg parliament, but was expelled from this body when he continued his agitation for reform. He emigrated to the United States in 1825.

After a tour with Lafayette of the eastern part of the country, he settled in Reading, Pennsylvania, became editor of a journal, and published in 1827 a pamphlet entitled *Outlines of American Political Economy*, in which he declared himself in hearty accord with the principle of a high protective tariff, then the leading political issue before the American people. In 1832 he accepted an appointment as United States consul to Leipzig, devoting the remainder of his life to the promotion of railway construction in Germany, the establishment of a German customs union (the Zollverein), and various literary labors, of which the best known is *National System of Political Economy* (1841). He planned to complete this work with two more volumes, but ill health and severe financial reverses combined to bring his restless career to an untimely end in his fifty-seventh year.

His collected writings have been published in three volumes. Throughout glows the fervor and highly polemical tone of a vigorous propagandist zealous for the unification of his native Germany, then a heterogeneous assemblage of states large and small. As befits a practical man of affairs, he wrote forcefully. His style is sometimes repetitious; curious contradictions are found here and there.

The *National System of Political Economy*, fortunately available in several English translations, is a volume of moderate size in four parts entitled History, Theory, Systems, and Public Policy. His treatise attacked the free trade doctrines of the "School," as he termed Adam Smith, J. B. Say, Ricardo, and other exponents of the classical faith. He endeavored to show how other nations could make themselves the commercial and industrial equals of Great Britain. Throughout he emphatically stated that the causes of wealth are much more important than wealth itself.

In a striking and original argument he developed the theory of productive forces, only hinted at in *The Wealth of Nations*; he showed that an increase of productive powers augments the real wealth of a nation to a much greater extent than any mere heaping up of material commodities. The training of talents and aptitudes, furthering of the arts and sciences, promotion of religion, morality, free speech, freedom of the press, transportation, and so on, he insisted, had inconceivably more to do with expanding a country's prosperity than the factors enumerated by Adam Smith.

"The power of producing wealth is therefore infinitely more important than wealth itself.— The present state of the nations is the result of the accumulation of all discoveries, inventions, improvements, perfections, and exertions of all the generations which have lived before us ; they form the mental capital of the present human race, and every separate nation is productive only in the proportion in which it has known how to appropriate these attainments of former generations and to increase them by its own requirements." Never were truer words written.

How, then, can the productive powers of a nation be increased ? By the intelligent intervention of the state, he insisted, since the productive powers of the individuals who compose the nation are more or less at the mercy of the administrative and legislative governmental heads to whom the guiding policy has been entrusted, especially when business and industrial life grow in complexity. Statesmen are at fault if they adopt a do-nothing procedure ; they "will know and must know," he stated, "how the productive powers of a whole nation can be awakened, increased, and protected."

List's ideas on economic evolution.— What must statesmanship do ? Simply see to it that division of labor applies to the entire population. Without a national division of labor and national co-operation of productive powers, no matter how extensive the division of labor among individuals may be, no nation can hope to attain a high level of prosperity and power. Every nation possessed of at least a modicum of potential moral and material resources, in his opinion, might reasonably look forward to reaching that level. In his opinion the economic life of every nation in the temperate zone, blessed with a suitable physical endowment, could be divided into five stages of growth.

The first and lowest, characterized by hunting and fishing, is followed by the pastoral, and that in turn by the agricultural stage. In the first two of these, free trade should prevail with other nations, in order that foreign manufactured articles might more easily be obtained in exchange for the home country's raw products. At some time in the agricultural stage, protection for native manufacturing enterprises should be provided by duties on imports ; shipping should be fostered by subsidies. Only in this manner can one nation render itself independent of others, and deserving infant industries be built up to adult stature. This is the fourth stage. The fifth he calls the "agricultural, manufacturing and commercial stage." Whenever a nation reaches this point and is powerful enough to compete on terms of equality with any other country, free trade should be reintroduced in order that agriculturists, manufacturers, and merchants should not relax their efforts. Whatever a nation might lose for the time being during the protective period would be more than offset in the long run by the harmonious development of all branches of economic development.

This fivefold classification of Friedrich List has long since been shown to be both inaccurate and vague. Hunting is not necessarily the first stage. Moreover the sequence of stages is not always as pictured above. His generalizations are much too broad. Nor is it always possible to share List's enthusiasm for manufactures and commerce as opposed to agriculture. Yet he rendered invaluable services in behalf of the growing science of economics, and undoubtedly ranks among the most influential of German economists.

He formulated a theory of the relativity of economic policy, faulty though scholars today consider it. List's protest against the absolute formulas of the "School," seems legitimate enough, but he treated Adam Smith unjustly, and himself fell into the error of laying down universal rules. He rightly stressed the development of the entire nation as all-important, no matter what might be the effects upon the immediate advantage of some individuals ; he focussed attention upon productive forces ; and in his contemplation of the ultimate union of the nations of the world into an all-embracing federation, promoted by true freedom of trade, he foreshadowed the existing embryonic League of Nations.

He was, in truth, a rare combination of business leader and scholarly genius. Correctly appraising the real state of affairs in his day and age and looking upon protection as a strictly transitional phase (a point too often forgotten by his detractors), he assisted considerably in placing the science of economics upon the path which it must follow, if it is ever to justify the hopes and devotion of those who thoughtfully study its intricacies.

The German "Triumvirate."—The conventional account of the German Historical School tends to minimize or even ignore the contributions of List, and to present Wilhelm Roscher (1817-1894), Bruno Hildebrand (1812-1878) and Karl Knies (1821-1898) as having independently worked out this particular line of thought. Roscher, for nearly half a century professor of economics at Leipzig University and the most erudite of the three, is commonly regarded as the founder. Author of many learned works, including the most extensive history of economic thought written up to that time, and a treatise on economics which dealt with the subject much after the fashion of the English classicists, he is now best remembered for a little book with a long title, *Outline of Lectures on Political Economy according to the Historical Method* (1843).

Here were stated, though haltingly, the fundamental principles of the school. He proposed, for instance, that economics be regarded as the science of the development of society, that current facts and opinions be studied from the standpoint of their historical evolution, that abstract deduction from ideal postulates be avoided and economics be made as realistic as possible, and that national rather than cosmopolitan economics be emphasized, since, in his opinion, the people of any one historical stage have had their own peculiar economy. These were, of course, valuable though by no means original suggestions. For some reason, however, he did little himself to act upon his own advice or to discover through historical study the wished-for laws of the economic development of nations.

Hildebrand.—Nor can much more be said for Hildebrand, man of travel and of many interests and activities, whose career culminated in the holding of the professorship of political science at the University of Jena (near Leipzig). His chief contribution was probably the establishment in 1863 of the *Yearbook for Economics and Statistics,* one of the most respected of German periodicals and one that still maintains its existence. Whereas Roscher had been most influenced by the achievements of Savigny in the field of historical jurisprudence, Hildebrand found his inspiration in current developments in philology. His attitude toward the classical economics, more or less evident in his many historical monographs, is most clearly perceived in *The National Economy of the Present and Future*, of which only the first of several promised volumes ever appeared (in 1848). He went somewhat farther than Roscher in attacking the methods of the classical writers, and hoped, indeed, to recreate the science, but never actually carried his plan into practice.

Knies.— Knies, ablest of the triumvirate and teacher of such American scholars as Professors J. B. Clark and E. R. A. Seligman, was professor of political science at Heidelberg University from 1865 to 1898. Like his two contemporaries, he wrote at length on a considerable range of topics ; like them, also, his connection with the historical method is best observed in one book, published in 1853 under the title of *Political Economy from the Standpoint of the Historical Method* (changed to *"from the Historical Standpoint"* in the second edition in 1883 in order to indicate that he did not favor but one method only). At once a greater sceptic and a more profound student than either of his fellows, he nevertheless did little more in the way of constructive effort. He carried the doctrine of relativity almost to an extreme, however, and even questioned the existence of natural laws. An irritatingly ponderous style marred most of his writings. One of his sentences, incidentally, covers two whole pages.

These three men were so different in their work, that it is no easy task to summarize their criticism of classical economics. In a very general way, they tried to trace the historical course of economic life (without falling into the error of becoming primarily historians). They held that there are no laws of economic science which hold true for all times and at all times. They stressed inductive as opposed to deductive logic. They moved away from the individualism and cosmopolitanism of the classicists toward a spirit of nationalism, and explored the connection of economics with such kindred fields as geography, jurisprudence and philosophy. Their doctrines, it must be emphasized, sprang from the environment in which they lived. The Germany of their time seethed with political ferment, as the numerous German states struggled toward their unification in the German Empire that came into being in 1871. The economic thinking of any age is ordinarily a creature of that age.

The "younger" school.— The essential features of the historical method are found much more fully in the writings of students of Roscher, Hildebrand and Knies, than in the foundations laid by the triumvirate itself. Among these students Germans naturally predominated; in the course of time the "younger" historical school made its appearance in Germany in contradistinction to the "older" school. Those who prefer to mark off the German historical school into two divisions, assert that the members of the older school were content merely with supplementing the classical theories, whereas the younger group proposed to throw overboard the entire classical approach to economics, to have nothing to do with deduction, and to reconstruct the science by the historical method alone. Whatever the merits of this argument may be (and the issue has not even yet been settled to the satisfaction of all), the younger group began about 1870 to assemble historical materials and to turn out a seemingly endless stream of monographs, with the express intention of postponing the drawing of generalizations by induction until a vast bulk of systematized data had been accumulated.

Schmoller.— Leader of this movement was Gustav Schmoller (1838-1917), long a professor of economics at the University of Berlin, and author of the most outstanding treatise of the historical school. His *Outline of General Economic Theory*, of which the first volume was published in 1900 and the second in 1904, is most interesting and valuable. Unfortunately this *Outline*, consisting of over one thousand pages in the latest editions, is not yet available in English. It contains an enormous mass of information, not too solidly welded together, we must admit, and yet so ample and rich in texture that it constitutes a comprehensive survey of society from the viewpoint of the economist. The range of topics is much greater than might properly have been expected from an ardent adherent of the historical method. Indeed the field treated is considerably broader than is the case in the majority of treatises written outside of Germany in recent decades.

The Outline of General Economic Theory reveals that

Schmoller had departed very considerably by 1900 from the program which the younger historical school had set for itself in the eighteen seventies. He saw, in other words, that economics must be much more than a mere branch of historical learning, and that if he were to deal adequately with all the variegated aspects of the economic life of mankind, every method employed by his predecessors and contemporaries must be employed. The treatise has a curious classical tinge. Not only does pure historical observation (induction) seem to yield precedence to deduction, but the psychology is that of the classicists; discussions of appropriate public policy are introduced, quite in line with good classical models, at every opportunity.

The Influence of Germany.— Coupled with Schmoller, egotistical but erudite spokesman of the younger historical group, are numerous other writers, many of them distinguished figures. Ever to be associated with historism are Georg Friedrich Knapp, scholarly student of German agriculture, and Karl Bücher of Leipzig, revered teacher of the present author. Bücher skillfully blended induction and deduction. He is deservedly famed for his *Industrial Evolution* (1893) in which he brought to light the forces that lead to the transition from one economic stage to another. Not to be overlooked in the work of reconstruction are Adolf Wagner, Erwin Nasse, Gustav Schönberg, Hans von Scheel, Adolf Held, Lujo Brentano, Gustav Cohn and Johannes Conrad.

A striking tribute to the work of these scholars and of hosts of others is that, during the eighteen seventies and eighties, men from most parts of the civilized world, who wished to equip themselves for professional work in economics, flocked in large numbers to Germany for post-graduate study. Momentous was this migration of ambitious youth in search of higher professional training. The German historical school was then at its apex; it stood unrivalled in the number and high quality of scholars who were devoting themselves to research and teaching in various branches of economics.

The influence of the school, therefore, was by no means confined to Germany, and is especially noticeable in the writings of Italian and American economists. This influence has not been as undiluted as the German preceptors would in all cases have wished, inasmuch as their protégés, though at first filled with zeal for German methods and ideals, upon their return to their native country, have tended in their mature years toward a very considerable use of the abstract method.

Summary.— The chief service of the historical method, undoubtedly, was to counteract the overabstract tendencies of the classicists. Laborious special investigations are absolutely essential for the creation of sound economic theory. In their enthusiasm for the gathering of exhaustive collections of economic facts, it is hardly surprising that the historical school all too often forgot that correct thinking necessitates both induction and deduction. But the men of this group did clarify the evolution of the major stages of economic organization. They reawakened interest in nationalism and pointed out the folly of an exaggerated individualism. They stressed the significance of non-economic as contrasted with purely economic motives. In short, they established beyond all question the relativity of economic theory. Although the historical school is now defunct, the historical method is firmly intrenched as an invaluable tool in economics, and its fruits are found nowadays in the researches more especially of those economists who perhaps may be described as institutionalists and statisticians.

CHAPTER XII

MARGINAL UTILITY ECONOMICS

UNTIL quite recently, the problem of how to spend income caused no worry whatever to the great mass of people. Throughout most of recorded history, the working classes were paid in kind (commodities), and barter was rather universally depended upon to secure goods not obtained in the form of wages. Since the productive system was extremely primitive by modern standards, the range of purchases was narrow to a degree almost inconceivable to civilized peoples today. Only when the practice of paying workingmen in money developed, toward the end of the Middle Ages, and the Commercial and Industrial Revolutions later on vastly increased the amounts and kinds of commodities available for purchase, did that freedom of choice arise which is one of the rarely noticed marvels of the modern world.

Value and Price.— With specialization of tasks and the consequent mutual exchange of products through the medium of money and credit, it naturally followed that nearly all problems in economics became either directly or indirectly problems in price. Indeed there is now no more universal phenomenon than valuation. The necessity of making choices, even though these choices may be determined largely by tradition, inevitably precedes all economic activity. Thus the subject of value and price has become fundamental, and value has been said to be the very essence of economics. Perhaps the theory of value engages the attention of economists nowadays more than any other phase of the science. In economics, it must be remembered, the word *value,* which in common usage has many different shades of meaning, means *the power which a thing has of commanding other things in exchange for itself.* This power in exchange arises because the thing is wanted by someone. If a commodity or service is not wanted, it will have no economic value and hence no price.

Granted that the value of a thing is its power in exchange, what is it that gives to one thing a high value and to another a low value? The economist finds the answer in the scarcity of goods relative to the desire of mankind for them. Air is necessary to life, and yet the supply of it is normally so abundant that nobody will pay for its use. On the other hand, even though the supply of a good may be very large, as in the case of wheat, the demand for that good may be so large as to make it scarce in the economic sense. Wheat ordinarily sells for some price, because there is not enough to suffice for free distribution. Wheat costs something in time and effort to produce, there is an insistent demand in many parts of the world for it, and he who has produced a part of the supply can therefore command other goods in exchange for wheat.

Utility.— From these simplified examples, it should be apparent that all economic values rest not only upon labor or cost but upon scarcity as well. They arise not because of anything inherent in a good, but as a result of human judgment. Such indeed was the opinion of keen thinkers for an untold number of centuries in the past. To go no farther back than Greece, Aristotle, unlike Plato, correctly discovered the standard of value in the usefulness of commodities. "In the truest and most real sense," he stated, "this standard lies in wants." Similar suggestions, to list but a few typical writers, are scattered in the works of Cicero, Aquinas, the mercantilist philosopher Hobbes, the anti-mercantilist Barbon, the semi-physiocrats Condillac and Turgot, and in the first half of the nineteenth century such Britishers as Bentham, Senior, Craig, Longfield and Lloyd, the Frenchmen, J. B. Say, Dupuit, and Auguste Walras, and the Germans Hufeland and Thomas.

In the course of time, it was inevitable that some genius would proceed farther than merely to emphasize the fundamental significance of wants in the determination of value and price, and would endeavor to erect a comprehensive system of economic theory upon this novel basis. So far as is now known, the signal honor of first formulating such a system belongs to the obscure German writer Hermann Heinrich Gossen (1810-1858).

Gossen.— A native of southwest Germany, Gossen entered government service, but retired in 1847 to devote himself to economic problems. In 1854 appeared his only book, *The Development of the Laws of Human Exchange,* a short volume of less than three hundred pages, which failed to arouse the slightest public interest. The sadly disillusioned author with- drew the entire stock shortly before his own death in 1858 and ordered the books destroyed. One copy, however, was miraculously discovered in the 'seventies by an English scholar, and the text is now available in a seldom-consulted German reprint (1889). Its predominantly mathematical character greatly detracts from its interest.

If there be any central doctrine in this nearly unreadable and formless volume, it is the idea that the source of value is to be found in men and not in things, and that value is deter- mined by margins psychologically measured. Gossen clearly formulated the now familiar principle of marginal utility, and made that principle the cornerstone of his economic system.

In his opening sentence, Gossen stated that "man wants to enjoy life and makes it his chief aim to maximize happiness." Upon this somewhat debatable assumption, he set forth a principle of diminishing satisfaction, arguing that the amount of satisfaction derived from the utilization of a good declines progressively (as in the case of some particular article of food) down to the point of satiety, and that maximum satisfaction is obtained when the enjoyment of different goods is discon- tinued at the points where the intensity of enjoyment is the same. Upon this principle of diminishing satisfaction, in turn, he based his theory of value, maintaining that goods have value only in proportion to the satisfactions which they yield. The first "atom" of any consumption good (the first piece of bread, for instance) thus has the highest value of any of the "atoms" of that good, and each additional "atom" has a progressively smaller value until the point is reached where no net surplus of satisfaction remains and the value is nil.

This was a tolerably clear explanation of the differences in value of consumption goods, of those goods, in other words, which afford satisfactions directly, and which he termed "goods of the first class." He was hard put to it to account for the value of all other goods, but attempted ingeniously to solve the difficulty by including in a second class so-called "complemen- tary goods" (for instance, the pipes in which tobacco is smoked), and in a third and final class all production goods such as tools and machinery, and by ascribing to goods in the second and third classes such value as was represented in the assistance which they lent to preparing the way for the use of consumption goods.

Careful examination of Gossen's book shows that many other essential ideas and much of the method of the founders of the modern marginal utility school are to be found in this still-born volume. More important writers press for attention, however, more important in the sense that their influence upon the main current of economic thought has been overwhelmingly greater.

Jevons.— Of the later writers who rediscovered and popularized the doctrines concerning marginal utility of ill-starred Gossen, William Stanley Jevons (1835-1882) stands out as the foremost English representative. So important were his contributions, that by common consent he is ranked among the first five British economists. Developing even as a boy an interest in various fields of learning, he entered University College at London, specialized in chemistry and interrupted his college career to assume the position of assayer of the government mint at Sidney, Australia. After five years he returned to London to resume his studies, read widely in philosophy, undertook statistical researches, and soon after graduation became tutor in logic and political economy at Owens College, Manchester. In 1876 he was called to a professorship at his alma mater, University College, resigning his chair four years later for reasons of health. Death by drowning, when only forty-seven, put an untimely end to a most promising career.

Considering his relatively short life, Jevons did a great deal of research and writing. In 1863 appeared *Pure Logic* and in 1865 *The Coal Question.* Six years later he published his most weighty book, *Theory of Political Economy.* Later publications include *The Principles of Science* (1874), *Money and the Mechanism of Exchange* (1875), *The State in Relation to Labor* (1882), and (posthumously) *Methods of Social Reform, Investigations in Currency and Finance, Logic,* and the fragmentary *Principles of Economics.* Gifted in many ways, he is eminent not only as a profound economist but as also an accomplished statistician, mathematician, and logician.

Many of his ideas and illustrations have become classics in economic literature. He advanced the theory, for instance, that the periodic appearance of spots on the sun cause such variations in the sun's energy as to affect the growth of crops and thus business conditions in general. In harmony with his laissez-faire views, he stated the oft-quoted proposition that the government may properly interfere with private business in four cases alone: (a) where the best co-ordination of numerous scattered operations may only thus be attained; (b) where the processes involved are of a routine nature; (c) where the work is done under the public eye; and (d) where little capital is required.

Theory of Political Economy.—He took the same large view of economics as Mill. Yet despite this belief, and certain inductive studies of specific problems already noted, he confined himself in his *Theory of Political Economy* to a rather narrow range of topics. He felt that he could make an original contribution to economics more by specializing in certain fundamental theoretical inquiries than by attempting to cover the entire range of the science. Hence his *Political Economy* deals only with problems of consumption, exchange and distribution; these, furthermore, are analyzed in a strictly scientific manner by limiting their application to what he called a "static state,"—a state of society in which no changes of any sort were taking place. As to method, he believed that if economics were ever to become a true science it would have to be mathematical. Yet in practice he did not realize this ideal. His work was essentially non-mathematical in character.

Jevons created his system expressly upon psychology, and this basis he adapted from the pain and pleasure calculus of Bentham. By no means, however, did he take over bodily all of Bentham's somewhat artificial notions, for to him it seemed clear that the fundamental influence of pleasure and pain upon man's conduct could be put in a much more simple and reasonable form. He denied the necessity of exact measurement of pleasures and pain, assuming that we can easily enough decide which of two pleasures or of two pains is the greater, and know when pain exceeds pleasure.

Jevons sincerely believed that economic life rests in last

analysis upon calculations of pleasure and pains, and that it was necessary to reinterpret the pheonomena of consumption, production, exchange and distribution from the standpoint of psychology. Thus he went beyond his classical predecessors in definitely making economics a calculus of pleasure and pains. Great was his dismay, several years later, when he learned that in the exposition of this novel theory he had been anticipated by Gossen.

In his "mechanics of utility," he asserted that the central problem of economics is that of exchange value. Holding that utility is the pleasure derived from the use of a good, and that the most significant law in all economics is the tendency toward satiety, he pointed out that utility tends to decrease as the amount used increases. This led him to the dubious distinction between the utility of *all* the amount used (total utility) and the utility of *any one* unit of the supply. For the utility of the last unit used, he coined the phrase "final degree of utility," a term still useful in economic literature even though the misleading phrase "marginal utility" has now replaced it in common usage. The final degree of utility might be ascertained, he added, by dividing the utility of the final increment by the quantity of the final increment.

It was this final degree of utility which, in his opinion, determined the course of exchanges and value in exchange. He disliked the word "value," in view of its varied meanings, and preferred the expression "ratio of exchange." To use his own language, therefore : "The ratio of exchange of any two commodities will be the reciprocal of the ratio of the final degree of utility of the quantities of commodity available after the exchange is completed." In other words, the value of any good is arrived at by a comparison on the part of consumers of the final degrees of utility of two or more goods.

However confusing to the reader this brief discussion of Jevons' views on value may seem, the significant point is that his greatest contribution to economic theory was made in the field of exchange. Had he followed up a suggestion in his preface that distribution is entirely subject to the principles of value, and proceeded to build up a theory of distribution upon his theory of exchange, he would have foreshadowed the practice now standard in modern treatises on economic theory, and attained an even more considerable reputation. But unfortunately and unaccountably he failed to discuss rent, wages, interest and profits in terms of final utility, and it fell to a contemporary Austrian to systematize in marginal concepts Adam Smith's "component parts of price."

Austrian school.— The dry mathematical illustrations used by Jevons, the omnipresence of the classical school in current thinking, and the apathy of British professional economists toward the marginal utility analysis, all conspired to withhold from him that influence which he so earnestly desired. No "Jevonian" school sprang up to accept and improve upon his fundamental notions, and it was only with the publication of Alfred Marshall's *Principles of Economics* in 1890 that his particular brand of theory began to make an impression upon the public.   Not in Germany or in England but in Austria did utility theory rise to dominance and thence to world-wide recognition. Together with Karl Menger, the illustrious Austrian, and Léon Walras (1834-1910), son of the Frenchman Auguste Walras and author of *Elements of Pure Economics* (1874) in which his father's views on utility were elaborated into a system involving the use of the historic term *rareté* (the intensity of the last want satisfied), Jevons must be content to share honors as one of the founders of modern utility doctrine.

Menger.— First in point of time and in significance among the scholarly Viennese triumvirate of Menger, Wieser and Böhm-Bawerk was Karl Menger (1840-1921), founder and undisputed leader of the so-called Austrian school of economics.[1] Born in Galicia, he studied economics and law at Vienna and Prague, entered the Austrian civil service for a brief period, and became professor of economics at the University of Vienna in 1873. Save for several years when he tutored Prince Rudolf of Austria, he retained this university connection for three decades, retiring in 1903 to devote his talents more fully to scientific research. In 1900 he was created a life member of the Austrian House of Peers. So great was his reputation for both teaching ability and scholarship, that students from all over the world thronged his class-

[1] *See* "Carl Menger" by F. A. von Hayek in *Economica* for November, 1934. Also "The Economics of Carl Menger" by George J. Stigler in *The Journal of Political Economy* for April, 1937.

room much as previously they had flocked to the lectures of representatives of the German historical school.

None of his writings has been translated into English; this, coupled with the fact that his leading theoretical work has long been out of print, explains why his theory has not been popularized. This inexcusable injustice has been in part remedied in recent years by the issuance of his collected works in four volumes in the series: *Reprints of Scarce Tracts,* published by the London School of Economics.

Menger's fame rests primarily upon his labors in the field of economic theory; yet his contributions to methodology and to other provinces of the wide domain of economics were by no means inconsiderable. In 1871, the same year in which Jevons published his *Theory of Political Economy,* appeared the *Foundations of Economic Theory* in which, working independently of Jevons, Walras and the luckless Gossen, he put forth the same general views. He intended in due time to supplement this short volume of four hundred pages with three others, but this comprehensive project never came to fruition.

Foundations of Economic Theory.— Adam Smith and Ricardo had concerned themselves almost exclusively with material wealth in their discussions. Menger, on the contrary, argued that things which possess the power of satisfying wants properly include useful human activities as well as useful material commodities, and hence he broadened the term "goods" (want-satisfying things) in a direction which more and more finds acceptance with economists today. Goods which can be consumed directly, like bread, were considered the most important; these he defined as "goods of the first order." In a manner reminiscent of Gossen, he distinguished all other goods as "goods of higher order." Thus with bread as a first-order good, flour became a second-order good, wheat a third-order good, and so on *ad infinitum* up to goods of the very highest order.

The significance of this division into consumption goods, on the one hand, and production goods, on the other, is that the want-satisfying power of higher-order goods (production goods) was dependent solely upon the want-satisfying power of goods of the first order (consumption goods). Hence whatever value goods of the higher orders may have is a value reflected back from the value of goods of the first order. In this way did he enunciate the theory of *imputation* by which he is best known to posterity.

He thus concluded that value (the power in exchange possessed by goods) must be a judgment of the mind. It could have no necessary connection with the amount of labor or capital used, he argued, inasmuch as things often sell at far above or far below their cost of production (for example, rare paintings and out-of-fashion goods) while diamonds discovered by mere chance may command fabulous prices. Value accordingly must depend upon the relation between wants and the supply of goods available for the satisfaction of those wants. And since people esteem things not in accordance with their general significance, but rather from the standpoint of the number of the units contained in the supply, it must be true that the want-satisfying power of a good decreases as the supply of the good increases, and increases as the supply decreases. Were diamonds as abundant as coal, they would be little esteemed, while if bread were scarce, its price would mount to fantastic levels (as in fact it sometimes does).

On the assumption that all the units of any commodity are alike, Menger asserted that equal value must attach to each one, and that hence the least important use of any one unit determines the value of that good. This was the same conclusion arrived at by Jevons when he spoke of final degree of utility and by Walras when he coined the expression "rarity." The concept of value of all these three writers thus rested upon the significance of the least important satisfactions yielded by the units of a supply.

Obviously people value any one unit of the supply of a consumption good (as a loaf of bread) according to the satisfaction derived or expected from the use of that particular unit. But when Menger and his fellow Austrians attempted to deal with the problem of the value of production goods they encountered nearly insuperable complexities and difficulties. Menger contented himself with the explanation that the value of goods of a higher order is always dependent upon the prospective value of the goods of a lower order in whose production they have assisted.

However one-sided and defective his discussion of value may seem to the reader, he surely rendered a profound service in deducing from his value theory a general theory of distribution. This indeed was perhaps his greatest contribution. Not a few economists before him had pondered the relation of distribution to value, and a few, like Jevons, had suggested that distribution should be considered as a value problem.

But it fell to Menger to be among the first to take the forward step of actually making a theory of value the basis of a discussion of distribution. He emphasized that the problems which arise regarding the rent received by landowners have to do with the value of the services of land; that problems concerning the wages of laborers have to do with the value of the services of laborers; and that problems as to the interest received by capitalists involve the value of the services of capital.

It was enough that Menger attempted the task of tying a theory of distribution to his theory of value; one could hardly expect that in the formulation of his general principle he would avoid all or even most of the traps to which his daring procedure exposed him. He laid down the proposition, accordingly, that the value of any one unit of a productive resource (labor, for instance) will depend on the use of the least important unit of that product, expanded his argument somewhat in connection with wages and rent, made a very slight beginning in the development of a theory of interest, and left to others the amplification and correction of the groundwork laid by Adam Smith in his component parts of price.

So firmly established was the Historical School in Austria as well as in Germany, at the time when Menger published his *Foundations of Economic Theory,* that more than ten years elapsed before any considerable amount of support was accorded his theories in the press. During this interval, furthermore, his own energies were all too largely consumed in a bitter quarrel with Schmoller over the merits of deduction versus induction. This controversy has become of such historical importance that it is generally known to present day economists as the "Methodenstreit," as Schmoller's German contemporaries baptized it. No substantial additions were made to the marginal utility doctrine propounded by Menger in 1871, until the appearance in 1884 of Wieser's *Origin and Leading Principles of Economic Value.*

Wieser.— Friedrich von Wieser (1851-1926), son-in-law of Menger and second in point of time of the Austrian trinity, received his higher education at the University of Vienna, spent a short time in the civil service as befitted his aristocratic lineage, became professor of economics at the University of Prague and succeeded his father-in-law at his alma mater in 1903.   During the World War he served for a time as Minister of Commerce in the Austrian cabinet.   In 1889 he published his second major treatise and the one by which he is probably best known to his foreign audience, since it was soon translated into English under the title of *Natural Value* by the robust Scotch popularizer of the marginal utility theory, Professor Smart of the University of Glascow.

Many years later von Wieser was induced to bring out the ripened reflections of a lifetime in a general treatise on economic theory (1914), now available in a recent English translation by Professor Hinrichs, entitled *Theory of Social Economics*.   This volume, the first truly comprehensive presentation of marginal analysis by any member of the Austrian school, stands as a leading achievement of that group.   Essentially non-mathematical in method, like the *Foundations* of his predecessor, lucid in exposition, mature in judgment and unchanged in fundamentals from the views expressed in his earliest work, this treatise is a great book indeed.[2]   It is in truth the classic statement of Austrian doctrines.

Theory of Social Economics.— In essence, his reasoning reaffirmed Menger's position.   In place of the latter's "least important" use, Wieser introduced the debatable term *Grenznutzen,* ever since known to English speaking students as "marginal utility."   More fundamentally he departed somewhat from his predecessor's analysis of imputed values. Menger had held — as already stated by Gossen — that value exists primarily in goods which directly satisfy the wants of consumers, and that the value of production goods is something that is reflected back to production goods because of

[2] See "Wieser's Theory of Social Economics" by W. C. Mitchell in *The Political Science Quarterly* for March, 1915, reprinted in *The Backward Art of Spending Money,* by W. C. Mitchell, McGraw-Hill, 1937.

their assistance in making possible the existence of these consumption goods. A cobbler's tools, for instance, have such value as may be imputed to them because of their use in making boots and shoes.

Wieser by a vastly elaborated argument tried to discern the principles in accordance with which a share of the value of consumption goods may be imputed to production goods, that is to say, goods of the higher order. His discussion is so subtle and so long-drawn-out that any simplification is virtually impossible. But we may say, in a very general way, (1) he analyzed the imputation of value under varying conditions of demand, supply, and quality of goods, (2) maintained in a series of equations the necessity of attributing a separate portion of any good jointly produced to all factors of production (land, labor, and capital) taken singly, (3) distinguished between reproducible cost instruments and non-reproducible specific instruments of production, (4) argued that in value-analysis the decisive consideration is not the part of the output which is lost through the failure to use this or that unit of a good, but rather the part which is gained through the employment of the unit, and (5) applied his laws of value to the explanation of rent, wages, profits and — to a much less degree — interest on capital. In brief, marginal utility was declared to be determined by marginal contribution.

Thus he seemed squarely in opposition to the classical doctrine that value rests upon cost of production, especially since he asserted that costs have no determining influence upon value. "Value sanctions costs," he stated, in a passage which forms his most notable addition to Menger's utility theory, "and is not caused by costs." Yet elsewhere he admitted that costs do have an indirect effectiveness in the determination of value, inasmuch as the costs incurred by business enterprises place more or less rigid limits upon the supply which they will bring to the market for sale.

Some critics, therefore, believe that, circular though his reasoning may appear, he was in reality endeavoring not so much to discard the cost of production theory as to supplement it and make it complete. At all events, he took occasion in the preface to his *Theory of Social Economics* to express high regard for the work of the classical economists. The classical doctrine, he stated, is "one of the most splendid and practically significant achievements of the scientific spirit, and despite all opposition it will not wholly lose its influence upon theory and practice so long as its place is not filled by a maturer doctrine."

Most important and interesting was Wieser's position on what he deemed to be the central problem of economic theory. He held that economics should concern itself not so much with the satisfaction of wants as with providing the means whereby those wants might be satisfied. To him, accordingly, the goal of economics was the maximizing of the utility derived from goods. Stressing in his *Social Economics* the decline of competition and the rise of monopoly since the days of Adam Smith and Ricardo, he advocated a reduction in the enormous inequalities in wealth and income then prevalent, through resort to increased government intervention in business affairs. He could not quite bring himself to endorse socialism ; instead, he championed reforms which would do away with the inequalities that result from unfair competition. He pleaded, in short, for what he considered to be economic rationality.

His volume is thus another in that long line of economic epics which have grappled with phenomena both from the viewpoint of what is and what ought to be in the realm of human behavior.

Böhm-Bawerk.—Last of the Austrian triumvirate was Eugen von Böhm-Bawerk (1851-1914), although Menger survived him by seven years, and Wieser, whose sister he married, by twelve. After taking his degree in law at the University of Vienna he studied in Germany under Knies, Roscher and Hildebrand, became professor of economics at the University of Innsbruck, resigned in 1889 to assume a responsible position in the Austro-Hungarian department of Finance, served subsequently on three different occasions as Minister of Finance, and returned to academic life in 1909 as professor of economics at the University of Vienna. Likewise of noble birth, he was long a member of the upper house of the Austrian parliament.

His more important writings spanned a period of twenty years (1881-1900), during which, with one remarkable exception, he followed fairly closely in the path marked out by Menger and Wieser. His was an acute and original mind, however, and economists of the present era are greatly indebted to him for many searching criticisms and much independent exposition in not a few divisions of the science, including a slashing attack on the Marxian system. Of chief interest to students of economic theory are two companion volumes dealing with capital and interest, each of them a complete unit, which the indefatigable Professor Smart turned into English soon after their publication, under the titles of *Capital and Interest* and *The Positive Theory of Capital*. In between these two works appeared a monograph entitled *Outlines of the Theory of Commodity Value* (1886).

Böhm-Bawerk agreed with his two predecessors in their concept that the value of a good, generally speaking, is measured and determined by the importance of that want which is least urgent among all the wants satisfied, yet he endeavored to develop an even more complete theory of value. To this end he suggested the replacement of the time-honored division of value into the terms use-value (utility) and exchange value by the expressions *subjective value* and *objective value*. Distinguishing, furthermore, between subjective use-value and subjective exchange-value (ideas much less formidable than they appear on the surface to be), he explained the transformance of subjective valuations into price. His long and somewhat tedious course of reasoning finally resolved itself into the statement that objective exchange value (price) rests upon individual valuations. With the aid of so-called "marginal pairs," and on the assumption of frictionless two-sided competition, he elaborated the fallacious idea that the market price will be determined within the upper and lower limits set by the subjective valuations of marginal buyers and sellers. Hence his conclusion that market price is marginal price and is the result of subjective valuations.

Valuable though these suggestions were, they were far overshadowed by his contributions in the field of distribution to the theory of interest. Classical economics had become hopelessly confused in its approach to the interest problem, and in particular had failed to explain interest as a rate of return upon capital. Jevons had made a brilliant attack upon all cost theories, and had thrown out hints in which some commentators find the nucleus of a marginal productivity theory.

Menger had sought a solution by means of what may be termed "negative imputation." Wieser had formulated a well-rounded marginal utility theory of distribution, in which the idea of positive imputation was made to apply to all the shares in the distributive process, and in which he looked upon interest as a ratio between the productivity of capital goods and their money cost. Böhm-Bawerk was not satisfied with any of the explanations hitherto offered, and made it his life work to dig deep into this baffling problem.

First of his publications was a volume entitled *History and Critique of Theories of Interest* (1884), more generally known as *Capital and Interest,* in which he presented an historical and critical account of interest theories beginning with the medieval canonists and ending with Knies. Classifying these various theories under the heads of the *productivity theory* (interest is the productive power of capital), the *use theory* (interest is the price paid for the use of capital), the *abstinence theory* (interest is the reward for abstinence), the *labor theory* (interest is the wage for labor undergone by the capitalist), the *socialist* or *exploitation theory* (interest is the gain from exploited labor) and minor systems, he acknowledged a small core of truth in some, but in general disapproved of all.

Positive Theory of Capital.—His own theory was expounded at excessive length in *Positive Theory of Capital* (1888), in which he set forth ideas which he asserted had been independently developed, although in fact they have much in common with those of Jevons. This theory is variously known as the *agio* or *discount theory.* Starting with the legitimate assumption that people as a rule systematically discount the future, in that they tend to prefer today's goods to future goods of a like kind and amount, he accounted for the emergence of interest by pointing out the technical superiority of so-called roundabout processes of production. Capital goods used in modern production, such as tools and machinery, have a relatively low value, he held, because they are not available immediately for consumption. But in the course of time, these capital goods "ripen" into consumer goods, much as automobile factories pour forth their streams of finished automobiles ; these consumer goods represent a growth of values in excess of all costs incurred. In thus demonstrating why roundabout methods of production produce a larger volume of consumer goods than does direct production, he clearly explained why borrowers *can* afford to pay interest.

But he failed to show why borrowers *must* ordinarily pay for the use of funds or goods owned by others. On this score his argument has had to be supplemented by theories which stress the cost of production of capital goods. There is furthermore ground to believe that his theory is in reality a productivity theory, inasmuch as it apparently rests not so much on preference for present goods, as on the possibility of productive return through the use of capital goods. At all events, his line of approach has provoked a great deal of discussion, and has frequently served as a point of departure upon which more recent economists have erected interest theories, such as the *time preference theory*.

Summary.—The labors of Menger, Wieser and Böhm-Bawerk in assigning to the consumer the place formerly occupied by the business man as the center of the stage in the discussions of the classical economists, have aided immensely in producing a remarkable revival in economic theory. The Austrian triumvirate emphasized demand and utility in the explanation of value, just as strongly as the classicists had stressed supply and the pain and sacrifice involved in labor. They held to the novel belief that value determines cost of production instead of being determined by that cost. So trenchant were their arguments that many economists have since busied themselves in making detailed analyses of cost of production on the supply side of value, and of the nature of consumption on the demand side. The conflagration which the Austrians kindled still blazes, and no end to it is in sight.

A most impressive array of followers has arisen in many parts of the world to fill out and supplement the bold outlines sketched by the leaders. Included in this group are notably Sax, Launhardt, Phillippovich, Schumpeter, Cossa, Pantaleoni, Wicksell, Pierson, and Smart on the European continent. In the United States the marginal utility approach has been welcomed by prominent thinkers like Patten, Fetter, Fisher, and William A. Scott, and in the person of J. B. Clark has achieved an independent development. The vast majority of economists, however, unable to share the Austrian enthusiasm for the rôle played by the consumer, have pursued a middle-of-the-road policy. The rank and file of business men, ignorant as they are of theoretical controversies, still cling to the time-honored conviction that the determinant of value is cost of production.

In the past half century and more, numerous economists have come to the belief that Jevons and the Austrians opened up a novel approach to the problem of value, and more or less completely outmoded the line of attack taken by their classical predecessors. As the new ideas were sifted and settled down in the body of economic thought, however, other economists have stated it as their conviction that marginal utility was implicit in John Stuart Mill's discussion of the laws of demand and supply. These critics, with whom the present writer ranks himself, feel that the contributions of the Austrians lie chiefly in greater refinement and clarity of exposition. The whole marginal utility concept partakes grievously of error by reason of the fact that no difference actually exists in the importance of different portions of the same supply. As for Jevons, his genius has all too long gone unrecognized by an altogether too large proportion of students of economic doctrine. His greatness, despite his unfortunate insistence that economics must be based upon a pain and pleasure calculus, is attested in not a few ways, and in none more strikingly than by the circumstance that he was fully aware that the marginal analysis merely expressed the laws of demand and supply more adequately.

CHAPTER XIII

ALFRED MARSHALL

HUGE though the output of writings on economic topics had become by the time of the appearance of the Austrians on the economic stage, the rush of publications in the past seventy-five years has surpassed in quantity everything written in all previous centuries. Economics, fortunately or unfortunately, tends for the most part to use the common terms of business. Like other sciences, it is true, it has its own peculiar jargon. But of all sciences it has the fewest technical terms, and hence it is possible for nearly anybody to pose as an economist merely by using the language of the economists.

Economics, furthermore, is inextricably identified with business because it deals with business and business problems, and for this reason untold numbers of business men have not hesitated to break into print on a wide variety of economic topics. Considering the extensive popular interest in the social sciences in recent decades, and the new and larger vistas revealed by the colossal upheavals of two world wars and recent depressions, the wonder is that the deluge has not been of even more prodigious proportions. It is indeed desirable that people should ruminate upon economic matters, but that economics should in time become everybody's science is decidedly a "horse of another color."

Almost anybody can read Adam Smith with pleasure and profit, but it is to be doubted whether the average person is equipped by training and experience to add to the general body of economic knowledge in a manner that will even remotely measure up to the standard set by the author of *The Wealth of Nations*.

Neo-classicism.— In all this torrent of economic literature one name has indisputably come to the fore among the ranks of English-speaking orthodox economists of the past two generations.   The mantle of Adam Smith, Malthus, Ricardo, and John Stuart Mill has fallen, by nearly unanimous consent, upon the shoulders of Alfred Marshall (1842-1924), for many years professor of economics in Cambridge University, England. The "neo-classicism" of which he is easily the ablest exponent is the most generally accepted body of economic thought in the world today.   His is the doctrine that is taught to college youth in the vast majority of American class rooms as well as in Great Britain.

Most professional economists in the United States are his followers, and many of the economic textbooks studied voluntarily or otherwise by American college students are attuned to his ideas.   In Europe and elsewhere his theoretical system still enjoys considerable prestige.   The neo-classical revisionists are constantly at work on the clarification and more logical interpretation of his doctrine, and bid fair to perpetuate his pre-eminence in orthodox circles for years to come.

Biographical data.— Born in London into a middle class family, Marshall early gave evidence of unusual intellectual capacity.   With Adam Smith and John Stuart Mill he was a born student.   Unaccountably attracted to mathematics he turned aside from further conventional study of the classics upon completion of his secondary schooling, entered Cambridge University, and graduated in 1865 with high honors in his chosen field.   Soon after taking his degree, he accepted an appointment at Cambridge as lecturer in mathematics with the intention of becoming a physicist.

Association with a group of brilliant colleagues soon aroused in him a profound interest in problems of philosophy, ethics, and biology, an interest which was in great part transferred to economics by the chance reading of Mill's *Principles of Political Economy*.

In 1868 his friends managed to have him appointed to a special lectureship in the moral sciences, and for nine years he read widely and deeply in economic works, although publishing nothing.   Upon his marriage in 1877, he was required by university regulations to relinquish his lectureship, and accordingly assumed, somewhat reluctantly, the principalship of University College in Bristol in the west part of England.   Two years later he published his first book, *The Economics of In-*

dustry, a comparatively small volume in the preparation of which his wife rendered him valuable assistance.

In 1883 the death of Arnold Toynbee opened the way to his appointment as professor of political economy at Oxford University, and the following year another death, that of Henry Fawcett, prominent leader of the later classicists, made possible his return to his alma mater. From 1885 to 1908 he held the most honored professorship of political economy in the entire world, retiring from Cambridge in 1908 at the age of sixty-five in order to devote himself to research and writing. His death occurred in the summer of 1924 shortly prior to his eighty-second birthday.

Marshall's works.— In common with Adam Smith, Marshall was a very methodical and cautious writer. The main conclusions which sooner or later appeared in book form were present in his mind for many years before he permitted their publication. The treatise by which he is best known, *Principles of Economics,* developed in a most deliberate fashion, and it was not until 1890, after the manuscript had long been subjected to the keen criticism of his students, that the completed product was published as the first volume of a proposed two volume work. Three more editions were called for prior to the close of the century, and the eighth and final edition appeared in 1920, all bearing witness to his meticulous scholarship.

He had hoped in 1890 to put out the second volume within a reasonable time thereafter, but his plans were interfered with by the rapid tempo of the age, engagements of various sorts, and undue solicitude for the state of his health, so that the appearance of *Industry and Trade* was delayed until 1919. He had long since abandoned hope of completing his allotted task in two volumes, and thus a third volume was published in 1923 under the title of *Money, Credit, and Commerce.*

At the time of his death, he had collected material sufficient for three more books dealing with the topics of conditions affecting unemployment, the economic functions of government, and the economic conditions of progress,— works never published, however. In 1925 many of his letters and shorter writings, together with an admirable biographical sketch by Professor J. M. Keynes, appeared in *Memorials of Alfred*

Marshall, edited by Professor A. C. Pigou. One year later Professor Keynes edited his testimony before royal commissions and his formal government reports under the title of *Official Papers of Alfred Marshall.*

Rehabilitation of economics.— In the writing of his *Principles*, Marshall set for himself a task which only the very ablest of economists should essay. He attempted to "present a modern version of old doctrines with the aid of the new work, and with reference to the new problems of our own age." "The new doctrines," he remarked, "have supplemented the older, have extended, developed, and sometimes corrected them, and often have given them a different tone by a new distribution of emphasis ; but very seldom have subverted them." In short, he took it upon himself to do for his own generation what Mill had attempted to do for his.

Building, like Mill, upon classical foundations, he strove to bring up to date a science which had deservedly fallen into considerable disrepute, and which was greatly in need of reconstruction at the hands of a master workman. The Ricardian structure, dominant for more than five decades in the thinking both of economists and of lay devotees, had been seriously undermined in the course of the 'sixties and 'seventies by events of an academic and non-academic nature. Mill had made his classic recantation of the wages-fund theory in 1869. The exposition by Jevons and the Austrians of the subjective theory of value had thrown a bombshell into the camp of the orthodox theorists. The historical school had also put the classical system under fire.

The writings of American economists such as F. A. Walker, and of von Thünen and Cournot, users of the mathematical method on the continent, had raised disturbing questions bearing on vexing theoretical issues. Sismondi, Carlyle, Ruskin, and others of the social economic reformers, together with socialists of various stripes and hues, had drawn attention to the increasing complexity and evils of economic life. Startling developments in the field of biology, associated primarily with the names of Charles Darwin (*On the Origin of Species*, 1859) and A. B. Wallace, and the theme of evolution through natural selection, coupled with the popularization of the evolutionary doctrine—most significant of all theories of life—through the industry of Herbert Spencer in his *System of Synthetic Philosophy* (1860-96) were wielding an ever growing influence upon economic concepts.

Furthermore, changed economic and social conditions compelled a marked revision in the perspective in which economic problems had to be viewed. The Malthusian theory of population had seemingly been disproved by the slowing up of the rate of increase in the population in many countries. Agricultural distress in Great Britain, as elsewhere in Europe, had thrown a cloud of doubt upon the Ricardian theory of rent. The gain in strength of the trade union movement ; the passage of protective factory legislation ; the world wide decline of the general price level during the 'seventies and 'eighties with the accompanying swing from prosperity to relative depression ; the re-establishment of barriers to free trade ; the rapid growth of monopolistic practices ; increasing regulation of economic life by various agencies of government ; unparalleled invention, and a host of other movements necessitated a fresh analysis of economic phenomena. In this environment, Marshall, in all modesty, sought to reinterpret the fundamental aspects of economic theory.

Economics a means to an end.—The eighth and latest edition of *Principles of Economics,* bearing the appropriate sub-title "an introductory volume," is a book of some nine hundred pages, including thirteen thoughtful appendices. The tone of the entire treatise is revealed in the very first sentence where he declared in an oft-quoted passage that "Political Economy or Economics is a study of mankind in the ordinary business of life ; it examines that part of individual and social action which is most closely connected with the attainment and with the use of the material requisites of well being." Elsewhere he stated that "the dominant aim of economics in the present generation is to contribute to a solution of social problems."

These are very significant observations. They disclose the real nature of a man to whom economics was far more than an abstract study, to whom, in fact, economic theory and principles were not ends in themselves but rather means to practical ends. They uncover the humanitarian interests which pervade all his writings, and which probably more than anything else served to turn his attention early in life from mathematical pursuits to the study of the amelioration of the lot of mankind. Feeling a profound respect for the doctrines of his classical predecessors he looked upon economics as, on the one hand, a study of wealth (defined by him as ordinarily consisting of the external goods of a person which are capable of a money measure, but at times including also certain immaterial goods) and, on the other, much more importantly, as a study of man himself.

To Marshall, accordingly, economics was explicitly a study of human behavior in society from the standpoint of factual data and environment and progress. This point of view was quite the correct one, since not only ought economics to be a study of certain aspects of human behavior but in truth it always has been that kind of a study.

Was Marshall a hedonist ? — Is human behavior in any way related to motives ? Are there forces which impel men to act in the way in which they do ? The answer of Marshall was that economics "concerns itself chiefly with those motives which affect, most powerfully and most steadily, man's conduct in the business part of his life." On the basis of this phrasing and of other similar expressions, many scholars infer that Marshall's conception of human nature was essentially hedonistic. As one critic says, "It appears to be only the ethics, not the theory, of human motivation of hedonism that he succeeded in avoiding." Other critics aver that, despite the use of modern words and modern terminology, his fundamental notions regarding the factors which control human behavior were those which Adam Smith accepted and Bentham expounded in his elaborate calculus. In brief, they charge that he erected his economic theory in terms of pleasure and pain assumptions which modern psychology has long since shown to be false. They endeavor to prove that when he divided the conscious motives of mankind into desire for gratification, as opposed to the desire to avoid the sacrifice involved in labor and in waiting for gratification, he was in reality merely operating upon a pleasure and pain foundation.

Other scholars, equally authoritative, either maintain that Marshall's theory, whatever its shortcomings, is in no way tied up with hedonism or with any other kind of psychology, or else insist that, so far as his value theory is concerned, modern psychology leads to substantially the same conclusions as does hedonism. In the words of Professor J. M. Keynes : "The solution of economic problems was for Marshall, not an application of the hedonistic calculus, but a prior condition of the exercise of man's higher faculties."

Value as the hub of economics.—Whatever the merits of this controversy (and the weight of opinion now absolves him from the charge of hedonism), Marshall introduced a novel thought in the statement that "the center around which economic science clusters" is money. He did not mean to imply by this proposition that money is the motive behind economic activity but simply that money is the most available means at the disposal of the economist for measuring whatever sets of forces control human conduct. Had he declared that money is the best measure of the center around which economic science clusters, he would have been more clear and accurate. At all events, he wisely emphasized the fact that money is a factor of the utmost significance in the analysis of economic theory. Adam Smith, Ricardo, Mill and even Jevons had failed to raise this issue.

Not only did Marshall aver that money is the center about which economics clusters, but his treatise revolves around this fundamental notion in such a manner that the entire volume may properly be considered a study in the determination of value. He was not the first, of course, to make value problems a central theme of his economic thinking. To mention no others, Jevons and the Austrians had attempted to reveal the apparent unity of the economic system through the medium of value. But Marshall integrated his material as no previous writer of importance had done.

The determination of value he regarded as a problem of equilibrium between the forces of demand on the one side and the forces of supply on the other. Hence after the *Preliminary Survey* of *Book I* and a *Consideration of Some Fundamental Notions* in *Book II*, he passed in *Book III* to *Wants and Their Satisfactions*, in which he discussed the factors which give rise to a demand for goods, continued in *Book IV* to an account of *The Agents of Production* and thus to a survey of the factors responsible for the supply of goods ; analyzed the *General Relations of Demand, Supply and Value* in *Book V*, and closed in *Book VI* with the application of the relations between demand, supply, and value to *The Distribution of the National Income*. In his whole analysis, it goes without saying, the existence of the capitalistic regime is assumed.

Analyses of the *Principles*.—To retrace our steps, the first two short books are introductory to the main body of the treatise. With the third book, likewise a short one, Marshall really got under way. In the insertion of a book on consumption (although, to be sure, the heading runs *On Wants and Their Satisfaction*), Marshall broke with the English classical tradition. This is not to imply that he made any considerable contribution to economics in this book ; in truth he based it mostly on the work of the Austrians, prior to whose appearance and that of Jevons the study of consumption had been all too neglected.

Only in recent decades has this subject received adequate attention by such writers as John A. Hobson, and inspired separate volumes. Marshall's treatment of wants and demand is conventional and deductive in character, and not at all to be compared with the inductive inquiries of today. Perhaps the most curious feature of the book is the discussion, original with him, of what he called *consumers' surplus,* one of the least useful expressions with which he has enriched economic terminology. Consumers' surplus is incommensurable, yet very real, he stated. The truth is that it is altogether too unreal to be of any great significance.

Very simply, consumers' surplus means the surplus satisfaction felt by a buyer of an article or service for less than he thinks it is worth to him. It is the difference between what he actually does pay and what he would have been willing to pay rather than go without. This, then, was Marshall's concept.

Demand and supply.—Just as Marshall drew upon the Austrians in his treatment of consumption and demand, so did he draw upon Mill in the preparation of the succeeding book on production and supply, to which he gave the title of *The Agents of Production*. This book, save for the addition of a fourth agent termed "industrial organization," is pure classical economics. Without doubt he felt himself on much safer ground when dealing with the topic of supply than with that of demand. Whatever demand may or may not be, it is very closely related to the nature and sources of human desires, and the study of human desires is primarily the task of the sciences of psychology and biology.

A desire is a feeling directed toward the attainment of a certain definite object, and becomes demand, in the opinion of most economists, when this feeling is coupled with the means to gratify it. The desires and demands of most people originate, of course, in the requirements and necessaries of human life, that is, in what are called needs. Needs become wants when the needs have to do with the absence or comparative absence of something indispensable to existence, such as food and drink. Since the demand for goods results not only from felt needs but from imagined needs, by reason of the influence of fashion, advertising, and other forces, demand is a much more inclusive term than is sometimes recognized.

Marshall fully recognized the difficulties in which the discussion of wants, desires, and demand involved him. He frankly stated, indeed, that until the then-existing paucity of statistical information was remedied, but little headway could be made in a scientific analysis of demand. In the domain of supply, on the other hand, there were no such grave limitations as to data ; supply, much more than demand, can be made to revolve around the tangible factor of money-costs.

Four factors of production.— The fourth book is hence a sympathetic account of congenial subject matter. The agents of production, without whose co-operation no supply of goods would be forthcoming, are taken to be land, labor, capital, and organization (now rather generally termed enterprise or entrepreneurship). In the discussion of land, he wrote at length on fertility, but unaccountably failed to treat the equally important aspect of location.

In his study of labor he concerned himself much more with the qualitative than with the quantitative side of population, thus happily departing from previous practice. A hangover from medieval thinking occurs in the statement regarding the accumulation of capital that family affection is the chief motive for saving, whereas in truth the chief source of savings, now as in his time, is the surplus of corporations. His keenness of observation and breadth of interest are shown at their best in his lengthy and admirable account of industrial organization, wherein occur his references to internal and external economies and the introduction of a significant concept new to economics, that of the "representative firm." By this phrase he designated all those business firms which sell at, or just above, or just below, their costs, and are therefore typical of business as a whole, since lower-cost firms, because few in number, were held not to be representative of business as a whole, while higher-cost firms tended to be weeded out.

Value and price.— In the fifth book, General Relations of Demand, Supply, and Value, Marshall made a profound analysis of value and price. This is the fundamental part of his treatise ; all that had gone before merely prepared the way for the discussion of value, and all that came after, in the sixth and final book, was the application of his laws of value to the phenomena of rent, wages, interest, and profits. Jevons and the Austrians before him had likewise made value the center of their thinking, and others, as Adam Smith, had suggested this line of approach. But Marshall proceeded farther than any of his predecessors in bringing all economic processes within the range of value theory. The task which he undertook in the Principles was primarily the explanation of economic life in terms of the price system.

It is a familiar truism that in the vast interlocking system of modern economic life, the production of wealth is mostly for sale in the market, and that the wants of most people are satisfied in so far as they are satisfied at all, by goods which they obtain from the market. Public authority, monopoly and custom each play an important part in price determination. Yet when Marshall wrote, free competition was dominant ; and he explained value problems mainly on the basis of free competition.

Tendency toward equilibrium.— If there be any one key to this explanation, it is the interplay of demand and supply in the determination of prices, and the resulting tendency toward equilibrium in nearly all economic behavior. In a manner never before equalled up to this time, and probably never since surpassed, he deftly avoided the one-sided emphasis of the classicists on cost and of the marginal utility economists on utility, and admirably fused both concepts into one. Ingenious is his analogy of value to the keystone of an arch, the two sides of which are demand and supply, and to a pair of scissors, each of whose two blades is indispensable to the other.

In his analysis of demand he made use of such Austrian concepts as those of utility, marginal utility, the law of diminishing utility, and demand schedules. In his explanation of supply, as might have been expected, he freely availed himself of such classical doctrines as the law of diminishing returns in agriculture, the Malthusian theory of population, the division of labor in its relation to productive efficiency, and the concept of abstinence in its relation to the formation of capital. Combining the older theories with the new, he reconciled an age-long opposition between the cost of production and the utility viewpoints, in the most notable economic synthesis enunciated up to the present time.

Price as an equilibrating influence.—It goes without saying that mere *desire* for a commodity, as for an automobile, is not the same as *demand* for it. Marshall defined demand as the amount of commodities that will be taken by purchasers in a given market, at a given time, and at a given price. This definition, which at least has the merit of being specific, still holds the field in economics textbooks.

Marshall set up demand schedules, represented both by diagrams and by figures, and showing the different amounts of commodities that will be taken by purchasers in a given market, at a given time, and at a series of varying prices. Similarly, he defined supply as the amount of commodities that will be furnished by sellers in a given market, at a given time, and at a given price, and set up supply schedules showing the different amounts of commodities that will be forthcoming in a given market, at a given time, and at a series of varying prices.

Each individual would-be buyer was thus thought to bring to the market a demand price reflecting the equilibrium between the marginal utility to him of the particular commodity and his marginal utility (rich or poor) for money. Similarly, each individual would-be seller was considered to have a supply price reflecting the equilibrium between his total costs of production and his marginal utility for money.

The prices at which goods are bought and sold were therefore held to be an integration of the individual valuations of all would-be buyers and sellers. No one buyer or seller,

taken by himself, can normally influence to any great extent
the price at which he buys or sells, since for him the market
price is beyond his control.   Yet the price would not be whatever it naturally is, were it not that each buyer and seller contributes a part, no matter how infinitesimal, to the collective
demand and supply.

Demand and supply curves.— Deeming that value is a
resultant of an equilibrium between these series of demand
prices and supply prices, Marshall represented these prices
graphically by two curves, one with an upward and the other
with a downward slope.   At the point of the intersection of
these curves the marginal demand price and the marginal
supply price of the commodities exchanged were declared to
be approximately equal.   Prices tend toward a point of stable
equilibrium between demand and supply.

At any given moment, or from a short-time point of view,
he maintained, value is dominated by variations in demand.
Once the would-be sellers have placed their goods on their
market they are more or less at the mercy of consumers'
caprices.   As Marshall puts it, market values are but temporary equilibria which depend on present demand, on the
one hand, and the stocks of commodities already available,
on the other.   *Over short periods,* demand is hence a much
more significant factor than supply.   *In the long run,* however,
the situation is reversed, and the factor of supply is the more
decisive.

Over long periods the prices of commodities cannot vary
greatly from the expenses of producing them.   If prices temporarily fall below expenses, output tends to be curtailed, and
assuming unchanged conditions of demand, the prices of the
products in question will eventually rise because of the diminished supply.   If, on the contrary, prices temporarily rise above
expenses, labor and capital will gravitate toward these more
lucrative employments, and in due time, again assuming an unchanged demand, the increased output cannot find buyers except at a lower price per unit.

Thus did Marshall endeavor to trace the explanation of value
to certain long-run forces which respectively determine demand
and supply.   Day-to-day market prices vary for a number of
reasons from the normal prices fixed at the expenses of pro-

duction, yet tend constantly to oscillate about them. "In the long run," he declared, "the value of a thing tends to correspond to its cost of production." Hence it would appear that Marshall abandoned his conception of value as an equilibrium of co-ordinate forces, and stressed the influence of supply far more than that of demand. Seemingly, in declaring that normal value coincides with cost, and that the values of all reproducible goods tend toward the level of costs, he formulated his explanation of value in ultimate terms of cost.

Danger of over-simplification.— Yet such are but surface conclusions. The real Marshall frequently warns his readers that a simple statement of doctrine is necessarily false and mischievous. He is at pains to emphasize the infinite complexity inherent in the value problem, and to maintain that every factor in value determination is continually being reacted upon by changes in all the other factors. Cost of production does not determine value, he asserts, nor does marginal utility determine value, nor do even demand and supply determine value. Nor is the amount of the demand or of the supply controlled by price. No one factor in any given situation can be said to be the sole cause of any other one factor. The problem of value is at bottom a mighty complex of opposing forces, each one of which is mutually and continuously aiding in determining all of the others. In the principle of balance of forces, each cause is in turn effect and each effect in turn is cause. The equilibrium finally reached, whenever it is attained, is moreover seldom an exact balance but rather a more or less close approximation.

Into the vast ramifications of Marshall's value theory as expounded in Book V it is impossible to proceed farther. Illuminating and matured is his discussion of such topics as the investment and distribution of resources, joint and composite demand, joint and composite supply, marginal costs in relation to values, and the theory of monopolies.

Distribution.— In the final Book, "The Distribution of the National Income," and the longest of the six books of the *Principles,* he made two very considerable advances over his predecessors. In the first place he viewed distribution more as a human problem and less as a mechanical one. Secondly, he treated distribution as an application of the theory of value to special sets of circumstances. All the distribution problems, and many more besides, which Ricardo and Mill and others had discussed as separate in character from the laws of value, were taken up by him as part of the valuation process, a model quite generally followed by economists at present.

There is a certain annual dividend, he declared, composed of the material and immaterial goods produced within a country in the course of a year. This national dividend (substantially what Ricardo had in mind when he spoke of the annual produce of a country's workers, except that Marshall included the immaterial goods produced by lawyers, physicians, and the like) comes into being as a result of the co-operation of the four agents of production — land, labor, capital, and business enterprise. The problem of distribution is then briefly this : what forces determine the division of the national dividend between the four agents which have co-operated in its production ? In other words, how may we account for the rent received by landowners, the wages received by laborers, the interest received by capitalists, and the profits received by business men ? The answer of Marshall, as might have been expected, is that there is no simple solution for any of these problems. Aspects of distribution which arise during short periods are compared with those of longer (normal) periods ; the influence of demand, supply, and cost of production is carefully examined ; comprehensive use is made of the marginal analysis ; and all values are skillfully inter-related.

Theory of rent.— His theory of land rent is essentially that of Ricardo. With most of his contemporaries, he regarded land and capital as two separate categories ; he asserted that land has no cost of production, and that in settled countries its supply is fixed. He, therefore, held rent to be the surplus yielded by superior land because of greater fertility or more desirable situation. The modern practice among theorists is more and more to adopt the business man's point of view and to lump land and capital together as including all the durable material factors of production. Business men are accustomed, for example, to speak of the rent of a house as naturally as they do of a plot of ground. But Marshall broadened the classical rent concept by the introduction of a new concept, that of "quasi-rent," by which he distinguished the temporary surplus income yielded by certain man-made instruments of production.

He pointed out that over short periods of time factories, mills and machines sometimes yield returns to the capital invested in them above the current market rate of interest, and suggested that this income was analogous to the rent of land.

Theory of wages.—Wages he called the earnings of labor, and on this particular aspect of valuation he lavished a full measure of attentive inquiry. Rejecting the four "non-competing" groups of Cairnes, the theory that wages are determined by the marginal product of labor, and the notion of a general rate of wages, he held that no general proposition concerning wages can be wholly true. Demand, supply and other forces are influential in the determination of the price of labor, and mutually affect one another; yet Marshall placed most emphasis on the factor of supply, and explained wages more in terms of the cost of production of workers than of any other force. Here, too, he declared that, over short periods of time, wages, like interest on capital, may take on the characteristics of quasi-rent.

Theory of interest.—In its primary and narrowest meaning interest is the payment made for the use of money. Since money is usually borrowed in order that durable goods may be purchased for employment in production, interest is generally looked upon as payment for the use of capital. In the broadest sense, interest may be regarded as the return yielded by any kind of investment. The price that the borrower pays is commonly known to economists as *contract* or *gross interest*. This contract interest is nearly always larger than the pure interest representing the true productivity of the capital employed, inasmuch as the lender adds to the pure interest charge certain amounts to compensate himself for expenses involved in the making of the loan and its superintendence, for the risk he runs as to insecurity of payment of interest or principal, for the amortization required to restore whatever is loaned to its original condition, and for the chance that the purchasing power of money may vary to his disadvantage during the life of the loan.

All this had become fairly common knowledge by the time of Marshall. The problem confronting him was that of the determination of the rate of pure (or net) interest, for the peculiar thing about interest, as compared with rent, wages and profit, is that interest is the payment for the use of capital. This problem he handled in characteristic fashion. Recognizing that men offer a payment for the use of capital because of the gain which they anticipate from its use, and that they must offer such a payment because the supply of capital is limited, he again resorted to the familiar device of an equilibrium reached by the balancing of opposing forces of demand and supply. The rate will tend to be fixed at the point where the marginal lender's estimate of what ought to be paid to induce him to save equals the marginal borrower's estimate of the productivity of capital in his business. The demand of borrowers he held to be paramount over short periods and the supply of capital of chief importance over long periods. Thus no one theory of interest was stressed to the exclusion of any other, although emphasis was laid on the fact that mankind normally prefers present gratifications to those which are deferred, and that, in the long run, interest must conform to the costs of saving and waiting involved in the formation of capital.

Theory of profits.—No economic term is more open to misuse than that of profits. Not alone by economists, but by business men, accountants and others, the term is employed with many different meanings. The business man tends to think of his profits as the excess of his money income above all his money expenses. The economist endeavors to get beneath the surface, however, and deducts items other than money expenses before he arrives at what he considers real or economic profits. Thus he assumes that the business man should deduct the wage which he might reasonably receive were he an employee instead of an employer, and likewise the rent and interest which his land and capital would respectively return to him were they hired or loaned out to others instead of used in his own business. If allowance is made in this way, not alone for actual money expenses but also for what may be called imputed expenses, the economist is persuaded that business men will understand that all too often they are deluding themselves into thinking that they are receiving profits when in reality they are not.

Marshall added little to the theory of enterprise and profits. In his chapters on the profits of enterprise and business power, as he phrased it, he even failed to define profits, confining himself to the remark that all wages of management from foremen up to managing directors and owners of business enterprises should be classed as profits. To him the business enterpriser was essentially a capitalist, and profits a return on capital. In this connection, indeed, he barely distinguished enterprise as a fourth agent in production, drawing but a faint line of distinction between labor, capital, and enterprise. Profits nowadays are looked upon as the return which may accrue to the business enterpriser by reason of his superior direction of industry, and much more especially his assumption of risks that cannot be insured. Marshall rejected the risk theory of profits, and contented himself for the most part with the statement that profits are but one further instance of the equilibrium between demand and supply, the demand in this case being the demand for business ability and the supply the amount of such ability. In the short run, he averred, profits are a quasi-rent; in the long run, an inducement to enterprise.

Social progress.— The final chapter of the sixth book is devoted to the study of "progress in relation to standards of life." Here he wrote in his loftiest vein. After discussion of the advisability of shortened hours of labor and of the influence of trade unions on the standard of life of a nation, he passed to provisional conclusions as to possibilities of social progress. Keenly interested in the welfare of the masses, he believed that the wisest means of raising the wages of the army of unskilled workers lay in a thorough education of the character and faculties of all classes of people. Such education, obviously, would greatly increase the numbers of people capable of doing skilled work, and foster the development of that higher constructive imagination without which man cannot take more complete command over nature. The character which man now has is the product of long ages of selfishness and strife, he concluded, and forward-looking economic changes must await the slow transformation of that character.

Not the least remarkable part of this treatise is the thirteen appendices which occupy close to one hundred and fifty pages of fine print in the eighth edition. These appendices reveal on every page unmistakable evidence of enormous learning and brilliant insight. Much of the material appeared in earlier editions as portions of the main body of the volume.

Not a popular writer.—Marshall, like Adam Smith, Malthus and Mill, wrote for the general public, and the *Principles* did reach that public to a certain extent. Yet the book has never attained the immense popularity which greeted the productions of his classical predecessors. It is not in any real sense, particularly in the latter portion, a book for uninitiated readers. It must be studied intensively, not skimmed over, if even the general drift of his thought is to be caught. For though the rhetoric is unadorned, and nearly every sentence is simple, the style is by no means adapted to the intelligence of the average person. Page after page bears witness to what was perhaps his greatest weakness in exposition—an aversion, amounting almost to a phobia, to hard-and-fast statements.

The ordinary reading public demands precise formulations, unevasive narration, and clear-cut conclusions. It wants to know clearly what was in the author's mind. Here Marshall fails them. Seldom does he give an unequivocal answer to the problems which he propounds. His constant fear of being misunderstood and his striving for the acme of accuracy in expression lead him into such excessive caution in the phrasing of his thoughts that obscurity too often results. One must constantly turn back and occasionally forward in the attempt to piece scattered passages into a coherent whole. What meets the average reader is an unfortunate, although undeserved, impression of indecision.

The *Principles* is thus a work for the economic specialist, and for him it provides rich fare. Looking upon economic reasoning and laws not as a body of concrete truth in themselves, but as an engine for the discovery of that truth, Marshall rescued economics from the dogmatism which cursed it during the greater part of the nineteenth century, and restored it to a position of eminence comparable to the pinnacle attained in former days. He laid not the slightest claim to originality or novelty, holding merely that he had restated and reinterpreted the old and new doctrines in such a way as to make them conform more closely to the facts of his own age. Nor had he any illusions as to the permanency of his work. In all sincerity, when on one occasion he gave a copy of his *Principles* to a favored pupil, he inscribed it "to ——, in the hope that in due course he will render this treatise obsolete."

Summary.—Yet his contribution was invaluable. He was above all a scientist, nobly striving to place economics on its own foundations and to erect it firmly into a separate and independent discipline. For this enterprise he had the most extraordinary endowments. Keenly alive to the intricacies of economic problems, by temperament fitted for analysis and explanation, cognizant of the limitations of the deductive method, and deeply steeped in the lore of history, he combined the qualities of the true scholar in nearly unrivalled proportions.

Nothing attests Marshall's greatness more than his endeavor to bring within the scope of analysis the element of time and the factor of change. To this end he made a distinction between the short run, the long run, the normal, and the secular trend. We are thus enabled to comprehend somewhat better the significance of the forces in economic society which are working toward equilibrium and an adjustment of unbalanced situations.

His task was, of course, hopeless, since no one man, no matter how gifted, can unravel all the tangled skeins of economic theory. His reasoning and conclusions are incomplete and vulnerable, for at times he abandoned his rôle of scientist in order to show what was more or less immediately desirable and possible in matters of public policy. Hardly one of his concepts or doctrines has escaped attack in the past half century. Nevertheless, his system, though considerably shaken, still holds its position of primacy among contemporary accounts of the functioning of the competitive order of enterprise. Though he wrote for a generation that has now passed away, much of his doctrine is securely imbedded in the structure of economics. He could hardly have been expected to foresee the stupendous development of price limitation by governmental decree, by trade union activity, and by monopolistic agreements of every kind which are transforming the present era into one of price rigidity and collective action. He labored to analyze and explain economic phenomena as they then existed. Of a vastly different sort is the research connected with the future of the existing system. Most eminent lineal descendant of the classical masters, he is the father of economic science as it now prevails over a great part of the civilized globe.

CHAPTER XIV

SOCIAL ECONOMIC REFORMERS

PROPOSALS for the betterment of social and economic conditions have as a rule followed in the wake of those social and economic upheavals which have inflicted an extraordinary amount of misery on the unfortunate members of society most disadvantageously affected by the transformations. These proposals have usually appeared with increasing frequency during the past one hundred and fifty years as the effects of the greatest of all social and economic revolutions, the Industrial Revolution, have manifested themselves. With the coming of a new industrial order the most far reaching programs of reform have been enunciated by the socialists. Indeed, socialism goes to the extreme length of desiring the replacement of free, competitive enterprise by a co-operative and collectively organized society. Yet as regards the attitude toward practical problems of the moderate socialists and of social reformers, there has often been so little real difference that to draw a strict line of demarcation between them is difficult or impossible.

The status quo.— Broadly speaking, the reformers have looked upon the economic *status quo* as essentially healthy and have sought to improve society by altering merely some particular one of its phases. In their opinion the remedying of social and economic evils lies not in the overturn of the entire social structure, but in the modification of this or that existing condition or institution. Social reformers strive to steer a middle course between the two extremes of economic orthodoxy and socialism. To them the golden mean consists in that amount of state interventionism, as it is termed, which will normally ensure an increase in the economic welfare of the people. They believe that such orthodox principles as self-interest and free competition will work satisfactorily only when directed by social control.

As might be expected, the social reformers (or moralists or

interventionists, as they are sometimes called) cannot be grouped along consistent lines of development. In the case of some of these writers, moreover, their criticism of the scope or the method of the classical economics was as notable as their advocacy of government regulation in behalf of social reform. Rigid classification of the opponents of the orthodox doctrines is, to say the least, a thankless task. Of the hundreds, indeed, thousands of social reformers who might be cited, only a handful will be alluded to, and in this policy of rigorous and arbitrary exclusion much injustice inevitably results.

Sismondi.— Representative of this type of dissent from prevalent laissez-faire ideas, the first in order of time of a long line of economists or quasi-economists was perhaps the prolific Swiss writer Jean Charles Leonard Simonde de Sismondi (1773-1842). Of an aristocratic family originally Italian, he entered early in life upon the career of a scholar and writer. Visiting England in his youth, he published a treatise, *Commercial Wealth,* in 1803, in which admiration for the doctrines of Adam Smith is revealed on nearly every page. Thereafter he devoted his attention for years mainly to historical, literary, and political studies, the result of which was an almost incredible literary output. He wrote, for example, a sixteen-volume work on the history of the Italian Republics in the Middle Ages and capped this achievement with a history of the French people in twenty-nine volumes. He is thus remembered primarily as an historian.

Sismondi's pessimism.— After an interval of fifteen years he returned to the study of economics and published in two volumes in 1819 his *New Principles of Political Economy or of Wealth in Its Relation to Population,* the work upon which his fame as an economist rests. In startling contrast to his earlier mood he wrote in the gloomiest of language of a world cursed, as he saw it, by the application of the principle of division of labor to the employment of women and children, the evil influence of the introduction of machinery, the exploitation of laborers, the prevalence of low wages, and maladjustments of production and consumption resulting in recurring commercial crises and depressions, ideas which he reiterated in later economic writings.

Not that he completely disavowed the theoretical principles

of the orthodox economics. He disagreed, rather, with the views of Adam Smith and Ricardo regarding the purpose and method of political economy and the relation of the government to business. Economists, he affirmed, had concerned themselves all too much with the means of increasing material wealth and all too little with the promotion of human welfare through the use of this wealth. Terming the classical economics the science of *chrematistics,* he sought to put economics upon a new basis, since in his opinion the true wealth of a country consisted not in the extent and character of its tangible goods but in the enjoyment and happiness of its people. Of what use, he argued, was a study which calmly disregarded the fact that the rich were becoming richer and the poor becoming poorer, through faulty distribution of the rapidly increasing wealth of the community.

Accordingly, he strongly urged that thinkers turn their backs upon the concept of economics as the science of the production of wealth, and view the subject as the art of augmenting national happiness. "Political economy at its widest," he stated, "is a theory of charity, and any theory that upon last analysis has not the result of increasing the happiness of mankind does not belong to the science at all." To him the chief task of the economist was the discovery of that proportion between the population of a country and its wealth which would assure the highest possible well-being of its inhabitants.

Not alone did he level his criticism at the aim of the classical school, as it seemed to him, but also at the method employed. Hitting especially at Ricardo and J. B. Say, he asserted that economics must be erected on the foundation of the concrete and historical method. The true economist must perforce come to his conclusions primarily in consequence of historical study, and must eschew the indiscriminate use of broad generalizations made upon the basis merely of deduction. Analysing economic evolution, he divided industrial history into the three stages of slavery, feudalism and modern capitalism, stages in which some commentators have professed to discover the germ of the economic interpretation of history propounded somewhat later by Marx.

Most ironically, Sismondi found it necessary to use abstract analysis when he came to work out his own scheme of distribution, upon which his doctrine of the over-production theory of crises rests, and in the use of the abstract method he fell into errors fully as grievous as those which he charged against economic theorists with whom he did not see eye to eye. Like many another writer before and since, he was on much safer ground in his condemnation of the social and economic ills of society than in the reasoning with which he endeavored to support his indictment. In any event, in his emphasis upon the necessity of studying the evolution of economic institutions, he must be regarded as an important precursor of the historical school of thought.

Proposed reforms.— Deeply sympathetic for the sufferings of the underprivileged, Sismondi broke entirely with the doctrine of the spontaneous harmony of interests propounded by Adam Smith, and in an age of laissez-faire he raised a protesting voice in favor of government interventionism. He advocated such reforms, for instance, as the grant to workmen of the right of organization, curtailing of the hours of labor, abolition of all work on Sunday, limitations on child labor, and the curbing of production by restricting the progress of invention. Yet regarding the procedure by which the practical attainment of his objectives might be worked out, he confessed himself, in last analysis, pathetically at sea. Indeed he declared that the formulation of the necessary measures was much more the task of the legislator than of the economist. His was chiefly a negative criticism of industrialism, nor did he leave any important followers or disciples. Yet his influence upon economic thought and especially upon the socialists has not been inconsiderable. Louis Blanc drew freely upon him; Rodbertus is believed to have borrowed his theory of crises; and Marx appropriated his analysis of the increasing concentration of wealth in the hands of fewer and fewer capitalists.

Leading figure among the early so-called welfare economists, he drew attention to the necessity of enlarging the area of discussion with which economists must deal, anticipated in his method the approach of new schools of thought that were soon to emerge, and developed arguments which comprise much of what is nowadays included in trade-unionism, protective labor and social legislation, and social insurance. Almost alone in his attitude, and one of the forgotten men of his age, he has finally and deservedly come into his own, as economics has more and more inclined to the social point of view.

Literary propagandists.—Contemporary with Sismondi, there arose in Great Britain a large and distinguished group of literary figures vigorously opposed to certain aspects of the new industrial order and certain doctrines of its theoretical defenders. Outstanding in this revolt were the poets Byron, Coleridge, Shelley and Wordsworth; the essayists Arnold, Carlyle, and Ruskin; the novelists Dickens and Reade; and the pamphleteer Cobbett. In France, Georges Sand, in Russia Leo Tolstoy, and in America Ralph Waldo Emerson were representative of this far-flung esthetic protest, a protest that dramatically inveighed against the materialism and ugliness of modern industrialism, and yet for the most part proposed but little in the way of reform programs.

Most devastating of those who indicted the evils of the Industrial Revolution were probably Charles Dickens, Thomas Carlyle, and John Ruskin. In *David Copperfield* and other novels, Dickens drew attention vividly to the ruthless practices of the industrialists. Thomas Carlyle, like Dickens, was primarily a propagandist, thrusting at the stupidities of his time at first in allegorical style, as in *Sartor Resartus*, and, in later writings, blasting with bitter invective what he termed "the brutish empire of Mammon." John Ruskin, no whit less stinging in his reproof, assailed the classical economics as a science of "illth" rather than a science of wealth, showed clearly the superficiality of many of the current notions regarding wealth, and proposed paternalistic measures to bring about a more just distribution of commodities.

Pope Leo XIII.— In Catholic circles, many prominent men have actively urged upon the Church the promotion of social justice. Besides Bishop von Ketteler, Franz Hitze, and numerous others, special mention must be made of Pope Leo XIII, most socially-minded of all the popes of the nineteenth century. During the twenty-five years of his long pontificate (1878-1903) eight of his encyclicals bore more or less directly on matters connected with social justice. Of these encyclicals the one entitled *Rerum Novarum* (The Condition of the Working Classes, 1891) most thoroughly discussed the topic of remedial social legislation, and is regarded as his profoundest utterance on the labor question. The Catholic social movement received at his hands a sanction and a direction which up to that time had not existed. Reaffirmation of his pronouncements in favor of governmental intervention in behalf of the laboring classes was made in 1931 by Pope Pius XI.

Hobson.—In the long line of interventionists, no contemporary writer holds a more honorable place than does John A. Hobson, probably the most widely read of unorthodox British economists in the United States, and typical figure in the current world group of welfare economists. Born in 1858, he received a classical education at Oxford University where the reforming spirit of Ruskin inoculated him with the fundamental idea of the inadequacy of laissez-faire policies in a world of social and economic injustice. At the age of thirty, he began to give university extension lectures in English and economics to working class people later enrolled in The Workingmen's Educational Association, an organization which provides a high type of adult education seldom found beyond the confines of Great Britain. Toward the close of the century he became a journalist connected with liberal weekly journals. He died in 1940.

In addition to a vast amount of journalistic work, he somehow found time to publish the impressive total of thirty-seven books dealing with economic subjects, of which perhaps the best known is called *The Evolution of Modern Capitalism* (1894) and the most discussed is entitled *Work and Wealth : A Human Evaluation* (1914). He never occupied an academic chair, and until comparatively recently his lack of technical training in economic theory and the unorthodox character and seeming thinness of much of his writing caused him to be looked upon askance by large numbers of professional economists. With public recognition by Professor Keynes in 1931 of his theory of the business cycle, his unquestioned intellectual ability at last received a stamp of approval all too long withheld.[1]

Welfare economics.—Hobson differs from the rank and file of economists by his advocacy of welfare as the central problem of economics. Yet nowhere has he expressly defined

---

[1] *See* "J. A. Hobson" by J. R. Commons in *The American Economic Review* for December, 1923

what he means by welfare. He takes it for granted that welfare is synonymous with the good life, and that there is a large and growing body of agreement throughout the civilized world as to the meaning of this good life. Increasing economic welfare would hence connote such things as an increase in production, a bettering of the quality of the goods produced, a reduction in the relative amount of effort and material resources required to produce those goods, diminution of industrial accidents and the lengthening of human life, a higher degree of literacy in the population, improvement in standards of consumption, and an increasingly more equitable distribution of wealth. In brief, he holds that the production, consumption, and distribution of wealth must be analyzed primarily from the standpoint of human welfare.

What he has attempted to do is to translate the ideals of his master, John Ruskin, into an economic system of human valuation. Believing in the necessity of fundamental changes in the economic structure of society, and confident that such changes can be brought about, he has striven first to present a full exposure of the inhumanity and waste of modern industry, next to find some intelligible and consistent methods of human valuation for economic goods and processes, and finally to indicate the most hopeful measures of remedy. His procedure is most easily followed in his *Work and Wealth*. He is much more than a mere dissenter from the dominant body of economic theory, since he offers a concrete program of reform within the framework of capitalism. Not only does he seek the truth regarding certain economic phenomena but he wishes to see that truth applied in practice. To him, as to many other economists, economics is both a science and an art. The phrase, "economic art," is one which he frequently employs in his writings.

Hobson's indictments.—Hobson indicts current economic science on three counts. He asserts that it puts an exaggerated emphasis on production, that it sets up a monetary standard of values not related to human welfare, and treats human actions as simply a means to the production of marketable wealth. This he condemns as narrow and sordid. Instead he proposes an analysis of production from the standpoint of human costs, a similar analysis of the human utilities which emerge as a consequence of production, and the striking of a balance between these human costs and human utilities. In other words, he looks upon economics as a study of a broad field of human activity in which full consideration must be given to man the human being rather than to man the commodity.

Human costs.— Productive activities are usually discussed by modern writers on economics in connection with the four standard factors of land, labor, capital, and enterprise. Hobson will have none of these conventional categories, and offers a unique classification under the following heads : art, invention, professional service, organization, management, labor and saving. Landowners, he insists, are put to no costs in any way corresponding to the payments which they exact for the use of their land. Thus rent is in the nature of an unearned return ; the exertions of landowners represent no net human costs.

As for the saving which is responsible for the accumulation of capital, human costs arise only when the saving is done by people of small incomes, since there is no sacrifice involved in the saving practiced by the middle and upper classes. Hence, in his opinion, the human costs of production are almost entirely borne by the various kinds of labor. And yet he feels that even in the case of labor there is much activity that represents no net human costs. To be specific, he maintains that most of the work of the artistic, inventive, professional, official and managerial classes is so interesting and so agreeable that it would be carried on with zest provided only their "human keep," as he phrases it, were assured. Thus the sole kind of labor that involves net human costs is that of the manual worker, since the greatest strain upon the human organism is found in machine tending, ditch digging and the like, where monotonous repetition, often at a swift pace for a long working day, is the main characteristic of the job.

Classification of consumption.— With production disposed of and the human costs of production asserted to rest primarily upon small savers and those engaged in manual labor, Hobson turns to the human utilities of consumption or, in other words, the satisfactions yielded by consumption. He divides human needs into three categories : physical needs, industrial needs —

(needs which arise by reason of the nature of one's work, as the need of a college professor for books in his particular field), and conventional needs.

In connection with this third class of need, he lashes out at modern standards of consumption; to him conventional needs stand for useless and even harmful demands. He has in mind that part of the consumption of all the classes of society which is devoted to the gratification of human vanity and "cussedness." He is insistent that physical and industrial needs be satisfied, while convinced, on the other hand, that the satisfaction of conventional needs results in naught but an addition to the already large total of human costs.

Such obstacles to right standards of consumption as the lack of standardization of consumers' goods, the ignorance of consumers, the irrational character of many of our group customs and practices, the ostentatious manner of living of the rich and their emulation by the moderately well-to-do and even by the poor, and finally the partial control of consumption by producers through advertising and salesmanship, all combine to create an appalling amount of economic waste. Moreover, this wasteful consumption so reduces the productive efficiency of consumers as to prevent mankind from making the greatest contribution to production of which it is capable.

Redistribution of wealth.— Thus he clears the ground for the doctrine by which he is perhaps best known. Since much of production is mal-production, and much of consumption is mal-consumption, he proposes such a redistribution of wealth as will minimize human costs and maximize human utilities. His "human law of distribution" runs as follows: society should distribute the cost of production according to the ability of individuals to bear those costs, and should distribute the produced goods among consumers according to their capacity to derive utility from them.

In brief, "from each in accordance with his ability and to each in accordance with his needs as a consumer." The enforcement of this reform is necessary, he believes, because society fails to realize that business is a co-operative venture for mutual gain. This failure he ascribes to the growing subdivision of labor, which removes the producer from the consumer, the stress of competition which fosters antagonisms, and the anonymity of modern business inherent in the growing use of the corporation.

Social control.— The achievement of this goal, it goes without saying, requires the intervention of the state through various devices of social control. This does not mean the replacement of capitalism by collectivism, he avers, but simply such a curbing of the profit motive as will bring about a better distribution of what he terms the "unproductive surplus." He desires particularly a limitation upon exclusive property rights, such as land ownership, and upon the peculiar ability that some men possess to amass unearned wealth through the building up of monopolistic positions.

To this end, he would socialize all industries which tend toward monopoly, all which perform an essential public service, and all which are largely reduced to routine operations. He would likewise socialize most of the professions. He would accord a large measure of freedom to new or experimental industries, and would leave all artistic activity absolutely untrammeled. Minimum wage laws and the high taxation of inheritances and excess profits together with other social legislation would insure the payment of higher wages to the majority of the population without slowing up the rate of progress, would vastly raise the standard of consumption, and would permit the rendering of an increased number of social services.

The most important of all the contributions of the application of the human law of distribution, in his own words, "would lie in other fields of personality than the distinctly economic, in the liberation, realization, and improved condition of other intellectual and spiritual energies at present thwarted by or subordinated to industrialism."

Theory of business cycles.— It is not an oversight, furthermore, which leads Hobson to base his explanation of recurring business depressions upon the unequal distribution of wealth between labor and capital. In essence, his theory is a modification of the labor exploitation theory of Marx. He maintains that since the well-to-do are unable to consume all of their income in times of prosperity, they invest their surplus in productive capital, with the consequence that the output of consumers' goods increases, consumers cannot buy this continually growing flow of commodities except at lower prices, there is an excess of production over consumption, prices collapse, and profits decline. Industry curtails output while the surplus is disposed of at these low prices, consumption finally catches up with production, business revives, profits of the well-to-do once more reappear and are again productively invested, the output of industry once more becomes too large for consumers to absorb, and another collapse of prices brings on a new depression.

Thus he attributes business depressions to the failure of consumer demand to keep pace with the production of commodities. There are writers who agree with him in this analysis, while others suggest that no single explanation is adequate and seek to give recognition to each of many significant factors.

His criticism of the marginal analysis offered by Jevons and the Austrians is most penetrating. Rejecting their argument that the predictable element of one's expenditure is the marginal element, he maintains, on the contrary, that this is the very portion of expenditure most characterized by guesswork. He insists that money is generally expended on the basis of social convention, and that hence the bulk of expenditure goes for such things as housing, food, and clothing after calculated adjustment of income to social requirements. Whatever income is left is spent in a hit-or-miss fashion. His view is therefore that the average individual gives little consideration as to how the last (marginal) penny or dollar shall be spent, and that the economist does well to confine his attention to what is known as the intramargin expenditure.

Summary.— What sort of economics is it, if indeed it be economics at all, that Hobson presented in his thirty odd books and innumerable newspaper and magazine articles? Some have dignified his ideas with the designation of "social economics," as distinct from the traditional deductive and static economics of price, exchange, value, and distribution. He is concerned not with wealth as such but with welfare in terms of the biological and psychological traits of man. His main criticism is of those economic theories which accept the weights that price and control of money assign to human worth, and his chief constructive work is that of the social crusader who regards it as part of the task of the economist to throw more light upon the ultimate ends of life. True it is that he involves himself at times in faulty logic and philosophical difficulties. But what economist has not? Even in Adam Smith, Ricardo, and John Stuart Mill may be observed the influence of contradictory cross-currents of thought. Economists must perforce traverse ground where the footing, to say the least, is treacherous.

However debatable the assumption that any general theory of welfare can be postulated at this stage in the development of knowledge it must be granted that Hobson has rendered two distinguished services to the cause of economics. On the one hand he has demanded that professional economists take fresh stock of themselves, and has forced them in greater or less degree to reconsider the premises upon which they have been proceeding. He has raised anew the issue as to what is or should be the subject of economics, and has brought considerable pressure to bear in favor of a broad interpretation of the confines of this particular science. On the other hand, he has done vastly more than the average economist to interest the mass of people in at least some of the problems with which economists have to deal. In the main he uses the language of the common man, he drives home his points by means of frequent repetition, and he proposes specific solutions to certain fundamental questions. He has made economics live for countless thousands whose curiosity might otherwise never have been aroused, and for this no inconsiderable feat he deserves the plaudits of fellow-workers whose labored efforts have met with a response far short of his.

Chapter XV

PRE-MARXIAN SOCIALISM

THE earliest and most scathing indictment of orthodox economics was made by economic radicals who may conveniently, though somewhat inaccurately, be lumped together under the one head of socialists.

The word "socialist" is derived from the Latin *socius,* meaning comrade, and appears to have first been used in print, together with the term "socialism," in *The Poor Man's Guardian* in 1833. From England the employment of these two words quickly spread to the continent where they soon gained wide currency. The history of radical criticism of economic society is a very old record, however, reaching back to the ancient Greeks and to the Hebrew prophets.

History of Radical Socialism.—Of the utopian schemes proposed in antiquity, that of Plato in his *Republic* is beyond doubt the best known. Nearly two thousand years elapsed before another elaborate description of an ideal society made its appearance with the disintegration of feudalism and consequent social and economic unrest. Sir Thomas More's *Utopia* (*Utopia* is Greek for "Nowhere") which has given its name to all similar plans, pictured in 1516 one of the most discussed of all ideal city states. Somewhat later followed Tommaso Campanella's *The City of the Sun* (1623), Francis Bacon's *New Atlantis* (1627), James Harrington's *Oceana* (1656) and Jean Jacques Rousseau's *The Social Contract* (1762). In more recent times, utopian ideals were set forth in William Morris' *News from Nowhere*, Edward Bellamy's *Looking Backward* and H. G. Wells' *New Worlds for Old.* These pictures of an ideal society were no mere brainstorms of disordered minds, but came naturally from the unjust social and economic contemporary conditions. In no case, however, did socialist activity result.

The beginning of true social radicalism is sometimes attributed to a comparatively unknown Frenchman named Morelly and to the Abbé de Mably, both of whom wrote at about 1750. Yet the first direct steps toward an active socialist movement were undertaken by François Noël Baboeuf, who attempted unsuccessfully toward the end of that century to capture the government of France for the purpose of establishing social and economic equality. Modern socialism dates from two revolutions,— that in the world of ideas, resulting in the epoch-making French Revolution, and the second one, designated as the Industrial Revolution. Socialism as known today is a phenomenon of the nineteenth century. It arose from the new currents of philosophic thought in France, which stressed ideals of equality and fraternity, and from the unprecedented misery among the masses produced by the factory system. The socialist movement which appeared about 1800 has ever since had a continuous and widening development, until by now it has spread over much of the civilized portion of the globe.

Socialism in the nineteenth century.— During the first half of the nineteenth century, socialism was chiefly utopian in character. The utopian socialists differed from the utopians of previous centuries, in concerning themselves not with intellectual problems solely but also with the working out of methods designed to attain their ends. For this reason they are sometimes designated as "realistic" utopians. Motivated largely by ethical considerations, they set as their goal the establishment of a heaven on earth then and there instead of in some vague hereafter. Human nature, they asserted, is primarily the product of social environment; to do away with man's selfishness and greed, let us create a new social and economic order by means of human intelligence. For private property in the instruments of production (the cornerstone of the classical economy), they proposed the substitution of collective ownership to at least a considerable degree; for freedom of individual enterprise, fraternal co-operation; and for inequality in wealth and income, either outright equality or a drastic approach to it. Their socialism was thus a program of both economic and moral reform, designed to reconstruct all society, rich and poor alike; it assumed that the possibilities of reshaping human nature are infinite.

Most publicized of the utopian socialists were the Frenchmen, Count Henri de Saint-Simon (1760-1825), François Charles Marie Fourier (1772-1835), and Etienne Cabet (1788-1856), and the Englishmen, Charles Hall (1740?-1820) and Robert Owen (1771-1858). Saint-Simon, long regarded as the pioneer in this group, was more the teacher and scholar than anything else. Of all the socialists of that time, excepting Fourier, he alone contemplated the erection of a new science to deal with the novel social problems raised by the Industrial Revolution. His fragmentary ideas were later on worked up and greatly expanded by Auguste Comte, known as the coiner of the modern term, sociology. In his principal work, *The Industrial System* (1821), Saint-Simon demanded that society be organized on an industrial rather than a political basis, with gifted scientific leaders and industrial chiefs replacing the old feudal and theological bureaucracy as rulers of a new industrial world. In this reorganized society all were to work, and individual rights of competition, property, inheritance and personal liberty were to be subordinated to the common good. These ideas form the basis of twentieth century socialism. The colony established by his disciples soon dissolved.

Fourier.— Fourier, unlike Saint-Simon, did not wish to reform society in one gigantic turnover. He is known, along with Cabet, Owen and others, as an *associationist*, or, in other words, as an advocate of socialist associations with limited memberships. He possessed a none-too-well-balanced mind. It is alleged, for example, that from middle age on he never knew the day of the week, or the month of the year, or even winter from summer. None the less his influence places him in the forefront of all French socialists.

After a checkered career as soldier and business man he voiced the thesis that, analogous to the law of gravitation in the physical world, there was a physical law of attraction applying to society. With all artificial obstacles to the working of this law removed, free play would be accorded the untrammeled exercise of the twelve human passions ; social harmony thus would result. To achieve this harmony society was to be reorganized into voluntarily formed autonomous communities of about four hundred families each. In these "apartment-house utopias," styled by him "phalanxes," all were to work within certain age limits, the highest rewards going to those who performed the most unattractive tasks. The "phalanxes" were more like joint-stock associations than pure communistic enterprises, since allowance was made for private property; after the deduction of a certain minimum for each member, five-twelfths of the surplus was to go to labor, four-twelfths to capital, and three-twelfths to talent (management). Alteration of family life was insured by the prohibition of monogamy, for he maintained that all social progress is proportioned to the progress of Woman toward liberty. The capital city of the world federation of these "phalanxes" was to be located at Constantinople.

In vain did Fourier wait for some philanthropist to finance his project. His books,—among them *The Theory of the Four Movements* (1808) and *The New Industrial World* (1829) were seldom read. Only after his death, did his influence make itself felt to any great extent. Certain of his criticisms of capitalist society were incorporated into the writings of Karl Marx and other socialists, and more than forty Fourierist communities were started, most of them in the United States where land was both abundant and cheap. Of the American colonies, the best known was the Brook Farm Phalanx, founded in 1841 near Boston and supported by many literary figures, including Horace Greeley, Nathaniel Hawthorne, Ralph Waldo Emerson, and James Russell Lowell.

Cabet's *Voyage to Icaria* (1840), in the form of a novel, pictured a socialist society approaching equality in distribution, and gained for him a following of several hundred adherents. As a result several "Icarian" communities were established in the United States, particularly in Texas in 1848 and in Illinois in 1849.

Robert Owen.— The utopian movement in Great Britain revolved almost entirely around the activity of one man, Robert Owen, since the British physician, Charles Hall, confined himself to an indictment of the private ownership of land, although he foreshadowed Karl Marx in enunciating a labor theory of value and the concept of surplus value. Owen, born in North Wales, early amassed a fortune in manufacturing in England and Scotland, and came to his socialistic views through close contact with actual industrial conditions. While manager of cotton mills at New Lanark, Scotland, he introduced what is now termed "welfare work." Successful in transforming a once poverty-stricken village into a model community of healthy and industrious people, and even in making his benevolence return profits, he was emboldened to consider the complete reformation of society. His proposal, unfolded over a period of years in works such as *A New View of Society* (1813-1814) and *The Book of the New Moral World* (1820), assumed that industrial and other evils were the products of the capitalistic system, of religion (although Owen himself was a deist), and of the institution of marriage. Hence he called for the establishment of ideal industrial colonies, somewhat similar to those favored by Fourier, in which the above barriers to man's natural goodness would be removed.

Putting his theory into practice, he organized the New Harmony community in the United States (Indiana) and similar communities in Great Britain. Returning to England in 1829, broken in finances but not in spirit, he set up Equitable Banks for Labor Exchange to which producers might take their commodities, receive labor notes in exchange, and in return for these notes obtain goods valued at a like amount of labor time, thus doing away with middlemen. With indefatigable ardor, he agitated for factory legislation, trade-unionism, and cooperative societies of various sorts. His publication *What is Socialism?* (1841) was probably the first book to make use of this new word in its title. In later years, he devoted himself almost entirely to propaganda. He died at the advanced age of eighty-seven in comparative obscurity.

"Father" of factory legislation, of the British co-operative movement, and of British socialism, Owen is an appealing and arresting figure. He left no sect; his colonies and other experimental projects failed. Yet in stressing the influence of environment on human character and the benefits of the co-operative association, with its emphasis on the abolition of profits, he left a most enduring mark. He was essentially a pioneer and promoter. His tombstone bears this fitting inscription in his own words: "It is the one great and universal interest of the human race to be cordially united and to aid each other to the full extent of their capacities."

However admirable the programs of the utopian socialists, the leaders woefully underestimated the difficulties in their execution; nor did they recognize the forces which underlie economic evolution. If any moral may be drawn it is : to withdraw from the world is not to change the world; any fundamental reformation of industrial society is extremely difficult without the aid of the government, society's most powerful institution.

Christian socialism arose during this period, in reaction against the atheistic proposals of many utopians. Its origins have been traced by some to the French Catholic priest Robert de Lamennais (1782-1854) and by others to Saint-Simon's *The New Christianity*. At all events, the title properly includes both Catholic and Protestant reformers. In Great Britain, Christian socialism developed under Frederick Denison Maurice (1805-1872), most brilliant member of the group; Charles Kingsley (1819-1875), well known for his novels, and Thomas Hughes (1822-1896), of *Tom Brown* fame, stressing, as elsewhere, the immoral character of the industrial system and seeking to govern economic society by the Golden Rule. Its most lasting achievement was the impetus which it gave to humanitarian legislation, and to the organization of profit-sharing and co-operative societies. The Christian socialism of the twentieth century continues to advocate changes in the social and economic environment, though marked by much diversity of opinion.

Ricardian Socialists.—Somewhat apart from the utopian socialists, stood a group of British writers termed "Ricardian socialists," chief among whom were William Thompson (1785-1833), John Francis Bray (died about 1840), John Gray (died about 1850), and Thomas Hodgskin (1787-1869). They advocated labor time as the standard of value and "anticipated" the Marxian concept of surplus value.

Louis Blanc.—A new note was sounded by the Frenchman, Louis Blanc (1811-1882), author of *Organization of Labor* (1841), and often classed as an associationist and a utopian. A separate classification is more logical, however, inasmuch as he depended not upon the spread of education for the success of his program but upon the aid of the government to establish what he termed social workshops. These shops, designed eventually to replace private industry, were to be subsidized and controlled by the state and united in one federation. Remuneration was to take place in accordance with needs or wants. His plan was given a half-hearted trial following upon the great proletarian revolution of 1848 in France and soon failed. His socialist creed significantly denied the efficacy of purely spontaneous associations, and held passionately to the idea of state socialism.

Proudhon.— Most difficult of classification is Pierre Joseph Proudhon (1809-1865). His was, in the main, a negative philosophy. Rarely has any one attacked socialism more vigorously. "It never has been and never will be anything," he stated in his greatest work, the *System of Economic Contradictions, or Philosophy of Poverty* (1846). Nor had he any higher regard for the capitalistic system, for to him property was theft (a borrowed phrase, incidentally), as he stated in a much earlier volume, *What is Property?* (1840). Bitterly, furthermore, he denounced all forms of government and authority, including the Church. Not for him any ready-made utopia! Yet when the revolution of 1848 forced him to declare himself constructively he proposed a reconstruction of society that was in effect but another utopian dream. Stressing the necessity of both liberty and equality he advocated an exchange bank where paper money would be issued for goods only in accordance with the labor time required for their production, and where producers might borrow freely without the payment of interest. Thus property would exist, but it would rest entirely upon the amount of labor performed. The rights and duties of all were to be mutual, hence the term "mutualism" which he applied to his program. Possibly the title of individualistic anarchist most aptly fits him.

Until about 1850, the center of the socialist stage was held by utopian socialism. With the year 1848 the scene in both thought and action shifted from France and Great Britain to another part of Europe. Leadership in economic radicalism passed to Germany. New types of socialism came to the fore and presently revolutionized the socialist movement. This change in emphasis arose partly because French visionary socialism was discredited by the failure of the revolution of 1848, partly because of the nearly virgin field which Germany offered to the introduction of reform ideas, but mostly because of the genius of several men, German born, all of them original thinkers.

Rodbertus.—Karl Johann Rodbertus (1805-1875), surnamed von Jagetzow from his estate, was a Prussian lawyer with a marked dislike for agitation and a horror of revolution ; he is considered by many as the founder of so-called scientific socialism. He spent most of his life in retirement, and became one of the most learned men of his times. His principal views are contained in one of his early writings, *To a Knowledge of our Economic Condition* (1842).

Starting with the propositions that labor produces all economic goods, either directly or indirectly (although he regarded intellectual labor, like land, as a free gift of nature), and that all goods ought to exchange in proportion to the amounts of labor that produce them, he stated that the main problem confronting the economist was that of distributive justice. Obviously production was being carried on solely for profit ; wage earners were getting only the cost of their subsistence, and were therefore receiving a continually decreasing proportion of the national income. With a diminishing wage share, the consumption of wage earners was bound to lag behind the increase in productivity, thus leading in time to market gluts, falling prices, unemployment and all the other familiar characteristics of crises (a theory originated by Sismondi).

A cure for these maladjustments lay in the ultimate attainment of political power by the masses and the ensuing ownership of the means of production by the state — an ideal which might not be reached in fewer than five or six centuries through a slow evolutionary process. For the time being, the evils of capitalistic exploitation could be immensely lessened by government establishment of a shortened working day, the determination of a normal amount of work per day, the readjustment of wages to correspond with changes in the productivity of labor, the fixing of prices, and their measurement in a labor currency. In this way the existing interests of the capitalists and landowners would be preserved, while, at the same time a much larger share of the annual product was assured the masses. Thus emerges the mild state socialism (or, if one prefer, state capitalism) of Rodbertus, second only to Marx himself in his influence upon the succeeding train of socialist thought.

Lassalle.—In marked contrast was Ferdinand Lassalle (1825-1864), the firebrand of German socialism. Of Jewish extraction, an aristocrat by inclination, possessed of remarkable endowments, and with little regard for the conventions, his short and stormy career was devoted alternately to militant socialism and to literary pursuits. In him as in few men were combined the student and the man of action. In his rôle as agitator he roused the workingmen of Germany from centuries of apathy and oppression, founding the Social Democratic Party (the General Association of German Workers) in 1863, demanding universal suffrage, and proposing the replacement of capitalism by co-operative producers' associations supported by the state. In order not to alienate the middle classes he stressed the subsistence nature of wages, and coined the phrase "iron (or brazen) law of wages." His attacks on capitalism and private property were based in great measure on the belief that mankind is ruled by chance (conjuncture) beyond the control of the individual, thus making it necessary that the government take over production and distribution for the sake of social welfare. When at the height of his reputation he was unhappily killed in a duel.

Chapter XVI

KARL MARX AND POST-MARXIAN SOCIALISM

From the state socialism of Rodbertus and Lassalle to the international revolutionary socialism of Karl Marx and Friedrich Engels is a mighty leap. Of these two men Marx was, of course, the indispensable partner; and yet the practical contributions of Engels must never be minimized.

Marx.— Karl Heinrich Marx (1818-1883) was born of middle class Jewish parents at Treves, near Coblenz, Germany, the third of nine children and the only son to live to maturity. When he was six years old, his parents embraced Christianity, which may or may not be the reason why Marx was something of an anti-Semite to the end of his days. After the completion of his elementary education with an excellent scholastic record, and in deference to his father's wishes he entered nearby Bonn University with the intention of studying jurisprudence and becoming a lawyer or entering government service. The following year he transferred to the University of Berlin where he applied himself after a fashion to a variety of subjects. Becoming attracted to the doctrine of the philosopher Hegel, then at the zenith of his influence, that society is constantly in a state of flux, he devoted himself to philosophy and received his degree as doctor of philosophy at the University of Jena in 1841. Barred by his radical views from securing a university appointment as lecturer, he entered journalism. Then ensued a tempestuous epoch of nearly ten years, during which he edited various radical journals in Germany and France, became a socialist, wrote several books, married Jenny von Westphalen after an engagement of seven years, and formed the beginning of his lasting friendship with Engels.

Engels.— Friedrich Engels (1820-1895), two years younger than Karl Marx, was the son of a wealthy German textile manufacturer. Brought up to his father's business he interested himself at an early age in radical movements and philosophies, and by 1844, when his close association with Marx began, he had already acquired considerable reputation as a writer.   Jovial, thoroughly loyal and self-effacing, he was exactly the kind of man needed to offset the fiery temper of his co-worker.

In 1845, the year in which Engels published his most important independent work, *The Condition of the Working Class in England*, and collaborated with Marx in writing *The Holy Family*, Marx was expelled from France and moved to Belgium, where he resided for the following three years.   In 1847 he replied to Proudhon's *Philosophy of Poverty* in merciless fashion with a book entitled *The Poverty of Philosophy*. Proudhon was then the best known radical on the continent. A year later, at the instance of the newly formed Communist League, an organization of workers, Marx and Engels drafted and issued in German the *Communist Manifesto* as the platform of that League.   At that time socialism included chiefly the adherents of various utopian programs.   Communism, on the contrary, was the term applied to the working class movement.

Communist Manifesto.— The *Communist Manifesto* (1848), a document of about thirty ordinary sized pages, and the most widely read of all socialist literature, consists of a short introduction and of four sections.   The first, and longest, entitled, "Bourgeois and Proletarians," treats of the rise of the class of modern capitalists (the *bourgeoisie*) and its struggle with the class of modern wage-earners (the *proletariat*).   Section two, entitled, "Proletarians and Communists," gives a philosophic interpretation of this class struggle and of the bourgeois objections to communism, predicts the inevitable triumph of collectivism (in its first stages, a dictatorship of the proletariat), and suggests the steps necessary to usher in the co-operative commonwealth (e.g., the abolition of the right of inheritance, the introduction of free education, and the extension of government ownership).   Section three, devoted to Socialist and Communist Literature, is a none-too-fair appraisal of previous socialist literature.   The final section, less than two pages in length, giving the Position of the Communists in Relation to the Various Existing Opposition Parties, declares that "the Communists everywhere support every revolutionary movement against the existing social and political order of things," and closes with the following words : "Let the ruling classes tremble at a Communistic revolution. The proletarians have nothing to lose but their chains. They have a world to win. Working men of all countries, unite !"

Das Kapital.— With the collapse in 1849 of the revolutionary movements initiated the year before in Germany and France, in the course of which he returned to those two countries, Marx sought refuge in England, there to pass the remaining thirty-four years of his life in exile, aside from occasional visits to the continent. During most of this time, he and his family lived in direst poverty, supported in the main by small yearly contributions from Engels. The drama of his life is most strikingly shown during this long period when he set for himself an almost impossible task of research, namely, the writing of a monumental treatise on socialist economics.

Year after year, assisted in his researches by fellow-exiles, he took notes from morning until midnight on a prodigious mass of original material in the British Museum in London. The practical fruit of this industry appeared first in 1859 in *Toward a Critique of Political Economy* and in much expanded form in 1867 in the first volume of *Das Kapital (Capital)*, one of the least read of the world's influential books and yet, strangely enough, one of the most often cited. The ponderous structure of the original German is in some part responsible for this situation. The volume made greatest headway in Russia, the country above all others, probably, where it has been perused with greatest respect and admiration.

Marx was also preoccupied at this time with the First International, formed in 1864 as the world's first great international organization of workers, and which lasted until 1871, when it virtually expired through internal dissension. Excessive toil and his long struggle with privation finally undermined a constitution once exceptionally rugged. After his death in 1883, Engels edited and published two more volumes of *Das Kapital* from the manuscript left by his collaborator, volume two appearing in 1885 and volume three in 1894. The three volumes attain the massive proportions of twenty-five hundred pages. Despite this, the treatise must be regarded as unfinished, not alone because the third volume ends with these words of Engels : "Here the manuscript breaks off," but also because the most important parts of this volume were written prior to 1867 and were never revised by Marx.

Marxian doctrines.— Any attempt at a simple statement of the Marxian doctrines with any pretense to accuracy is a matter of the utmost difficulty, for even today the numerous schools of Marxianism which have sprung up represent radically divergent interpretations of his thought. It is certain that he endeavored to analyze the trend of contemporary events, and that the *Communist Manifesto* — the first important pronouncement of modern socialism, and *Capital,* the "bible" of socialism, were both products of the times. Had not most of Europe seethed with unrest, had not men, women, and children been working long hours for pitifully small wages in unsanitary mills and factories operated by owners apparently for the securing of maximum possible profits, had not revolution followed revolution in the struggle of the working classes for better economic conditions and for greater participation in governmental functions, these volumes would very probably have never been written. He set for himself the task of showing the essential relativity of economic institutions, and of explaining in terms of natural laws the historical evolution of the capitalistic method of production and the inevitable transformation of the capitalistic system into socialism.

In pointing out what he deemed to be the influence of economic facts upon social and political activity, he wrote the lengthiest exposition and criticism of capitalism hitherto undertaken. Only indirectly can he be said to have written an exposition of socialism. The bulk of this treatise is concerned with an exhaustive analysis of the economic conditions of his day. Hence the title of his chief work, *Das Kapital (Capital).*

The essential doctrines of Marx appear to resolve themselves into three elements : (a) the materialistic (or economic) interpretation of history, (b) a system of economics, and (c) a theory of social revolution. The argument runs somewhat as follows :

Materialistic interpretation of history.— According to the materialistic interpretation of history, the evolution of society is explained in terms of economic factors. Not religion nor literature nor art nor morals nor even the government itself, but rather the economic environment is the determining factor in civilization. The all-important consideration in any historical period is the prevailing system of production and distribution. This principle was not original with Marx, yet it is the "fundamental proposition" of Marxism, as Engels himself expressly stated, although nowhere in his writings did Marx elucidate the point any too clearly. In the progress of history, furthermore, the chief moving force is class conflict.

Marx thought of economic institutions as not alone the dominant factor in evolution but as rooted in century-old struggles between economic groups. "The history of all hitherto existing society is the history of the class struggle." History, in other words, is primarily a record of continual and inevitable conflict between the rich and the poor, the exploiters and the exploited. In the remote past, masters had opposed slaves; in the middle ages, serfs and vassals clashed with knights and lords; in modern times, the bourgeoisie had overthrown the institution of feudalism, establishing in its place the régime of capitalism, and creating a new alignment in the opposition of the proletariat to the bourgeois capitalists.

Predecessors of Marx had attempted, in the main, to explain the most important events in human history, such as the Crusades, the rise and decline of empires, migrations and revolutions of all sorts in terms of the physical environment (soil, food, etc.), changes in political systems, religious beliefs, the rise of great men and so on. Marx would have little of this. He appears to have come by his belief in an economic interpretation of history through acceptance of the naturalistic interpretations of Ludwig Feuerbach and the doctrine of Hegel, that all change and growth occur as a result of the conflict of opposites, and, further, through other influences.

But he did not go to the extent of excluding the influence of all factors save the economic one, merely terming it the dominant explanation. As to whether the economic factor is or is not paramount, scholarly opinion is even today divided. Some believe that this is the one Marxian theory which has stood up best under the ravages of critical attack. Others, on the contrary, regard it as a wholly unjustifiable generalization of a partial truth. That Marx did pioneer work, however, in emphasizing the materialistic element is conceded by nearly all; yet, without doubt, the writers who nowadays make best use of economic interpretation are no longer the socialists.

Class struggle doctrine.— There is difference of opinion, also, as to the validity of the class struggle doctrine, the weight of opinion inclining to the belief that the theory is not tenable. Individuals belong to numerous groups, both social and economic, and are moved by countless ideas and interests. As yet no universal solidarity of wage earners has ever arisen. Conflicts of interests, on the contrary, have appeared between workers in the same industry, and between workers in different industries. The claim that comes first and foremost is nearly always that of one's country, as evidenced on innumerable occasions in the past in times of national emergency. Narrow class lines tend to yield to the tie created by common citizenship in the country of one's birth or adoption. Neither history nor logic seems to bear out the fundamental importance of the Marxian conception of the class struggle.

System of economics.— From the materialistic interpretation of history, Marx went on to analyze the existing economic system and to expound his system of economics. He liked to think of himself as an economist, and in a sense all of *Das Kapital* is an endeavor to give to the world a somewhat complete outline of political economy. The basis of this system is his theory of value. All wealth, in his opinion, was produced by the worker; land is a passive agent and capital is created by labor. Harking back to Ricardo, he contended that, with certain exceptions, the value of all commodities is measured and determined by the labor required to produce them (or, in more exact language, that commodities are exchanged for each other in ratios which measure the relative amounts of socially necessary labor power incorporated in these goods, including in labor cost a proportionate part of the cost of producing raw materials, tools, machinery and other capital instruments).

Labor and value.— All labor was reduced to "human labor in the abstract" and value became "a mere congelation of homogeneous human labour." In a primitive society and under purely competitive conditions, it is indeed certain that the products of laborers would tend roughly to exchange for each other in proportion to their labor cost. But that principle was not true of the society of his time, any more than of present day society. Even were it possible to reduce labor to an abstract fund, no value theory can hold water which approaches the problem from the supply or cost side exclusively. Value depends as much upon demand, upon the want satisfying power which commodities have, as upon their cost of production.

Marx next asserted that labor power, like every other commodity, has value—a value determined by the quantity of labor necessary to produce it. Consequently, labor sells in the market at a price equal to its cost of production. This was a restatement of the "iron law" of wages, according to which wage-earners receive as wages only enough for the minimum of existence and the propagation of the race. Thus arose the "surplus value" concept, the most familiar, perhaps, of all Marxian theories, yet essentially similar to one already propounded by the Ricardian socialist, William Thompson.

Exploitation of workers.—The worker, Marx declared, is at the mercy of the capitalist and the landowner who own the means of production. The worker toils a certain number of hours per day (six, for instance) in order to procure his necessary minimum of subsistence, but is not permitted by the employer to stop at that point. He is compelled, instead, to keep at his work, not necessarily because the employer wishes to exploit the worker, but because of savage competition with other employers for his own preservation. At all events, surplus products are produced by the worker during the additional hours for which he works for nothing, and these products are sold by the employer at a value determined by the amount of labor incorporated, thus giving rise to a surplus value which is appropriated by the employer.

It is the worker, by the way, not the consumer, who is exploited. And not all this surplus is pure profit for the employer, since out of it must come the rent due the landowner for the use of his land and the interest on funds loaned by the money lending capitalist. That part of the surplus value finally retained by the employer-capitalist may be termed industrial or commercial profit.

It would be idle to deny that an appalling amount of exploitation of workers on the part of employers has been perpetrated in the course of an untold number of centuries. Yet to account for this exploitation some explanation other than the Marxian analysis must be sought, since that analysis is self-contradictory.

If its validity be assumed, employers would tend to compete for additional workers in order to increase their respective shares of surplus value, and this competition would naturally force up wage rates and in time eliminate entirely all surplus value. Furthermore, since employers profit only from the labor employed and not at all from tools, machinery and other equipment by reason of the fact that these things exchange according to their labor cost, it would seem that those employers would prosper most who use relatively much labor and relatively few capital goods. That such is not the case in practice is obvious on every hand. The Marxian elucidation has long since gone into the limbo of discredited theories. If interest, rent and profits are unjustifiable incomes, the attack must come from another quarter.

Trend toward concentration.—The exploitation of wage earners, in the opinion of Marx, had other important consequences. He asserted, in the first place, that the law of the concentration of capital amalgamated industry into ever larger business units,—a prediction made, incidentally, as early as 1848 or sooner, before the modern trend toward large-scale production had manifested itself. That concentration has indeed proceeded apace throughout the civilized world needs no demonstration. To be sure, it is more a concentration in control than of ownership, inasmuch as the prodigious growth of the joint-stock principle and the issue of stock certificates carrying limited liability has made possible an undreamed-of extension of property rights in business enterprises.

The small unit still persists, and in certain fields of endeavor, as agriculture, is likely to persist for an indefinite period of time. But the definite trend involved in the superior efficiency of large industries is toward so-called "big business." Unfortunately for Marx, the law which he had in mind was concentration in ownership instead of in control. The second consequence which he believed he foresaw was the ever increasing number and misery of the laboring class.

With regard to this theory of increasing misery, as it is called', there is indisputable evidence that up to at least the early part of the twentieth century the position of the average worker improved rather than retrograded. Money wages and likewise real wages (the purchasing power of money wages) increased both absolutely and relatively by reason of protective labor legislation, the rise of the co-operative movement, the generosity of certain employers, and the growth of labor organizations in number and power — factors which Marx could hardly have been expected to take into account. No such comforting conclusion can be drawn for the period beginning with World War I. Authoritative data for unemployment and wages are lacking to establish the point one way or the other. Yet recent wars, business depressions, and other phenomena afford occasion for the gravest apprehensions.

Collapse of capitalism.— The capitalistic society set up by the bourgeoisie thus contains within itself the seeds of its own destruction. The employer capitalists, steadily increasing in power over the worker through the exaction of longer hours of work and the payment of lower wages, and forced by competition constantly to introduce improvements in production, have a larger and larger surplus of goods on their hands to dispose of if they are to remain solvent. Because of the growing smallness of their numbers they are unable themselves to consume this increased wealth except on a decreasing scale, and must plough back their earnings more and more into their properties. The pauperized workers are naturally not in a position to purchase as much as they would like, since they are paid in wages less than they produce in commodities. Their numbers are furthermore augmented as former bourgeois employers, bankrupted in the competitive struggle, descend to the status of employee and become candidates for jobs. Production thus tends constantly to run ahead of consumption, and gluts come periodically. Prices drop, often to a point where further production is unprofitable. Widespread unemployment ensues and during the accompanying depression and liquidation increasing thousands of the employing class are forced down into the ranks of the proletariat. Finally a sort of equilibrium is established, recovery sets in, and in time the whole vicious circle is repeated (reasoning borrowed from Sismondi and Rodbertus).

Depressions come more and more often and with ever increasing severity. The "industrial reserve army" of the unemployed grows to huge proportions; the gulf between the surviving employers and the hapless proletariat widens; the middle class completely disappears. Finally capitalism collapses; the few remaining capitalists are expropriated by the proletarian masses; and the socialist commonwealth is inaugurated.

Marx did not draw this picture because he necessarily believed in the superiority of a socialist over a capitalistic system. He simply stated that there were certain tendencies inherent in capitalism which would inexorably lead to its overthrow. Socialism was no empty utopian dream but an inevitable development. Heaping ridicule upon the various types of utopian socialism which had preceded his own particular analysis, he called the Marxian interpretation "scientific" socialism, and as such it has ever since been known.

Social revolution.— Of the very essence of his doctrine was the method by which the social revolution was to be effected and the proletariat placed in the saddle. By the term "revolution" he meant the dislodgment of the capitalist class from economic and political power. He appears to have countenanced any and every method which would aid in ushering in the proletarian state, although bitter debate has raged for decades around this point. According to the weight of evidence, he placed no great faith in democratic and constitutional means aside, possibly, from several countries such as England and the United States. He therefore looked forward to violence as the weapon by means of which the majority of workers would attain their objects. The proletariat would have to be armed; an independent military force built up; and everything possible done to hamper and attack the existing order. At some propitious moment the workers' leaders must strike and strike hard, overthrowing the capitalists by the use of all methods which capitalism has employed to preserve itself.

Then, during an intermediate period of uncertain length, would arise the dictatorship of the proletariat, inasmuch as the creation of the socialist commonwealth would take time to achieve. Further than this Marx did not care to predict, stating that the future would take care of itself. He took it for granted, however, that at some time after the institution of the régime of collectivism (the final revolution of history) all property rights would be abolished, control of the productive machinery and of natural resources would rest in society as a whole, and a classless community would evolve.

Whatever may be thought of the Marxian doctrines, it were less than fairness not to speak with great respect of Marx the man. Had he followed the conventional path of self-interest he might have risen to high estate along orthodox lines, because of his unquestioned and unusual endowments and energy. Instead, he chose to devote nearly forty years to championing the cause of the underprivileged masses. No disparagement can explain away those many years of prolonged and heart-breaking study, of firm resolution and courage, of exile and destitution spent in what he believed to be the noblest of human causes. Assuredly not a great man in many respects, much may be overlooked in the career of one in whom a calculating brain was joined to a warm heart.

Marx the prophet.—According to Marx, history is to pass through certain epochs, although he did not minutely mark them off : prehistoric communism, ancient slavery, feudal serfdom, capitalism, transitional state capitalism (the dictatorship of the proletariat), state socialism, and pure communism. He indeed is rash who would assert without qualification that the Marxian prophecy of communism as the final outcome of economic development is either absolutely right or positively wrong. In some respects Marx was a shrewd prophet ; in others he was not. He failed to foresee, for instance, that the lot of the workers in many countries was destined to be considerably alleviated by the tremendous progress of the labor organization movement, the rise of various forms of co-operation, and the widening of the functions of the government in the direction of more rigid regulation of private industry and private property rights. Nor did he foresee that concentration of ownership would make relatively little headway in the province of agriculture, and that the first important practical application of socialism would take place, contrary to his analysis, in one of the most feudal and least industrialized of modern nations (Russia).

On the other hand, some of his prophecies seem to be in process of partial fulfilment. The position of labor has been weakened by a vast increase in the army of the unemployed in most so-called civilized countries ; crises and depressions have become increasingly severe ; and world imperialism has caused recurring wars, two of which have shaken the present economic order to its very foundations.

Ironically enough, however, the conclusions of Marx were based not upon a truly scientific inquiry but upon a preconceived dogma. If capitalism is doomed, as he contended, in that it has fulfilled its historical mission, it is doomed on grounds other than those presented in the theories and generalizations of "scientific socialism." His reasoning was cogent, but hardly scientific, as many thoughtful socialists have reluctantly testified. Indeed no writer on economic phenomena, save possibly Malthus, has been so often "refuted." History rarely, if ever, fits formulae as neat as those which he so laboriously put together.

The essential weakness of Marxism.—What, then, is the essential weakness of Marxism ? Many have professed to find the answer in an alleged invalidation of the theory of permanent revolution, citing as proof the miscarriage of European socialism since the outbreak of the World War. The obvious reply to this argument is that international conquest by socialists may be a matter not of decades, as Marx imagined, but of centuries, preceded by an amount of revolutionary strategy and understanding infinitely greater than has up to now been expended in the undermining of capitalism. May not the dilemma in which the orthodox Marxists find themselves lie in the unsolved problem of preventing the revolutionary dictatorship from degenerating into a privileged bureaucracy !

To judge by the results of the Russian experiment, the Marxian theory of the growth of a classless society under a proletarian dictatorship, following upon the overthrow of the capitalist régime, has proved to have little basis in fact. The dictatorship of the proletariat is in practice simply the tyranny of a small minority over a large majority, a minority whose final interests, contrary to the reasoning of Marx, are not necessarily those of the workers whom it governs. In resolving capitalist contradictions, new class stratifications are created. Is it not asking too much of human nature to expect that the revolutionary leadership will dissolve itself voluntarily in the service of the socialist society? Is it not much more likely that dictatorships will strive to perpetuate themselves, so that in the long run a new slavery replaces the old? Can there be any greater fiction in the Marxian analysis than that of a disinterested dictatorship of the proletariat?

Yet nothing is more certain than that Marx is vastly more important at present than at his death in 1883, notwithstanding the almost unparalleled avalanche of condemnation which has descended upon his theories. His name has penetrated to the utmost corners of the globe to an extent surpassing even that of the recognition accorded the writings of Adam Smith, and daily his doctrines are defended or reviled, as the case may be, with a vehemence attaching to no other thinker in the history of social ideas.

As to his merits as an economist, opinion naturally differs. There are many eminent orthodox commentators, however, who assign to him a place among the most powerful and original intellects ever to grace the ranks of students of economic science. Other critics find his greatness in his endeavor to rationalize economics and to bring out the effect of changing institutions upon our present civilization. He was not the first to view the cumulative change of economic institutions as perhaps the central problem of economics, but no scholar of his day and age did more to stress the significance of the historical aspects of the problems to which economists devote attention. He is beyond doubt the most noted philosophic historian of the capitalistic system. By some, furthermore, he is accounted the father of so-called "institutional" economics.

To carry the argument one step farther, the "contradictions" of capitalism, as Marx would have it, are no greater than the contradictions of Marxian socialism itself. It is of the essence of his doctrine that the overthrow of the capitalistic order should first take place in those industrialized countries where capitalism had reached its highest state of development. He believed, therefore, that the earliest important victories of the working class would be won in some such advanced country as England or the United States or Germany. What would be his amazement, were he alive today, to discover that the first Marxian state has arisen in "barbarous" Russia, where the population is approximately eighty per cent agricultural, and that outside of Russia communism as a political force has made its greatest progress in parts of China and Spain where modern industry is relatively in its infancy! In truth the Marxian formula would appear to have been completely reversed as it is now working itself out in Soviet Russia. There power was seized by the revolutionists, a communist régime set up, and prodigious efforts put forth to create a working class and build up an industrialized state in support of the dictatorship. The workers' revolution calls, furthermore, for a world revolution and a perpetual conflict between communistic governments as they arise and surviving capitalistic powers. How different has been the actual course of development. What remains, accordingly, of so-called "scientific" socialism?

Influence of Marx.— Yet to uncounted millions of followers the world over, the vast majority of whom have never read a word of *Das Kapital,* and who know comparatively little of the dramatic portrayal in that treatise of the defects of capitalism, his is the name that unites under one banner a vast army of those who feel convinced that the only remedy for their economic ills is a social revolution. His proclamation that the reign of injustice must inevitably give way to the establishment of justice upon earth is the slogan that has captured the imaginations and emotions of man. Hope springs eternal in the human breast that the golden age is before and not behind mankind. To this in great part is due his influence. He found socialism in a state of demoralization and left it firmly intrenched as a political and economic movement of great significance.

Like most prophets Marx has been variously interpreted by various schools of followers. Inevitably the numerous contradictions in his writings gave rise to contradictory emphases and interpretations. In particular have the socialists differed regarding the tactics to be pursued in bringing about the overthrow of capitalism and the nature of the ultimate structure of the ensuring society. Until the rise of modern communism in

Russia, socialism, while more or less avowedly Marxian, was in general marked by what has come to be known as opportunism. Capitalism was found to have much that is good and to be so deeply rooted in the social and political fabric of mankind that a policy of piecemeal advance was adjudged the better part of valor. If socialism were ever to become a reality it was accordingly thought necessary to teach, advocate, and actively work for its principles, with actual accomplishment and partial amelioration of existing conditions in mind to an extent far outweighing strict logical consistency.

English Fabian Society.—This line of approach first appeared in England, shortly after the death of Marx in 1883, in the formation of the English Fabian Society, named after the cautious Roman general Fabius, famed for his campaigns against Hannibal. This society, at no time formally organized, has been largely educational in its functions and has never numbered, at any time, more than a few thousand in its membership. Led by a small group of intellectuals such as Annie Besant, George Bernard Shaw, Sidney and Beatrice Webb, Graham Wallas, Chiozza Money, Edward Pease, William Clarke, H. G. Wells, Philip Snowden, and J. Ramsay MacDonald, the Fabians have exerted an influence upon the course of events in Great Britain much greater than might have been expected. They have stimulated investigation in fields affecting labor relations, issued a voluminous pamphlet literature, thrice led the Labor party to control of the English government, and in general worked for remedial social legislation through the agency of existing political organizations.

The fundamental tenets of the Fabian creed, sometimes termed "administrative socialism," were introduced during the 'nineties into Germany under the name of "revisionism" by Edouard Bernstein. Believing with the Fabians that Marx had erred in several of his predictions and holding with them to the principles of education, co-operation, and gradual change he put his hope in the evolutionary processes of democracy. The two chief doctrines against which he inveighed were the inexorable progress of concentration and the self-destructive nature of capitalism. At the time of the outbreak of the World War revisionism had become the dominant type of German socialism. In every other civilized country except

Russia, revisionist socialism likewise gained the ascendancy over the extreme supporters of the Marxian philosophy.

State Socialism.— In its conventional usage there is implied the retention of the capitalistic régime with a considerable increase in the control of the state over industry. It contemplates, in this sense, therefore, no overturn of established institutions, but rather such extension of government activity as the regulation of railroads and other utilities and the setting of minimum wages and maximum hours. But to speak of state socialism as a species of capitalism is obviously a curious anachronism. It is truly unfortunate that the term state socialism does not universally connote some special variety of socialism. Some headway is happily being made in this direction in the growing tendency of thinkers to look upon state socialism as that type of socialism which provides for a division of the ownership of the means of production between the different political units of the state. As thus viewed, the central government would own and operate those enterprises, such as banks and railroads, whose ramifications extend throughout the entire nation. To the smaller governmental units, in turn, would be assigned the administration of the more purely local enterprises. By some, the terms "democratic state socialism" or "democratic socialism" are preferred.

Syndicalism.—Whatever state socialism may or may not be, no such difficulty arises in connection with syndicalism and gild socialism. Syndicalism is derived from the French word for industrial union (*syndicat*). The syndicalists aim to emancipate the working classes through seizure of the control of industry. To this end they pin their faith in the organization of all wage earners into industrial unions. By means of "direct action" (militant tactics such as the boycott, sabotage and strikes) they hope so to cripple the capitalistic system that a general strike of all labor will in time force the capitalist employers to turn over their industries to the workers. The industrial unions will then own and control the means of production in their respective fields, uniting in a federation of unions for such central government as may be deemed necessary. Syndicalism attained considerable strength in France and Italy prior to 1914 and is loosely represented in the United States by the Industrial Workers of the World. Certain of its elements have been borrowed by other types of socialism and by capitalistic labor organizations. The leading writer has been the Frenchman, Georges Sorel (1847-1922).

Gild Socialism.—This is a comparatively recent movement, chiefly intellectual in its nature, which received its greatest support in Great Britain immediately preceding and following World War I. The gild socialists, headed by S. G. Hobson, R. H. Tawney and G. D. H. Cole, propose a type of social organization characterized by a peculiar system of dual sovereignty. They would establish self-government in industry through national gilds (industrial unions). Much as the American Federation of Labor represents certain groups of workers so the members of the national gilds would be represented in a national gild congress. As consumers the members would likewise be represented in a second or political congress endowed with the power to control the prices charged by the national gilds, to provide for the administration of justice and to carry on diplomatic relations. This dual concept of the state, it is believed, would best create and maintain both economic and political democracy.

With the growth of the socialist movement prior to World War I orthodox Marxism steadily yielded ground to moderate socialism (*revisionism*) and by 1914 its adherents, outside of Russia, were in a very decided minority.

Anarchism.— Frequently confused with socialism is anarchism, a doctrine which is fundamentally the very antithesis of socialism. The ideal of the anarchists is complete freedom and non-compulsion. They would do away with government entirely in order to destroy the existing economic system with its accompanying inequality in wealth and income. That accomplished, they believe that individuals will of their own accord form co-operative and self-sufficient communities where all work will become pleasant and absolute equality and complete freedom will prevail. Philosophical or individualist or Christian anarchists (Godwin, Tolstoy, Tucker) advocate a peaceful policy of non-resistance. Communist anarchists (Kropotkin, Bakunin, Emma Goldman), at present dominant, favor revolutionary tactics in the attainment of their goal. The movement is of relatively little significance except in some of the Latin countries of Europe.

Socialism since 1914.— Socialism has grown from a mere philosophical project into an active political program throughout the world. Emerging first in Germany under the leadership of Lassalle, the socialist movement gradually increased in strength in most of the nations of Europe. Elsewhere national socialist organizations sprang up in many parts of the civilized area of the globe. By the time of the outbreak of the World War the various socialist bodies had attained a very considerable measure of success, not alone from the standpoint of the growth of political parties but also from that of the adoption into the social laws of the time of numerous planks of the socialist program.

The resort to arms in 1914 split the socialists in the vast majority of countries into two or more irreconcilable groups. Up to that time Marxian socialists of all varieties may be said to have been strong believers in internationalism, and to have held that workers had nothing to gain in any war save in a war against capitalism itself. In line with this opinion the Second International had been inaugurated in 1889 to replace the defunct First International, and under its auspices numerous international socialist conferences were held. As the World War progressed, however, the Second International broke down after feeble attempts to put a stop to the conflict, not to be revived until several years after the cessation of hostilities.

Contrary to what might have been expected, most of the European socialist groups promptly rallied to the support of their respective governments. The more radically minded members, bitterly denouncing their conservative brethren for betraying the Marxian cause, set up new parties under the name ordinarily of communism. In Russia the communists, successful perhaps beyond their wildest dreams, began in 1917 one of the most gigantic social revolutions and experiments ever undertaken. In March of that year a popular uprising under the leadership of moderate socialists (the Mensheviks) deposed the czarist régime and established a revolutionary government, only in turn to be overthrown in November by the communist branch of the Russian socialists (the Bolsheviks). This latter group, which has since assumed the name of the Communist Party, had for many years held no belief in the doctrine of Marx that socialism could only be established in those countries in which capitalistic institutions had come to maturity. Led at first by Lenin and Trotsky and subsequently by Stalin, communism in Russia has set out to demonstrate that even in backward countries the dispossession of the capitalist classes is possible if carried through by force and maintained by a ruthless dictatorship of self-appointed leaders at the head of well-disciplined proletarian armies. The Third International, created in 1919, and meeting occasionally in congress in Moscow, proclaims itself the true representative of Marxism.

Conservative socialists meanwhile came into power in various parts of Europe at the conclusion of World War I or shortly thereafter, as in Germany, Austria, and Great Britain. Before far-reaching programs could be put into effect the conservative socialists, with rare exception, were either defeated at the polls or were curbed in their influence by the rise of military dictatorships and fascist or semi-fascist governments. Today the factionalism engendered in the ranks of socialists by the crucial test of the World Wars still persists. The clash between communism and moderate socialism is at times apparently as bitter as that between the upholders of capitalism, on the one hand, and all opponents of the capitalistic order, on the other.

The seemingly insuperable economic problems of the post-war era have furthermore been responsible in goodly measure for the rise of fascism in Italy, Germany, and elsewhere, with the result that the present situation is almost unbelievably complicated. It is barely possible, however, that in view of the triumph of Russian communism and the blotting out of moderate socialism by fascist dictatorships in not a few countries the chief current in today's socialism is more in harmony with revolutionary than evolutionary Marxism. In a world given over to hatred and suspicion the forces of reason may conceivably for an undetermined period have to yield precedence to those of force and revolution.

Chapter XVII

AMERICAN ECONOMIC THOUGHT

STRANGE indeed had been the neglect until recently of the nearly virgin field of the history of American economic thought. Happily the period from 1606 to 1918 is now revealed in the full sweep of its economic and social development in the truly monumental work in three volumes by Professor Joseph Dorfman of Columbia University, *The Economic Mind in American Civilization* (1949). This eagerly awaited publication uncovers a mass of new material and corrects numberless wrong interpretations of long standing. Professor Dorfman is currently at work upon the completion of his research.

Early thought.—During the colonial period, economic writings dealt chiefly with agriculture, trade, taxation, money and banking, and were generally similar to the discussion of contemporary Europeans. The most pressing problem had to do with the sufficiency of money, both coin and paper ; in this respect the colonists first threw off the shackles of a transplanted European theology. Benjamin Franklin, the most prominent name in American economic literature prior to the Revolution, brought his powerful intellect to bear on a number of questions such as currency, wages, and particularly population, where to a certain extent he anticipated Malthus. His ideas on productivity were somewhat vitiated by his long residence in Europe and his personal contact with certain physiocrats.

With the declaration of independence in 1776, economic problems came more than ever into the foreground. Of contributions by statesmen, undoubtedly the most significant were those of Alexander Hamilton in his state papers dealing with finance and trade. Arguing for a national bank, for the use of

---

[1] *See* "The Development of Economic Thought in America" by E. R. A. Seligman, in *Economic Forum* for Fall, 1933 (Vol. I, No. 4). Also "Essays in Economics" by E. R. A. Seligman, Chapter IV, *Economics in the United States,* MacMillan, 1925.

public credit, and government encouragement of industry, he exhibited unsurpassed powers of sustained reasoning. Other arresting writers, unrecognized by their generation, were Pelatiah Webster, Samuel Gale and Tench Coxe. It is worthy of note that the first American edition of *The Wealth of Nations* appeared in 1789, first year of the new republic of the United States of North America.

Well into the nineteenth century, exposition of economic doctrine took the form mainly of slavish allegiance to the classical theories then dominant in Great Britain. Closing their eyes to the great differences in the social and economic institutions of the United States as compared with Europe, American writers aped the explanations of economic organization as formulated by Adam Smith and Ricardo. Sharp dissent from British economists, however, was registered earlier in the western hemisphere than in France or Germany or other parts of the old world as a growing number of Americans began to look about them and thus to form a realistic conception of economic life in a new country. This reaction, initiated late in the previous century by Hamilton and others, was continued by such publicists as Daniel Raymond, author of the first distinctly American treatise on economics (*Thoughts on Political Economy,* 1820) ; A. H. Everett ; Williard Phillips ; Hezekiah Niles ; Matthew Carey ; Jacob Newton ; N. N. Cardozo ; George Tucker ; Friedrich List, the eminent German economist, who drew upon Raymond for his well-known theory of nationalism during his sojourn in the United States ; and John Rae, Scotch immigrant to Canada and later to the United States, whose *Statement of Some New Principles on the Subject of Political Economy* (1834) displayed marked originality in stressing invention and governmental interference as the true source of wealth.

Henry Charles Carey.— All these writers must yield precedence, however, to the man who was "the first American economist," Henry Charles Carey (1793-1879). Son of Matthew Carey, he took over his father's publishing business while still a young man, soon acquired a fortune, and devoted the last half of his long life of eighty-six years to writing. Thirteen octavo volumes and three thousand pamphlet pages, besides an amount of matter supposed to be twice as lengthy contributed to news-

papers, attest his industry.   Some of his work has been translated into eight languages.   Chief among his writings were
Principles of Political Economy in three volumes (1837-1840) ;
The Past, The Present, and The Future (1848) ; and *Principles of Social Science,* likewise in three volumes (1858-1859),
in which his complete system was expounded.

Prior to Carey, most American writers were clergymen,
lawyers, or teachers who looked upon economics as one of the
arts with which educated persons should be at least casually
familiar.   Like his predecessors and the great majority of his
contemporaries, for that matter, he was much more the amateur
than the professional economist.   Widely read in history,
sociology, philosophy, psychology, mathematics, physics, chemistry, and biology, he labored mightily to elevate economics to
the level of a social science.   The laws of physical science, he
maintained, were likewise those of social science, inasmuch as
the same harmonious laws govern mind and matter.   Man, he
said, is the molecule of society.

Carey is much better known for his economic optimism, however, than for his somewhat unsystematic contributions to economic science.   He lived at a time of phenomenal prosperity for
the United States as a whole.   The population increased during his lifetime from four to fifty millions ; roads, canals, and
railways with incredible rapidity opened up an immense new
territory; a flood of inventions lowered costs of production
and raised standards of living; land was cheap and abundant; wages high; and the price of food low.   Startling,
indeed, was the contrast between European and American en-
vironments of those decades, between an economy founded,
in the one instance, upon scarcity, and, in the other, upon
abundance.   Rarely, and with good reason, has an economist
been so influenced by his surroundings.

Accordingly, while professing highest admiration for Adam
Smith, he broke entirely with certain classical doctrines.
Heaping scorn upon the Malthusian principle of population,
the law of diminishing returns — and with it the Ricardian law
of rent, the Ricardian theory of wages, and the classical belief
in free trade, he formulated a cost of reproduction theory of
value and proclaimed "a perfect harmony of real and true
interest among the various classes of mankind."   As a country

progressed, he averred, the shares of income received by land-owners, capitalists and wage earners all increased in the aggregate, but wages increased relative to the other shares, and thus this tendency toward equality among the industrial classes made for balance and harmony.

This happy outcome was held dependent, however, upon his "principle of association." Deeply impressed with the wealth of city populations as compared with the poverty of the frontier, he was convinced that increasing national wealth and efficiency depended upon a proper balance between agriculture and manufacturing, and relatively equal prosperity in these two groups of economic activity. He asserted that when agricultural products were consumed by a city population near the place of production, the costs of transportation were considerably lowered, and capital was properly devoted to fixed improvements, buildings especially, instead of being used for trading and for transportation. This reasoning was greatly colored by the fact that the manufacturers in Philadelphia, his home city, were forced to pay high wages to employees to prevent them from taking up cheap land in the West. Thus Carey, originally a free trader, blossomed forth as an advocate of the home market idea and as an ardent protectionist.

So extensive was Carey's influence that the term "American School" is often applied to himself and his adherents, including E. P. Smith, William Elder, H. C. Baird, Charles Nordhoff, Horace Greeley, Robert Ellis Thompson, and Francis Bowen, besides scholars in Germany and in Italy. To succeeding generations, however, his significance has somewhat waned. Indeed, his real claim to fame is rooted chiefly in his uncritical reaction against the equally uncritical acceptance of the British classical doctrines by the Americans of his day. He is a shining example of the oft-stated dictum that an economist tends to reflect his environment.

Meanwhile the tardy development of a general theory of economics was far overshadowed by discussions of practical economic problems. Tariff controversies, land tenure, taxation and debt, currency and banking difficulties, public improvements, the workingmen's movement, slavery, communistic programs and experiments, the rise of big business,—these and other special subjects were ardently debated by numerous writers, few of whose outpourings had more than a passing value. Of the more prominent figures of this somewhat indefinite period some, like Davis A. Wells, analyst of Civil War fiscal problems, have been adequately appraised. Others, like Horace Greeley, long editor of the New York *Tribune*, have never been sufficiently studied. Of greatest popular appeal was undoubtedly the self-taught social reformer, Henry George (1839-1897), the sale of whose books has far exceeded that of any other American economist living or dead and of all European economists except Adam Smith and Karl Marx.

Henry George.— Living in California and later in New York City at a time when land values there were rapidly rising he was deeply impressed by the paradox of vast riches side by side with poverty and squalor. Convinced that the fundamental cause of this inequality was the retention by landowners of the increase in land values, he published a pamphlet in 1871 entitled *Our Land and Land Policy*, in which he advocated the replacement of all existing forms of taxation by a single tax on the private receipt of land rent. After much study, this general theory was much elaborated in his memorable work *Progress and Poverty* (1879). This book met with unexpected public favor, due in part to its graceful style; some two million copies have been sold. In succession followed *The Irish Land Question* (1881), *Social Problems* (1884), *Protection or Free Trade* (1891), *A Perplexed Philosopher* (1892), and *The Science of Political Economy* (1898), completed after his death by his son. These books did little but repeat his fundamental ideas, and are of interest chiefly in indicating the wide range of his reading in economic literature after the publication of *Progress and Poverty*. Twice he campaigned unsuccessfully for the mayoralty of New York City. At the time of his death he was a celebrated international figure.

As his starting point, George stressed his conviction that land is a free gift of nature and the rightful heritage of mankind. With the growth of population, however, all the land of a country tends to become occupied, newcomers being forced to settle upon inferior plots. As land is thus reduced to private ownership, labor is kept in a state of poverty because it must pay for the use of land on terms laid down by the landowners. Progress in the arts of production makes for a larger total product of industry, but "all the advantages gained by the march of progress go to the owner of land."

The remedy for this simple cause of poverty was obviously to deprive landowners of their rent. To accomplish this, George proposed, not outright government ownership of land, but a tax upon the full annual rental value of the land, with permission to the landowners to retain the title to their land. In reality, he aimed ultimately to make land common property, and he so expressly stated. He proposed, furthermore, the discontinuance of all other forms of taxation. Hence the revival of the physiocratic expression, "the single tax," in connection with this plan of reform. He was perfectly well aware that the suggestion of a tax solely on the rent of land was by no means novel, and he made grateful acknowledgment to the physiocrats. In fact, he regarded himself as their doctrinal descendant.

George maintained that all vacant land would be put to productive use, all people previously supported by their rent incomes would be compelled to go to work, that the tax would be easy to collect and would not be shiftable, that the total income of the community would be vastly increased through the encouragement of production, inequalities in the distribution of wealth would be reduced to a minimum, unemployment and depressions would disappear, and the causes of poverty would tend to disappear.

The announcement of this panacea for economic and social evils was greeted with more interest and approval abroad than in his native country. In Great Britain, Australia, and elsewhere several large-scale attempts have even been made to put his theories into practice by means of legislation. In the United States countless enthusiastic followers have sought to popularize his doctrines by the means of Henry George clubs. In recent years several single tax colonies have been started, and the Henry George School of Social Science has come into existence in New York City.

Academic economists at first met the appearance of *Progress and Poverty* with nearly complete silence. When at length they could no longer ignore the veritable furore occasioned by public debate over his theories, they assailed both his method and the doctrine as a whole with merciless severity. They endeavored to show that "the natural rights" theory is entirely without foundation in fact ; that the single tax is too inflexible ; that it would fall far short of meeting the expenses of government ; that the administrative difficulty of distinguishing between land and the capital invested in permanent improvements would prove nearly insuperable ; that wages and profits, instead of rent, absorb most of the increase in income made possible by progress in production ; that the tax would unjustly discriminate against those who had invested in land instead of in other forms of property ; and that if economic rent were to be taxed on the ground that it is an unearned increment, common justice demands that other unearned increments, such as monopoly incomes, chance business gains, stock market profits, and inheritances should also be taxed to the full. The single tax can in no way be regarded as the sole remedy for modern social problems.

Yet these same economists rather generally support the view that at least partial taxation of future increases in land values is highly desirable as a supplement to other forms of taxation. They freely grant that George performed a distinguished service in bringing to the fore the issue of justice in distribution, and commend him for his keen thinking on certain theoretic aspects of the relation of wages to rent. Although he cannot be included in the ranks of scientists, Henry George will long be remembered as one of our great liberalizing forces.

The teaching of economics.— In the meantime, the teaching of economics had gone through a curious evolution. In 1800, when economics began to be touched upon in courses on moral philosophy, instruction was generally in the hands of active or retired clergymen. Academic recognition of the science appears to have first occurred in 1817 when the Rev. John McVickar was appointed to the chair of moral philosophy and political economy at Columbia College (now Columbia University). Not until 1865, when Professor Perry assumed the chair of political economy at Williams College, Massachusetts, was economics accorded the distinction of an independent professorship. Soon thereafter economics chairs were established with increasing frequency. Charles F. Dunbar became the first professor of political economy at Harvard in 1871, and the next year William G. Sumner and General Francis A.

Walker took over respectively the first chairs of political economy at Yale University and the Sheffield Scientific School (Yale). Walker was the distinguished son of a distinguished father, Amasa Walker, whose leading work, *The Science of Wealth*, attained wide popularity as a textbook.

During most of this time the realities of American economic life were virtually ignored in the classroom. Teachers of economics tended at first to rely upon the treatises of Adam Smith, Malthus and Ricardo for whatever textbook material they imposed upon their long-suffering students. These classics were gradually abandoned for J. B. Say's *Treatise of Political Economy* which, in various American and English translations, became the leading textbook for a period of some forty years ending in 1880. When eventually they came to write their own texts, they continued in the main in the same classical tradition. Incredible though it may now seem, the great majority of these teachers discussed in their books the same problems of economics which had been formulated by French and British writers in the light of a French and British environment. Whatever independent thinking was devoted to slavery, to the rise of labor organizations, to tariff protection, and many other live topics was ordinarily undertaken by non-professional economists like Carey. Especially in periodicals did the best qualified men apply their wits to these questions so strangely neglected by professional teachers.

This sterile period in academic scholarship fortunately terminated with the Civil War. One aftermath of that conflict was a marked change in economic conditions. Free lands in the West were gradually taken up, at the same time that the tentacles of modern capitalism began to spread rapidly over an ever enlarging territory. The archaic economic training then offered at American colleges was totally unfitted to prepare earnest students to cope with the gigantic problems raised by this transformation. In consequence there began a migration of students nearly unparalleled in the history of modern scholarship. At that time the best teaching and most thorough methods of research were to be found in Germany. It was mainly toward that country, accordingly, that young American scholars made their way, there to work under the leaders of the historical school. Probably the first to leave, in 1873, was John Bates

Clark, a man who was later to rank with the greatest economic theorists of the world. By 1880, E. J. James, J. F. Johnson, H. W. Farnum, S. N. Patten, R. T. Ely, A. T. Hadley, E. R. Seligman, F. W. Taussig, H. C. Adams, and a few others had crossed the ocean for further study. During the 1880's and 1890's, and even in later years, this hegira continued in considerable proportions, with occasional digressions to Vienna to Menger, Wieser and Böhm-Bawerk. Upon their return to the United States, these pioneers obtained teaching or research positions, assumed a rôle of leadership, and laid foundations for the scientific study of economics which have endured and are now nationwide.

The American Economic Association.— Fired with enthusiasm these younger men initiated a movement to organize American economists into a professional association. Such a step had already been taken by German economists in 1872. Moreover, the American Statistical Association had been founded in 1839, and the American Historical Association in 1884. The American Economic Association was finally launched in 1885. Its guiding spirits were Professors Ely and Seligman, the former of whom served as its unpaid secretary for the first seven years. Francis A. Walker, then president of the Massachusetts Institute of Technology and the leading economic thinker of the day in the United States, was persuaded to become the first president of the association. Walker's fame as an economist rests in part upon his work as superintendent of the ninth and tenth federal censuses, in part upon his criticism of the wages-fund doctrine and his origination of the residual claimant theory of distribution. During his seven years' incumbency, the Association was placed on a firm footing. Thereafter the presidential tenure was reduced to two years until 1908 when annual terms were instituted. In the past fifty years, most of the outstanding American economists have been honored by election to the office.

The founding of the American Economic Association marked the close of the first epoch in the history of American economics and the beginning of another. The Association owed its formation primarily to the desire of the newly returned men from Europe to protest collectively against the current laissez-faire attitude of economists in the United States, and to further the

factual approach
historical school of Germany

use of the "look and see" method. In the statement of principles adopted by the first meeting in 1885, the German point of view was much in evidence. Article III, for instance, ran as follows : "We regard the State as an agency whose positive assistance is one of the indispensable conditions of human progress." This statement of principles was discarded in 1888 ; the main objects of the Association have continued for the past half century to be the encouragement of scientific economic research and entire freedom of discussion on every aspect of economics.

It might reasonably have been supposed that the men trained in Germany would turn their back on theoretical discussion and go in for historical studies. To some extent this did happen. But the abler members of the new group devoted their talents toward developing economics as an abstract science. Deductive reasoning became dominant toward the end of the nineteenth century. The reasons are easily comprehended.

First was the controversy which raged when the fundamental issues raised by the European marginal utility theorists began to penetrate deeply into American thought through English translations of the Austrian masterpieces. With the publication of Marshall's *Principles of Economics* in 1890 more fuel was added to an already extensive fire. Secondly, the economic training received by these men in Germany was more theoretical than is sometimes imagined. The German masters, in addition to stimulating their students in the ways and means of historical research, found themselves obliged to answer speculative inquiries, and thus reasoned about economic phenomena much as the classicists had done. Finally, the two most gifted of these American students happened to possess a natural aptitude for abstraction ; John Bates Clark and Simon Nelson Patten were the first American economists worthy of mention in the same breath with Ricardo, Mill, Jevons, Marshall, Menger, Schmoller, and others of the aristocracy of economics.[2]

John Bates Clark.— Born in Providence, Rhode Island, in 1847 Clark graduated from Amherst College at twenty-five, and

[2] *See* "John Bates Clark" by R. T. Ely in *The People's Money* for November and December, 1936, and "Simon Nelson Patten" by the same author in the same periodical for March-April and July, 1936.

repaired to Europe for nearly three years of further study at the Universities of Zürich and Heidelberg. At Heidelberg he was a fellow-student of Böhm-Bawerk under Karl Knies, eminent teacher of Wieser, Ely, Seligman and of numerous others who were later to rise to positions of distinction. Upon his return to the United States, Clark taught economics successively at Carleton, Smith, and Amherst Colleges, was called to Columbia University in 1895, and served there until his retirement in 1923. He was the third president of the American Economic Association.

His first published volume, *The Philosophy of Wealth* (1885), was a collection of scattered essays, most of which had previously appeared in periodicals, in which, with a grace of style not always evident in his later writings, he showed marked originality in the field of pure theory. Of the many interesting ideas advanced in this book, several must at least be mentioned in passing. Asserting that the classicists had grievously erred in imputing to mankind the sole motive of material self-interest in economic activity, in favoring unrestricted individual competition, and in refusing to view society as an organic whole rather than an aggregation of individuals, he commented upon certain economic evils of the times and pleaded for the application of the moral law to economic progress to the end that a "true law of distribution" might be ascertained and put into effect. Of more immediate importance, he announced to the world the application to value theory of the notion of marginal utility, using the expression "effective utility" to denote the additional services of marginal units. He always maintained that this conception of value existed in embryo with him before his departure for European study, and that although he was greatly indebted to Knies for fruitful ideas on the theory of value, he elaborated the fundamental importance of utility as a factor in the price fixing process in utter ignorance of similar work done by Jevons, the Austrians and Walras. At all events, the marginal utility doctrine which he developed was couched in a terminology different from that of the other originators, and it was the statement of this doctrine which brought him in striking fashion to the attention of his contemporaries.

There were many among his friends who hoped that he would

carry the dissatisfaction with the traditional economics manifested in *The Philosophy of Wealth* to the point of entering the lists as an active crusader against the ills of society so warmly assailed in his book. But Clark was much more a man of meditation than of action, and actions do not always speak louder than words. He continued his quiet reflections year after year, publishing much of his thought in periodical form until the polished product appeared in book form in 1899 under the title *The Distribution of Wealth*.

The Distribution of Wealth.— In this epoch-making volume, which firmly established his reputation as a theorist, he strangely departed, except for one particular — and that of the highest significance, from the position which he had taken in his first book. He wrote *The Philosophy of Wealth*, in his own words, for "readers and thinkers who have long been in revolt against the general spirit of the old political economy." In that volume he inveighed against the premises laid down by the classical school and was especially caustic in his condemnation of the working of competition. In *The Distribution of Wealth*, on the contrary, he reversed his stand and made those very premises the basic assumption of his reasoning. In the earlier work he portrayed competition as a harmful and possibly dying institution ; in the later volume he wrote of competition as not alone an inextinguishable but a beneficial force.

A partial explanation for this seeming right-about-face lay in the fact that in the interim he had resolved to use his marginal analysis as a point of departure for the formulation of a scientific theory of distribution, that is, to subdivide the labor of inquiry into two parts. He deemed it best, first of all to attempt to discover the laws governing the determination of values and distribution in an imaginary static state, and next to present somewhat tentative answers to the problems of distribution under dynamic conditions (those of progress). This latter part of the burden he regarded as much the more difficult and important of the two, so much so that its execution would "occupy generations of workers." *The Distribution of Wealth* is therefore mainly an "heroically theoretical" endeavor to elucidate a "natural law of distribution" in a society free from all disturbances caused by progress or change.

The economist who attempts to develop generalizations applicable to economic life is unfortunately estopped from using the method so freely available to workers in the physical sciences. The chemist or the physicist, for instance, comes to his conclusions after isolating and experimenting with selected phenomena. With him, in a sense, everything is under his control. Not so the economist. With him little or nothing is controlled, for he is dealing with a world full of constant change. He may therefore seek a way out by setting up an imaginary world in which economic life goes on under certain assumed conditions, hoping that such a course will aid him in comprehending what is actually going on. This, in effect, is what Clark did, and none has surpassed him in the subtlety with which he carried through his self-imposed task. His static state, in which economic forces are permanent, is somewhat similar to the state of normal equilibrium pictured by Marshall. It is that "natural" or "normal" state which society would assume "If labor and capital were to remain fixed in quantity, if improvements in the mode of production were to stop, if the consolidating of capital were to cease, and if the wants of consumers were never to vary."

Under such circumstances Clark concluded that the factors of production would receive a share of the total service income corresponding to what they had contributed to that income. Labor would receive what labor had created, capitalists what capital had created, and business men (entrepreneurs) what the co-ordinating function had created. In the analysis that led him to accept this as the "natural law" of distribution, as he termed it, he went through the following procedure (very briefly stated). He ruled out land as a separate factor in production, including land under the head of capital. Then he took the business man's point of view with regard to capital, holding that capital is simply the amount of money invested in such material productive goods as factories, tools, machinery, farms and city lots. Thus he reduced capital to an abstract mobile capital fund (called by him "social capital"). In order to bring a similar homogeneity to labor he reduced all laborers to productivity units ("social labor"). This so-called *funding* of labor and capital, incidentally, was not an idea original with him.

That accomplished, he applied the doctrine of marginal

utility to the price of labor and capital. Exactly as the values of ordinary goods are fixed by the values of the marginal (or final) units of those goods, he asserted, so the value of labor and capital is fixed by the values of the marginal (or final) units of labor and capital. The return on capital is set by the productivity of the marginal unit of capital, and wages are fixed by the productivity of the marginal laborer. This marginal laborer is not necessarily the last laborer hired in point of time, but simply any one of the laborers of the entire labor force, since Clark made the assumption that all the laborers were of equal efficiency (and further that all the units of capital were alike). Clark also assumed that each employer, in his greed for maximum profits, would so apportion his use of labor and capital that the value of the increment of product attributable to the marginal unit of labor and capital would about equal the expense incurred for that unit. In other words, the marginal unit of labor and capital is the unit which just pays for itself.

This, then, is the popular textbook marginal productivity theory of distribution which is to be found incorporated in so many modern textbooks on economics, especially as it relates to the determination of wages. The theory rests upon the premises of the free play of competition, the supremacy of the self-interest principle among men, and the superiority of the régime of private property over any other economic order. Whatever may be thought of the theory from a strictly scientific standpoint, it is a most comforting doctrine in its assertion that in the static state free competition among employers assures to the employee the full value of his product. Some critics have gone so far as to suggest, wholly without verification, that Clark advanced this particular theory in order to show that the problem of distributive justice is as capable of solution under a capitalistic as under a socialistic system.

Clark had hoped to devote himself as earnestly to what he called "social economic dynamics" as he had to the study of static social phenomena, but the project never materialized. Two more works came from his pen, *The Problem of Monopoly* in 1904 and *Essentials of Economic Theory* in 1907, but they added not a great deal to the sketch of the field of dynamics with which he closed *The Distribution of Wealth*. *The Problem of Monopoly* is of interest chiefly in displaying his over-emphasis on potential competition as the principal factor in the control of industrial combinations and monopolies. In *Essentials of Economic Theory* he stressed his opinion previously stated that the dynamic laws of society were based upon and varied but little from his static laws, thus affording a reasonably optimistic outlook for the future.

In appraising this economic system some economists look upon it as but a work of art, while others maintain that Clark projected an essentially scientific explanation of the economic world as it existed at the time when he wrote. All would presumably agree, however, that in both his method and his achievement he approaches Ricardo more closely than any other American economists. At the time of his death in March, 1938, he was possibly the most highly acclaimed by the profession of contemporary economists.

Simon Nelson Patten.— In sharp contrast is Simon Nelson Patten (1852-1922), tenth president of the American Economic Association, and called by the late Professor Seager of Columbia University "the most original and suggestive economist that America has yet produced." Born in New York State, reared on an Illinois farm and gifted with a youthful mind at once inquiring and undisciplined, he departed in his early twenties for Germany in search of further enlightenment in the field of philosophy. For three years he pursued his studies at Halle under Johannes Conrad, signal member of the historical school, receiving the degree of doctor of philosophy in 1878 despite his limited knowledge of the German language. Thereafter ensued years of maladjustment toward the end of which he somehow managed to write and have published his first book, *The Premises of Political Economy*. Such was the recognition acquired through this penetrating reexamination of classical economics that he was appointed in 1888 to a professorship of political economy at the University of Pennsylvania where he remained until his retirement in 1917.

During his university career he was a most prolific writer, although he never learned to write with facility and many of his books were in the nature of pamphlets. Most significant for the economist are the following: *The Consumption of Wealth* (1889); *The Economic Basis of Protection* (1890);

The Principles of Rational Taxation (1890); *The Theory of Dynamic Economics* (1892); *The Theory of Social Forces* (1896); *The Development of English Thought,* his longest book, (1899); *The Theory of Prosperity* (1902); *Heredity and Social Progress* (1903); *The New Basis of Civilization* (1907); and *The Reconstruction of Economic Theory* (1912). Shortly after his death some of his periodical writings were published under the title of *Essays in Economic Theory* (1924). Much of his later work bordered on the line between economics and other social sciences, and he even ventured into the fields of mathematics and biology, to say nothing of a novel, *Mud Hollow,* which he published in 1922. He was one of those rare individuals who attempt to take all knowledge for their province.

Patten's genius lay in his acuteness of observation. Of him Clark once remarked that at one time or another he had anticipated all the later developments in economics. This is indeed high praise. Yet if any one economist ever deserved to be known as the great "anticipator" Patten was that one. With his feet on the ground he continually looked into the future, and the glimpses that he caught were those which the subsequent course of events has proved to be truly prophetic. Long would be that list of his forecasts of what either has since happened or is in the process of taking place. But as Clark further stated, Patten never completely worked out his ideas. The limitations of the human mind are such that only rarely is it given to one man to excel both in intellectual originality and in systematic perfection of his thought. In Patten's case there was further the circumstance that many of his theories required many subsequent years of social and economic development before it was possible to build them up into a state of completion. His thought was a continuous and orderly growth but it never culminated in any one well rounded volume comparable to *The Wealth of Nations* or Clark's *Distribution of Wealth.*

Back of the brilliant fragments of his thinking were certain environmental influences. There was, for instance, his paradoxical personal nature, in which were combined the moral enthusiasm of the Scotch Presbyterian, the perverseness of the Irish, the persistence of the Scotch and the independence

of the prairie landowner. To the end of his days he showed
traces of the awkward farmer boy. There was likewise
the influence of his German contacts, for in Germany he was
especially impressed with the intelligent consumption habits
of the Germans and the way in which they made economical
use of their wealth. The emphasis of his German professors
upon the interactions of economic with non-economic motives
in human action, and their insistence upon the wide extension
of the powers of the state were also influential.

But more fundamental were the characteristics of the American environment in which he grew up and in which he moved
as an adult, keen observer of the rapid economic and social
changes going on about him. His was no mere book learning,
steeped though he was in the classical economics and especially in Mill's *Principles of Political Economy,* which he is reported to have reread year after year. He was pre-eminently
the American economist, ever seeking to re-examine the concepts of his predecessors in terms of American economic
phenomena. Most important were the indelible impressions
which swept over him during his formative years on the Illinois
prairies. There he noted the apparently inexhaustible bounty
of nature, the increased efficiency of labor as larger amounts
of capital were applied to the land, and the boundless optimism
of the frontier people in their struggle with the elements of
nature.

Patten's dynamic economics.—Patten thus had little or
no use for static theory, viewing it as utterly devoid of
realism when tested in the crucible of experience. If there
was any one economic law in which he believed it was surely
that of social change. Knowing the present he yet lived in the
future. He was the reformer, the revolutionist, ever working
for the reconstruction of the world. His was a pragmatic
philosophy, similar to that of William James and John Dewey,
which organized itself around the constructive forces of
America. No pessimist was he. To him economics was never
the "dismal" science, but rather the science of optimism, a
vital, creative force.

Hence his attack on traditional beliefs. He denied the existence of a law of diminishing returns, assailed the classical
laws of rent and population, regarded monopoly and not com-

petitive conditions as the normal situation, favored protection to home industry as a permanent national policy, and stressed the desirability of social planning through the medium of governmental interference in private affairs. The exertions of labor, he maintained, were the only costs of production, nor did the rate of profits tend toward a minimum. Economic rent, in his opinion, was a differential return going not alone to the owners of better land, but also to superior workmen, and technicians and the more capable employers.

Of the utmost significance was the high position which he assigned to the field of consumption, since he elevated consumption in his economics to the place occupied by value in the classical thinking. He laid down five laws of consumption, such as those of harmony and variety, the general effect of which was to indicate how consumption might be so improved as to yield maximum satisfactions to consumers, were only habits of consumption brought into conformity with the new products and the inestimable potentialities of the United States. He campaigned, for instance, in favor of corn bread as opposed to wheat bread, holding that the country was better adapted to the growing of corn than of wheat. And he was continually urging people to eat to live instead of living to eat. He himself set the example by living the life of an ascetic. In this connection his concept of the transition from a deficit economy of pain to a surplus economy of pleasure is of note. Society tends to progress, he averred, from a stage of undiversified consumption and methods of production characterized by huge real costs to a stage where consumption is diversified and goods are produced with a minimum of real costs. The progress of society was thus to be measured by the surplus of utility yielded by goods of all sorts over the real costs of producing those goods.

Withal, like Clark, he was the deductive type of thinker, using the very method for which he so roundly took the classicists to task. Rarely did he use ordered facts in support of his conclusions or attempt with figures to disprove the theories of others. Such facts as he adduced were usually brought forward merely by way of illustration of theories which he propounded. Some of his untested assumptions thus turned out to be of a wholly ridiculous nature. But by and large his theories in the long run proved to have the saving grace of soundness. Facts appeared in due time which proved him right on such diverse matters as prohibition, teaching methods, religious developments, feminism, industrial control, technical advance, trade unionism, and problems of the American home. And he was greatest as a teacher, inspiring many who studied under him to continue working on the economic and statistical problems which he interpreted so brilliantly. Intellectual genius need observe no rules.

Pungent as were Patten's criticisms of not a few of the conventional economic doctrines they have been cast in the shade by the writings of one whose facile pen has done more than that of most other recent American thinkers to set new problems before the students of economic theory. In any list of the most influential American economists of the past generation must be included the name of Thorstein Veblen (1857-1929).

Thorstein Veblen.— Born of Norwegian immigrants on a Wisconsin farm Veblen early displayed abundant evidence of unusual mental vigor. After taking his bachelor's degree at Carleton College, where he studied economics under John Bates Clark, he pursued graduate work at Johns Hopkins and Yale Universities, obtaining his doctor's degree in philosophy at Yale in 1884. Weakened by several years of illness it was not until 1891, when he was thirty-four years old, that he began the teaching of economics. He was thirty-nine before he was promoted to an instructorship and forty-three before he became an assistant professor. He never attained the rank of full professor. From 1892 to 1906 he was a member of the faculty at the University of Chicago; from 1906 to 1909 he taught at Leland Stanford University, and from 1911 to 1918 at the University of Missouri. From 1919 to 1925 he lectured at the New School for Social Research in New York City, retiring then by reason of ill health from all scholastic work to California, where he died four years later. In common with Clark and Patten his teaching appealed almost exclusively to graduate students. Careless of the amenities of life, his academic career was much more checkered than might otherwise have been the case. In 1924 he was offered the presidency of the American Economic Association, but refused the nomination.

First of his long list of publications was *The Theory of the Leisure Class* (1899). Next appeared *The Theory of Business Enterprise* (1904), probably his most significant work. A long period of ten years elapsed before his third book, *The Instinct of Workmanship* (1914) and declared by himself to be his only important book, was published. In rather rapid succession there followed *Imperial Germany* and the *Industrial Revolution* (1915); *The Higher Learning in America* (1918); *The Nature of Peace* (1919); *The Place of Science in Modern Civilization, and Other Essays* (1919); *The Vested Interests and the State of the Industrial Arts* (1919); *Engineers and the Price System* (1921); and *Absentee Ownership and Business Enterprise in Recent Times* (1923). He contributed frequently to scientific and other periodicals.

Veblen's outlook.— Veblen's interests thus seem to have wandered far afield from those of conventional economists. He was indeed an omnivorous reader in most provinces of learning, possessed of what he called a "court plaster" memory which forgot nothing, and probably unsurpassed in erudition by any human being of recent decades. His extraordinary intellect probed deeply into the roots of ancient and modern civilization. So extremely difficult is it to pigeonhole him that many of his detractors have even denied him the title of economist. But a perusal of his various works establishes the fact that as a rule he dealt primarily with the economic aspects of whatever problem he approached.

He was further much more the critic than the reconstructor of economic science. His rôle was that of disillusionment with the economic theory that had preceded him, and particularly with the premises from which he deemed that theory to be deduced. For the logic of Adam Smith, Ricardo and many others of the classical economists he expressed his admiration, but with their assumptions of hedonism, freedom of enterprise, competition and private property he had no patience. Nor had he any respect for the marginal utility theorists or the doctrines of his former teacher, J. B. Clark. The historical school as represented by Schmoller met with some favor in his eyes, because engaged in a study into the origins of economic institutions. On Marx and Marxism he was indecisive.

This skepticism was heightened by a singular aloofness from

everyday life. An excessively shy figure, he lived a garret-like existence, never voted, travelled little, rarely spoke unless spoken to, was impervious to social pressure, and as he moved from one place to another left most of his possessions behind, despite the fact that he was twice married. He was little interested in purely American problems, and might almost have passed as readily for an Eskimo as for an American.

Whether or not he was impelled to it by his deep study of the newer anthropology and psychology Veblen came to center his interest in economics around so-called institutions which he defined as habits of action and thought widely current in a social group, or, more briefly, as widespread social habits. Illustrations of such habits he found in private property, absentee ownership, and so on. He set himself to ascertain how these institutions had evolved into their present-day form, and how it was that people in general had come to look upon them as desirable. Many writers before him had studied these institutions but usually had done no more than to examine them in operation.

Assuming that man is a creature of instincts acquired through heredity and of habits formed by the influence of environment he presented a theory of the process of the development of institutions, technologically speaking, through what he called the "savage," the "barbarian," and the "handicraft" into the "machine" age of the present. He laid stress upon the seeming strong contrast between the machine process and the business enterprise erected upon that process, asserting that the former was concerned with the satisfaction of human needs, the latter with the making of money. These two institutions he viewed as the two most characteristic economic institutions of the day, and since he regarded the machine process as under the domination of business enterprise he naturally concluded that business enterprise was the one most important characteristic and the one most worthy of analysis.

What struck him as paradoxical in this setup was that the farmers, the artisans, the engineers, the scientists and other expert workers were operating under the apparent direction of a special class of people interested chiefly, or even solely, in the largest possible net money returns rather than in the maximum production of goods. This seemed to him the more inconsistent since in his opinion the colossal gains of an economic nature during the course of the Industrial Revolution had been due wholly to the unexampled progress of the machine process.

With business men, as he thought, more concerned about the vendibility than the serviceability of their products there arose the tendency of business enterprise to become more and more anti-social. He pointed to the prevalence of parasitic trades, the huge growth of advertising, the establishment of monopolies and the rapid increase in businesses financed largely by borrowing, among other things, as ways in which "business" hampers "industry" and sooner or later lead to periodic breakdowns and depressions. These business practices more and more became "vested interests," he declared, or, in other words, "legal rights to get something for nothing."

Well, what of the future? Here Veblen was anything but satisfactory. He looked forward to an ever deepening rift between the directed and the directing class, each failing to understand the other because of the deadening influence of habit in causing people to continue thinking along old lines. He came eventually to desire a radical alteration in the existing economic structure, but perhaps anticipated no such transformation. Unlike Marx, however, he accepted Darwin's point of view that there is no discernible limit to the process of evolution. Only in one of his books, *The Engineers and the Price System*, did he venture to suggest what direction any change for the better ought to take. There he somewhat vaguely advocated a general strike of the "technicians" and the establishment of the control of business in a soviet of engineers, scientists and technical experts, by no means an original idea with him. Shortly before his death he is reported to have stated that he saw no solution for the shortcomings of capitalist society save control through communism.

In common with Patten he was given to long-distance prophecy, and in at least two notable instances his predictions have been verified. In *The Nature of Peace* (1919) he predicted what has recently come to pass in Germany. In *The Theory of Business Enterprise* (1904) he foretold in great detail the crash of 1929, warning business men of the collapse of their paper pyramids, their holding companies and what not, and arguing that recovery would only set in with the revival of the consumer goods enterprises (a moot point not yet definitely settled one way or the other).

He never secured a popular hearing, due in some measure to the highly professional language in which his ideas are imbedded. The man in the street has probably heard of Adam Smith, Karl Marx, and Henry George, whereas the voices of Clark, Patten and Veblen — conspicuous among American economists — are as those of one who cries unheeded in an economic wilderness. It is a sad commentary on the present state of cultural affairs that so little has been done to popularize the writings of America's most influential economists.

In the ranks of the professional fraternity appreciation of Veblen has run the gamut from the exclamation "Pish! Posh!" to the statement that he has been the greatest emancipator of the human mind ever known to the social sciences and the profoundest economist yet produced by America. In a very general way the orthodox economists have privately been little inclined to grant him a high standing.

The labor of disentangling the scientific from the satirical material, the dogmatic assertion of impossible generalizations, the circumstance that he has paid little attention to production, value and distribution problems regarded by them as the heart of economic theory, and the offense which some of his mannerisms and eccentricities have given has led them to conclude that he was neither a clear thinker nor a constructive guide, but merely occupied in dressing up old criticisms in new terminology. On the other hand, many of his younger contemporaries have looked upon him as possessed of inspired insight, and as having altered the course of American economic thought to an extent unequalled by any other man.

Guided largely by his suggestions they have undertaken to undermine and overthrow the conventional economy and to erect a new science of economics upon the basis of the institutional viewpoint. Only the passing of time will reveal to what extent his work is to partake of the quality of constructive permanence.

CHAPTER XVIII

RECENT AMERICAN ECONOMIC THOUGHT

The Period Prior to World War I.—American economic thought at the beginning of the twentieth century may be divided roughly into three groups which tended to shade through infinite gradations into one another. One group stood for the substantial validity of the doctrines of the classical or neo-classical school, stressing the teachings of John Stuart Mill or Alfred Marshall. A second and smaller group held to the doctrines of the Austrian School or of John Bates Clark. The third and smallest group was composed of the followers of S. N. Patten. A few stray rebels, including Thorstein Veblen, Richard T. Ely, John R. Commons and H. C. Adams, were dedicating themselves, like Patten, to the task of "liberalizing" economics, agreeing, if at all, only in their protest against the extremes of individualism.

But, in the main, the typical economist of those days was the college or university professor preoccupied with the instruction of college youth and in no way given to the political processes of social change. Stress was laid on the theory of value and distribution or on so-called "pure" economics, with occasional digressions to the practical problems of the day. Marginal analysis was looked upon as the chief tool of economic investigation. Such statistics as were available were of a rather rudimentary sort. Pathetically little was known, in fact, about statistical theory. As for textbooks the most widely used seem to have been the abridgment of John Stuart Mill's treatise by J. Lawrence Laughlin of the University of Chicago, President Hadley's *Economics* and Ely's *An Introduction to Political Economy*.

Training grounds of numerous economists of the next generation were to be found in the classrooms and seminars of such professors as Patten, Laughlin, Frank W. Taussig (1859–1940) of Harvard and E. R. A. Seligman (1861–1939) of Columbia.

All of these scholars displayed an admirable catholicity of thought in their dealings with their students. Particular reference must be made to Taussig and to Seligman, chairmen of their respective departments for roughly forty years. More students are reported to have taken their Doctor's degrees in economics with these two men than with any other two economists in the United States to date. Their reputation was further enhanced by the publication and wide use of textbooks bearing the identical title of Principles of Economics. Taussig's chief contributions in published form were in the field of international trade and those of Seligman were in public finance. Both were at home, however, in the vast domain of economics, both served on government commissions in the framing of public policies, and both were longtime editors of economic journals, Taussig of the *Quarterly Journal of Economics* and Seligman of the *Political Science Quarterly*. These two quarterlies, both established in 1886, were followed in 1890 by the *Annals* of the American Academy of Political and Social Science at Pennsylvania and the *Journal of Political Economy* at Chicago, the *Yale Review* in 1892, and the *American Economic Review* in 1911.

By 1900, therefore, economics in the United States had taken a long step toward standing on its own feet. In the ensuing half century the debt of many decades' duration owing to European scholars has finally been paid, and with interest. Leading American students of the science rank on a par with the most erudite representatives to be found abroad and, indeed, in several fields have assumed the lead in pioneering researches. The story of achievement is long and fascinating, worthy of a better fate by far than in the following all too brief condensation.

Several writers, in addition to those already mentioned, press for recognition in the period prior to World War I. There is, for instance, the name of Frederick W. Taylor, father of the technique and its application to industry which have come to be known as scientific management. Convinced that the responsibility for the prevalence of waste in industry rested primarily upon inefficient management he engaged in a series of laborious scientific investigations and experiments over the course of two decades in the endeavor to substitute knowledge for guesswork. His conclusions are best observed in his *Principles of Scientific Management* (1919).

Professor H. L. Moore, member of the department of economics at Columbia from 1902 to 1929, pioneered in the utilization of mathematical concepts, dating back to Cournot, in the preparation of much needed statistical studies. His pleas for statistical verification of theory fell in the main, however, upon deaf ears.

Professor Frank A. Fetter (1863–1949), for many years chairman of the department of economics at Princeton University, sought to establish economics upon a sounder basis by formulating, in his own oft-quoted language, "a quite new statement of the theory of value, eliminating entirely the old utilitarianism and hedonism which have tainted the terms and conceptions of value ever since the days of Bentham." Founder of the "American Psychological School" and defender of the point of view which insists that economics is in reality a psychological science, he has won a wide hearing for his doctrines of "psychic income" and "time value."

Professor H. J. Davenport (1861–1931) of Cornell University strove, on the contrary, to rid economics entirely of psychology by assuming prices as a base and by making marginal utilities and disutilities dependent upon them. Insisting upon the entrepreneur point of view, he came to view economics as the study of the private pursuit of pecuniary gain.

Lastly, Professor Irving Fisher (1867–1947) of Yale University, first American mathematician to become an outstanding economist, endeavored to reformulate economics in mathematical terms and to reduce all human and physical phenomena to pecuniary categories. Widely known for his "impatience" theory of interest and for his scheme of the "stabilized" or "compensated" dollar, he went on to champion numerous plans of economic and social reform. Question-begging though many of his assumptions were, he aided greatly, like so many of his contemporaries, in laying new foundations for the economics of the future.

When the First World War broke out, neo-classicism, long in the ascendancy in the United States, was at the zenith of its prestige. In the life and death struggle of the succeeding four years, economists in most of the countries at war were called upon by the governments concerned to act not only as technical advisors but as the holders of responsible positions in the economic mobilization of all available resources. Summoned all too belatedly and used all too inefficiently in the United States, such economists as did serve the government did much to bring back the vitality which economics had enjoyed in Ricardo's day. Nor did the influence of the war cease with the end of hostilities. Significant trends away from the traditional body of thought were set in motion which are still evident in the systematic thought of today.

The Challenge to Orthodoxy.—The challenge to orthodoxy in the United States, however, appeared long before 1914. Those who have endeavored to make economics a cultural rather than a formal science like to look upon their intellectual orientation as the joint product of such thinkers as Georg Hegel, Karl Marx, Charles Darwin and Herbert Spencer in Europe and Charles S. Pierce, William James, John Dewey and Thorstein Veblen in America. What they have had in mind is such a reconstruction of the science as will provide what seems to them a thoroughly realistic interpretation of the economic phenomena of the twentieth century. Interest in the renaissance of economic thought came to a head, so to speak, in the publication of a volume in 1924 entitled *The Trend of Economics*.

Under the editorship of Professor Rexford Guy Tugwell of Columbia University, thirteen American economists, drawn from a number of different schools, joined forces in a cooperative intellectual enterprise of exceeding interest. Obviously all phases of economic opinion current in those days could not be represented in so small a group of writers. But many phases are represented in what has come to be regarded as a sort of manifesto of the younger generation as of the early nineteen twenties. Of the thirteen contributors all but two, W. C. Mitchell and A. B. Wolfe, were relatively young in age; all had been trained largely in American colleges and universities, and most of them were specialists rather than general theorists. Noteworthy is the circumstance that seven of these writers had by 1950 attained the honor of the presidency of the American Economic Association—W. C. Mitchell, F. C. Mills, John M. Clark, Paul H. Douglas, Frank H. Knight, S. H. Slichter and A. B. Wolfe. Suggestive of the general tenor of the titles of the thirteen essays are the following: "Economics—Science and

Art," "Functional Economics," "Experimental Economics," "The Limitations of Scientific Method in Economics," "The Socializing of Theoretical Economics," "Some Recent Developments of Economic Theory," and "The Prospects of Economics."

In a period, however, when the economics of marginal equilibrium still held the field as the supreme orthodoxy, this volume of essays failed to receive the attention which its merits deserved. Economics was still in the grip of economists who were first and foremost teachers of economics. It could hardly be expected that men who were primarily teachers would react favorably to sweeping condemnations of existing theory. And thus *The Trend of Economics* has fallen into near oblivion, mute evidence of the indignities to which all but the greatest of books in the course of time must be prepared to bow.

Dissatisfaction with the established economics, smoldering during the illusory prosperity of the nineteen twenties, burst forth with renewed zeal with the onset of the depression of the nineteen thirties. To this critical movement the all too vague and elusive term "Institutionalism" has been rather generally applied. Institutional economics has come to denote in the United States a particular brand or branch of economics concerned not so much with economic laws as with so-called institutions. The criticisms of the institutionalists appear to have been directed chiefly against the assumptions by the orthodox economists that the production, exchange, consumption and distribution of wealth are determined by economic laws. The assertion is made, on the contrary, that these economic processes are regulated, not by economic laws, but by economic institutions.

This state of dissatisfaction with orthodox economics dates back at least as far as 1899 when Veblen's *Theory of the Leisure Class* was published. By many students Veblen is considered to have been the first to have given the world a well-rounded exposition of institutional economics. Others hold that Karl Marx was the originator of institutional economics in that he focused attention upon the processes of institutional change within the economic system. Still others hold to the view that the institutional approach is as old as economics itself. Be all this as it may, institutionalism came of age during the nineteen thirties. In 1931 one session of the December meeting of the American Economic Association was devoted to "An Appraisal of Institutional Economics." In 1933 a novel departure in textbooks appeared with the publication of *Economic Behavior* by members of the department of economics in the Washington Square College of New York University. Old line economists looked in vain in the pages of this text, if indeed they looked at all, for conventional assumptions and categories. Conspicuously absent, for instance, was any treatment of the factors of production as such, of hypothetical demand and supply curves, of marginal buyers and sellers, of functional distribution, of any sort of normative equilibrium. Instead, a most interesting picture was presented of the controls over economic processes exerted by habit, custom and tradition.

In 1934 Professor John R. Commons of the University of Wisconsin published his *Institutional Economics*, the first book in history, it may be assumed, to bear this intriguing title. At the same time institutional economics moved out of cloistered halls of learning into the pitiless glare of public life with the call to Washington of not a few adherents of the institutional approach as advisors to the "New Deal" administration of President Roosevelt.

With the outbreak of the Second World War in 1939, however, institutionalism, as such, may be said to have run its course. More and more the term is being confined to economic heterodoxy in the United States during the first three decades of the twentieth century. The attempted reconstruction of economics by those opposed to economic orthodoxy proceeds nowadays, in a very general way, under different terms. Very few of these so-called heretics will admit to being an institutionalist. They very much prefer the substitution of such expressions as "experimental" or "social" or "collective" or "holistic" as descriptive of their endeavors in the revamping of economic science. By far the most comprehensive survey to date of the work and goals of these men is contained in a volume by Professor A. G. Gruchy published in 1947 under the title, *Modern Economic Thought: The American Contribution.*

The issue raised by Professor Gruchy is a fundamental one. Is there in truth any such thing as the "American contribution" to the history of economic thought and, if so, has it been made solely or mainly by dissenters from so-called orthodox economics? The present author, privileged to have studied under Professors Taussig and Seligman, on the one hand, and under Professors Mitchell, John M. Clark and Tugwell, on the other, feels constrained to answer in the negative. To mark off the contributions of American economists since 1900 as falling into two mutually exclusive streams of thought is vastly to over-simplify the situation. Scholars should proceed with the utmost caution in labelling certain economists as "abstract" or "deductive" or "unrealistic," for instance, and others as "pragmatic" or "inductive" or "realistic." Taussig and Seligman were as much interested in the trends of economic life and perhaps as well informed as were Mitchell, Clark and Tugwell, nor did they neglect the dynamic, changing aspects of economic activity. "Heterodox" economists appear to have made as much use of such theoretical devices as abstraction, deduction, hypotheses and generalizations as those who are termed "orthodox."

What can be stated with certainty is that the "new" school, if it can be called such, has contributed valuable criticism in the general field of economics. In a negative way the limitations of economic "laws" have been sharply delineated. Positively, the emphasis on relativity, on evolution, on group behavior and on institutions (defined as widespread social habits) has served as a necessary corrective. Numerous monographs have given us much needed descriptive material. Books by such creative thinkers as W. C. Mitchell, John R. Commons and John M. Clark have aided not a little in revealing the enormous complexity of economic life. But the fact still remains that economics, no matter how the term is defined, deals with that particular province of human knowledge which studies, on the one hand, the character of man himself and, on the other, the natural environment in which man lives. The field of economics is marked off from other fields of knowledge by the known truths that man's wants, as regards their number and variety, are without limit and that the means for the satisfaction of these wants are limited. Hence economic activities are those which seek to acquire from the resources of nature the requisites for the satisfaction of human wants.

Since these activities are carried on for the most part through the medium of money making and money spending they tend to operate in terms of prices. The price system functions in a competitive system in a certain manner and it functions in a socialistic society, for instance, in a quite different manner. But the price system does function in all of the various types of economic systems and this functioning is the all important consideration. On the bases of this price system economists, in the course of centuries, have endeavored to draw conclusions—statements, in other words, involving approximations or tendencies regarding economic phenomena. Dignified by the term "principles" or "laws" these statements attempt to explain the working of institutions, man-made or otherwise, since the laws of economics work through institutions and are vastly more fundamental than these institutions. We tend to modify our statements, naturally, as conditions change. And most fortunately for the human race economic conditions are especially subject to alteration because they are in great part man-made institutions.

And thus it is that the appearance from time to time of various types of a "new economics" but serves to drive home the truth that what is needed is not an entirely new body of principles but rather such a testing of principles generally accepted as will either discard them or integrate them into the general body of economic doctrine. Economic study has never been nor is it today a closed body of dogma. Its objective is by no means solely the verification of particular economic theorems but also the introduction of such inductive evidence as will lead to revisions in the existing body of principles. The closing of the gap between economic theory and economic practice is a task for all economists whether or not they be members of so-called "old" or "new" schools of thought.

Economists in Government Service.—During most of the nineteen twenties the American people lived in a fool's paradise. When the "new era" of 1922–1929 came to its inevitable end and depression replaced prosperity, the party in opposition swung the electorate to the Democratic standard by its promise of a "new deal." And thus was inaugurated in the first administration of President Franklin D. Roosevelt a program the like of which the United States had never before experienced. The series of measures designed to bring about both economic recovery and economic reform under the label of the New Deal produced the most conflicting and contradictory attitudes imaginable. In an unprecedented rush to the printing press economists as well as laymen sought to explain the new regime or to arouse opposition to or support for it. Economists by the score, many of them of national reputation, were drafted by the federal government for positions involving admonition or regulation as law piled upon law and control upon control.

Enormous as government activities had become by the end of the thirties in the United States, they were completely dwarfed by the scope and magnitude to which they were forced by the exigencies of the Second World War. The decade of the thirties was characterized by a condition of idle resources, unemployed workers and falling prices, a condition which the government sought to alleviate by means of measures directed to the curtailing of production and the encouragement of consumption. With the outbreak of World War II, the government reversed its steps in mighty strides and employed its full resources in the waging of total war in the endeavor to increase production, curtail consumption and hold down the general price level. Never before had the role of government been expanded into such an all-pervading direction and control of the American economy. And never before had American economists taken such active participation in the formulation and carrying out of government policy. Government agencies literally swarmed with economists, academic and otherwise, seeking to deal with the problems of the war economy and of the reconstruction that would follow the conclusion of hostilities. For literally thousands of men and women this wartime experience represented the first leap from the classroom to the realm of reality.

Conclusion.—With the end of the war in 1945 came challenging demands of another sort. All out production, coupled with tremendous national resources and the requisite "know-how," had enabled the United States to emerge victorious in its global struggle with its totalitarian enemies. Yet the problems bequeathed to America by the economic distortions occasioned by World War II and by revolutionary tensions extending over much of the world were such as to stagger the imagination and give rise to the gravest concern for the future. Among the domestic problems were those of maintaining high production, full employment and economic stability, and of framing a satisfactory pattern of labor-management relations. In the field of international relations a generation which had already witnessed two world-wide armed conflicts and the rise and fall of great empires was now called upon by the swift rush of events to contain the rapid spread of the communist state in Europe and Asia. President Woodrow Wilson had pioneered in turning the United States away from a century and more of traditional isolation and had sought for the entire world a system of collective security. Presidents Roosevelt and Truman, following in his footsteps by choice or necessity, continued the fight which he had begun for an international conscience.

Thus at mid-century the peoples of the globe find themselves in a situation where World War II peace treaties have not yet been concluded; in which the "hot" war has been succeeded by a "cold" war; in which the United Nations, which officially came into existence in October of 1945 to keep the peace once it had been made, has done little except to mark time; in which two nations stand astride the world; in which the United States has embarked on the Marshall Plan, the Atlantic Pact and other measures for providing the resources needed for world recovery and of rearming numerous countries, especially those in Western Europe; and in which the Truman "Fair Deal" program is heralded as the one best way of expanding purchasing power, of raising standards of welfare and of conserving and developing resources in the United States. Truly, no greater task has ever been faced by Americans in times of so-called peace.

In all this deepening concern with problems national and international, economists found themselves flung into positions of prominence where all too much was expected of them by both the government and the general public. True it is that the devices at the command of the economist in 1950 were those which were either utterly unknown or else of a comparatively rude sort much earlier in the century. But economics as a science is still in its swaddling clothes. There is so much to be known and so little is known for sure. Despite the vast extension and improvement of statistical data in recent decades,

economists are still dealing with most of the problems confronting them on an inadequate basis of fact. Even where the data
appear to be adequate they must be tested repeatedly against
fresh observations. In this complex and rapidly changing world
economists must ever be ready, therefore, to reformulate their
conclusions in the light of newly discovered evidence. The
wonder is that their achievements have been as considerable
and substantial as they have been by comparison with the
modicum of truth known prior to World War I. Only by the
interplay of speculative reason and meticulously careful observation can economics in time be erected into a meaningful
structure. Little that is worthwhile in economic science has
ever been accomplished by the mere discovery and assemblage
of facts without the guidance of theory. Nor, by the same
token, can economic theory aspire to be looked upon as sound
reasoning without the constant testing of hypotheses as new
data are brought to light.

There was a time, not many decades ago, when theoretical
reflections upon economic and political upheavals were tardy
in making their appearance. Such a criticism can hardly be
made with any justice of economic thinking during the past
twenty years in the United States. In the early thirties, for
instance, interest in imperfect or monopolistic competition grew
apace as the depression of those years boldly revealed the shortcomings of the working of competition. As unemployment continued to mount, the influence of the full employment theory
enunciated by John M. Keynes was felt as American economists
divided themselves more and more into two opposing camps
on the issue of pump-priming. While most of the older economists continued to cling to what is increasingly termed micro-
economics, increasing numbers of the younger element ranged
themselves under the banner of the new macro-economics.
Finally, as an example, may be noted the central theme of most
of the sessions of the December, 1949, meeting of the American
Economic Association. With "A Stocktaking of American
Capitalism" as the nub of discussion, papers were delivered on
such topics as capitalism and monopolistic competition, planning compatible with a market economy, capitalism and economic stability, and capitalism and economic progress. Thus
the obligation of economists in America to appraise the opera-

tion of our capitalist system was brought before the membership of the Association.

So varied and complex has the concrete subject matter of economic study become that the day has long since passed when any one figure could encompass its length and breadth within the pages of an exhaustive treatise. Specialization is the order of the day and necessarily so. This is perhaps the reason for the truly unprecedented volume of output and sharpness of controversy in recent years. No previous decade can match the decade of the forties in these two respects. Division of labor has gone to lengths undreamed of in the nineteenth century. A dazzling variety of ingenious devices for the extension of economic analysis, furthermore, has aided mightily in meeting the mounting requirements for more exactness in economic knowledge. The combination of theoretical and statistical analysis, something relatively new in economics, has produced an economist's tool-chest of truly astounding proportions. Research, long conducted by college teachers only, has in recent decades become the province also of economists in government service, of economists employed by business units and by labor organizations, of research bureaus on the order of the National Bureau of Economic Research, of private foundations of various sorts and of a host of other contributors. The yearly output in the United States very likely exceeds that of all other countries in the world put together. Let us trust that the outcome of these quantitative studies will in the due course of events be a more dependable theory of the workings of the economy as a whole than any evolved thus far.

Of the more than fifty men who have been honored with the presidency of the American Economic Association a large majority are now dead. It would be unwise to single out any one scholar for special notice were it not for the circumstance that in late December of 1947, ten months before his death at the age of 74, Professor Wesley Clair Mitchell of Columbia University became the first holder of the Francis A. Walker medal. This medal, to be awarded not more than once in every five years to an American who "in the course of his life made a contribution of the highest distinction to economics," was touching evidence of the high esteem in which he was held by professional economists. No volume of Principles bears his name nor did he frame any speculative system. Yet his *Business Cycles* (1913) is truly one of the landmarks in the development of economic thought. Inspiring teacher, upholder of exacting scientific standards, lucid in thought and expression, without affectation or pretense of any sort, Mitchell will long continue as one of the shining lights in American and world economics.

And now we turn to another landmark—to *The General Theory* of Britain's John M. Keynes.

AMERICAN ECONOMIC ASSOCIATION

Organized at Saratoga, New York, September 9, 1885

Past Presidents

1886–91	Walker, F. A.	Massachusetts Institute of Technology
1892–93	Dunbar, C. F.	Harvard University
1894–95	Clark, J. B.	Columbia University
1896–97	Adams, H. C.	University of Michigan
1898–99	Hadley, A. T.	Yale University
1900–01	Ely, R. T.	University of Wisconsin
1902–03	Seligman, E. R. A.	Columbia University
1904–05	Taussig, F. W.	Harvard University
1906–07	Jenks, J. W.	Cornell University
1908	Patten, S. N.	University of Pennsylvania
1909	Dewey, D. R.	Massachusetts Institute of Technology
1910	James, E. J.	University of Illinois
1911	Farnam, H. W.	Yale University
1912	Fetter, F. A.	Princeton University
1913	Kinley, David	University of Illinois
1914	Gray, J. H.	University of Minnesota
1915	Willcox, W. F.	Cornell University
1916	Carver, T. N.	Harvard University
1917	Commons, J. R.	University of Wisconsin
1918	Fisher, Irving	Yale University
1919	Gardner, H. B.	Brown University
1920	Davenport, H. J.	Cornell University
1921	Hollander, J. H.	Johns Hopkins University
1922	Seager, H. R.	Columbia University
1923	Plehn, C. C.	University of California
1924	Mitchell, W. C.	Columbia University
1925	Young, A. A.	Harvard University
1926	Kemmerer, E. W.	Princeton University
1927	Adams, T. S.	Yale University

1928	Taylor, F. M.	University of Michigan
1929	Gay, R. F.	Harvard University
1930	Hammond, M. B.	Ohio State University
1931	Bogart, E. L.	University of Illinois
1932	Barnett, G. E.	Johns Hopkins University
1933	Ripley, W. Z.	Harvard University
1934	Millis, H. A.	University of Chicago
1935	Clark, J. M.	Columbia University
1936	Johnson, Alvin	New School for Social Research
1937	Sprague, O. M. W.	Harvard University
1938	Hansen, Alvin	Harvard University
1939	Viner, Jacob	University of Chicago
1940	Mills, F. C.	Columbia University
1941	Slichter, Sumner	Harvard University
1942	Nourse, Edwin	Brookings Institution
1943	Wolfe, A. B.	Ohio State University
1944	Davis, Joseph	Stanford University
1945	Sharfman, I. L.	University of Michigan
1946	Goldenweiser, E. A.	Institute for Advanced Study
1947	Douglas, P. H.	University of Chicago
1948	Schumpeter, J. A.	Harvard University
1949	Ellis, H. S.	University of California
1950	Knight, F. H.	University of Chicago
1951	Williams, John H.	Harvard University

Chapter XIX

JOHN MAYNARD KEYNES

On Easter Sunday, April 21, 1946, occurred the death of one of the most controversial figures of all time in the realm of economics and practical economic policy. Named first Baron of Tilton four years previously in recognition of his outstanding war-time services, John Maynard Keynes was undoubtedly the most discussed of all the economists of his time during the last fifteen years of his life. Some there are, indeed, who maintain that no one else, living or dead, has so profoundly influenced economic theory or policy as has he. Others assert, on the contrary, that what is true in his doctrines is not new and that what is new is not true. Whatever the merits of this controversy there can be no question but that students of economics and informed citizens owe it to themselves to have at least a nodding acquaintance with the so-called New Economics of Lord Keynes.

Early Career.—Keynes was born on the fifth of June, 1883, in Cambridge, England, the eldest son of John Neville Keynes, an economist and logician whose *Scope and Method of Political Economy* (1891) still commands the admiration of scholars, and of a mother, one-time mayor of Cambridge, in whom charm and ability were most happily combined. The son early displayed a veritable prodigy of intellect. Upon his graduation in 1905 from Cambridge University, where he excelled in mathematics, philosophy, economics and debating, he entered the India Office of the Civil Service. The fruit of his keen interest in money and foreign exchange problems, and in Indian finance in particular, appeared in his first book, entitled *Indian Currency and Finance* (1913), a work in which his opposition to orthodox monetary theory was clearly foreshadowed.

In 1909, however, he had returned to Cambridge University as a teaching fellow in Economics and in 1912 he had succeeded

Professor Edgeworth as editor of the *Economic Journal,* a post which he filled uninterruptedly and with the greatest distinction until 1945. His unflagging devotion to detail and his flair for constructive suggestions were never more in evidence than in his editorial performance as well as in his secretaryship of the Royal Economic Society.

In 1915 he took a leave of absence from Cambridge in order to serve as advisor to the British Treasury. Four years later he abruptly resigned from the Treasury's mission to the Paris peace conference on the ground that the Treaty of Versailles would in time prove to be more harmful to the nations dictating this treaty than to vanquished Germany and would in fact only breed more conflict. The reasons for his opposition were soon set forth in a book, *The Economic Consequences of the Peace* (1919), which brought him instant international recognition. Seldom has any book by a scholar created such a storm of controversy or met with such a phenomenal sale. Five editions were shortly called for and translations into eleven languages soon appeared. Much better written than any other of his works, this volume is little short of being a masterpiece. Most of his predictions, furthermore, in time came true.

After his resignation from the Treasury, Keynes returned to his teaching and research and to a multitude of extracurricular activities. As bursar of Kings College, chairman of the *Nation* and later of the *New Statesman and Nation,* founder and chief financial supporter of the Cambridge Arts Theater, chairman of the National Mutual Life Assurance Company, and manager of an investment company, to mention no other activities, he put as much energy into each of them as if any one activity had been his only one. Nearly surpassing belief were his power of concentration and his capacity for work. Rejoining the Treasury in 1940 he became a director of the Bank of England, made several trips to the United States in connection with various economic matters, headed the British delegation to the Bretton Woods monetary conference in 1944 and became co-author of the plan for an international monetary fund and a world bank. Hardly had he returned from an international monetary conference in the United States than he died suddenly of a heart attack at the early age of sixty-two. No man could have been more pleasant in his dealings with his fellows, more thoughtful of the interests of others, more generous in his time and money.

Keynes was never the cloistered scholar that so many economists have been. The wonder is that the quality of his work did not suffer more than it did from the innumerable interruptions in his research occasioned by his manifold outside interests. He was far more the fertile than the logical writer. The harvest which he attempted to garner was more often than otherwise far from completely ripe before he put the sickle to it. Comparatively few are writers like Alfred Marshall who strive in unhurried fashion for the impossible in perfection.

Break with Laissez-Faire.—As early as 1913, in his book *Indian Currency and Finance,* Keynes had given evidence as to his concern both with current economic problems and the content of traditional economics. Karl Marx had coined the term "classical economists" with reference to Ricardo and his British predecessors, including Adam Smith. Keynes, on the contrary, preferred to use this term in connection with Ricardo and his followers, going so far as to place Marshall and particularly Pigou, Marshall's successor at Cambridge, in this all embracing category. His quarrel with the classical doctrines related, furthermore, not to scope or method but to the assumptions made by the classicists.

Be all this as it may, he broke with laissez-faire economics in his recommendations for a managed currency in India and boldly announced in *The Economic Consequences of the Peace* that laissez-faire capitalism had died with the outbreak of war in August, 1914. This onslaught was continued in a *Tract on Monetary Reform* (1923), wherein he pleaded for monetary management in Great Britain and in a pamphlet, "The End of Laissez-Faire" which appeared in 1926. In all this he was merely belaboring the obvious inasmuch as laissez-faire, in the meaning which Adam Smith had attached to it, had not even survived the passing of the nineteenth century over the face of the globe. In abandoning laissez-faire, however, he by no means cut himself adrift from the main ingredients of what has come to be called capitalism. To the end of his days he remained its staunch defender, seeking not to destroy but to preserve the foundations upon which capitalism rests: freedom of choice, the allocation of resources through price incentives and the driving force of the profit motive. As he once put it, capitalism, though in many ways extremely objectionable, if "wisely managed can probably be made more efficient than any alternative system."

During the decade of the twenties his main interests in research seem to have centered around important post-war European controversies on economic policy. True it is that *A Treatise on Probability* (1921) displayed a vast erudition in the philosophical foundations upon which the mathematical theory of probability rests and gave new proof of his many-sided genius. But the problems attendant upon the enormous dislocations in business and finance following upon World War I were those to which he chiefly addressed himself. Persuaded that the economic and social evils of his day were mostly attributable to wrong thinking and that monetary instability was at the bottom of the major evils of British capitalism, he argued eloquently for the stabilization of the internal price level by means of a managed currency. To his dismay his arguments went unheeded, though by the end of the decade nearly all his predictions had been verified. The conservative British government restored the gold standard in 1925, an increasingly larger share of the national income continued to go to the "rentier" (capitalist) class, and industry and trade languished and unemployment mounted to new high levels.

A Treatise on Money.—In the midst of Britain's depression, a Britain in which the return of peace had occasioned economic disturbances more serious than elsewhere in Europe, Keynes published his most exhaustive piece of research up to that time. *A Treatise on Money* (1930) is in two volumes, the first entitled *The Pure Theory of Money* and the second *The Applied Theory of Money,* the whole work running to slightly under eight hundred pages. The scope of this work is much narrower than the title would seem to indicate. It is, indeed, in no sense a complete treatise on money and it was never intended to be. If there be any central theme it is the concept of the theory of money as the all-pervading theory of the economic process as a whole. His discussion tended to center around the effects of the quantity of money in circulation (primarily bank deposits) upon productive activity, the distribution of income, the progress of profits and the creation of capital. Admirers hailed these two volumes as a masterly analysis; opponents tempered their criticism with words of genuine respect for his uncommon erudition.

Keynes himself was far from satisfied with the reception accorded his work and accordingly set himself afresh at his task. As the depression deepened and Britain became engulfed in what to him appeared to be "the greatest economic catastrophe of the modern world," his break with what he termed "the classical theory" became more and more pronounced. By 1935 his matured convictions on the nature and prospects of capitalism had taken constructive form. Early in 1936 appeared in print the last important book that he was ever to write, the volume that is hailed by many scholars as the one great classic work of our time, *The General Theory of Employment, Interest and Money*.

The General Theory.—*The General Theory* was published in an age unparalleled for bold and vigorous theoretical speculation. The only close approach to the present era in this respect is that of the Ricardian period in the early nineteenth century when discussion was rife as to whether the government should foster the economic prosperity of landowners or of the up and coming manufacturing class. Since 1936 the attention devoted to Keynes in the non-communist world has undoubtedly surpassed that given to Ricardo in the one hundred years succeeding the publication of his writings, or even to Alfred Marshall in the fifty years following upon the appearance of his *Principles of Economics* in 1890. The furor wrought by Keynes' major work is in truth without precedent. Never within the space of so few years has a work in the field of economics received such microscopic examination or called forth such a flood of articles, pamphlets and books.

In fewer than four hundred pages frankly addressed to his fellow economists, rather than to the general public, Keynes traversed ground for the most part disregarded by the conventional economics which had preceded him. Adam Smith, for example, had concerned himself basically with the size of the national income; Ricardo, with the distribution of incomes; Marshall, with the interaction of demand and supply. To Keynes the principal problem of economic theory affecting his own generation appeared to be the problem of unemployment in a capitalistic economy, and it is to this problem of unemployment that he devoted himself in the six books into which *The General Theory* is divided. Book I is by way of an Introduction, Book II deals with Definitions and Ideas, Book III considers The Propensity to Consume, Book IV, longest by far of the six Books, concerns itself with The Inducement to Invest, Book V discusses Money-Wages and Prices, and Book VI concludes the account with Short Notes Suggested by the General Theory.

It was high time, in truth, that economists of high professional repute directed their critical attention to the all-important problem of peacetime unemployment. Conventional economics from the days of Adam Smith, with few exceptions, had assumed that there is always a tendency in the free enterprise economy toward full employment of labor and material resources. Economic processes in such a society were held to be self-regulating and self-perpetuating. The normal situation was understood to be stable equilibrium at full employment. Through the free movement of prices, wages, rates of interest, mobility of workers and choices of business men economic forces were always tending to put to work all who wished to work. Frictional unemployment, accounted for by such imperfections in the labor market as immobility of labor, ignorance of job opportunities and shortages of materials, was in no sense a major problem since in the space of a few weeks or months employable people temporarily out of work would again find work. All that was needed was a restoration of the balance between price on the one hand and costs, particularly labor costs, on the other. The constant tendency, therefore, was stable equilibrium at full employment.

Mass production and chronic mass unemployment are phenomena of comparatively recent decades. To this circumstance more than to any other may be attributed the extremely sketchy nature of the treatment accorded the problem of unemployment by the conventional economics from Adam Smith through Marshall, J. B. Clark and others. The connection between idle men and idle money was, to be sure, well understood. It was clearly recognized that the wages and profits created by production must all be promptly spent on consumption or promptly invested in new enterprise if the original production were to be sustained. Not until the early part of the twentieth century, however—though stray passages in the works of Malthus, Ricardo, Hermann, and possibly others heralded the way—did the notion take root that the above equation could balance and still leave millions of people unemployed. In the popularizing of this new concept in Britain Keynes led the way.

The General Theory opens in the preface with an attack upon classical theory (construed by him to include even the doctrines of his contemporary, Arthur Pigou) and sustains this assault almost without interruption through the final chapter. The principal argument is to the effect that the long-accepted orthodox view, according to which economic forces were always tending toward full employment, was merely an account of a highly special situation. Rarely, Keynes argued, were economic forces really in so-called equilibrium at the point when no further pull toward more employment existed. His contention was therefore that the normal or general situation was that in which full employment did not prevail, and that in fact there can be an equilibrium at all levels of employment. Hence the title of his book, *The General Theory of Employment, Interest and Money*.

Classical Foundations.—Now the curious thing about this book-length attack on classical theory is that Keynes really built his own doctrines on classical foundations. These foundations are two in number: the aggregate supply function and the equality between national income and the value of the output.

As to the first foundation, his concept is basically similar to the supply function of the classicists. The "aggregate supply function" is but a generalization of the classic theory that the higher the price the greater the output, and, conversely, the lower the price the lower the output. He measured total production in terms of total employment instead of in physical units, and wrote of businessmen's expectations of gross income in place of offer prices. But the essence is there nevertheless.

Secondly, though sensibly rejecting Say's law of markets that supply creates its own demand, he held with the classical economists that supply is the source of all income and that the national income is equal to the value of current output—a statement long recognized as true by national income statisticians.

Since the value of the output can be measured in only one possible way—by what buyers pay for the output—the national income for any given period will equal the spending of all buyers of current output for that period. Output and employment will then vary directly with total purchasing or, if one wishes, with total spending. Hence output and employment vary directly with the national income or, in other words, with aggregate spending on current output.

But is it not wise to divide this spending stream into its component parts? Keynes properly maintains that it is and proceeds to separate buyers into four groups. There are first of all the consumers; their spending is very naturally termed consumption. There are secondly the business enterprisers; their spending is termed private investment. There are thirdly the various agencies of government; their spending is characterized as public investment. And lastly come foreigners, if any, whose spending is characterized as foreign investment. Thus total spending on current output must equal consumption plus the three kinds of investment. And inasmuch as total spending on current output equals the national income, the national income must equal consumption plus investment.

Employment.—Employment is thus determined by demand, and by "demand" he means the aggregate demand of the entire economic system. The "aggregate demand function," as he puts it (in more familiar terminology, the aggregate demand curve), is a demand schedule representing the proceeds expected from the sale of the output at varying levels of employment. If the amount of employment rises the aggregate demand price increases and if the amount of employment falls the aggregate demand price decreases. At the point on the schedule where the aggregate demand function intersects the aggregate supply function the actual amount of employment at any given time is determined. The point of intersection represents what he terms effective demand.

Now an equilibrium will exist only if the total of the effective demand equals the price of the goods produced. If the effective demand is to continue to equal the value of the goods being produced in the face of increased investment by the community, then its expenditure for consumers' goods must be correspondingly decreased. Likewise, an increase in consumption must be offset by a corresponding decrease in investment if the effective demand is to remain unchanged. In other words, stable employment takes place only when any change in the rate of consumption is accompanied by a corresponding change in the opposite direction in the rate of investment or when any change in the rate of investment is offset by a corresponding and opposite change in the rate of consumption.

If employment is determined by aggregate demand, and aggregate demand consists of consumption plus investment, which is it then, of these two elements, Keynes inquires, which is the more important in maximizing employment? It cannot be the factor of consumption, he asserted, since consumer expenditures, in his opinion, tend to be relatively stable. He realized, of course, that consumer expenditures rise and fall as community income rises and falls. This was not at all what he had in mind. What he did stress was that the consumption habits of individuals are not as a rule very flexible. As he saw the picture, the amounts by which consumption rises and falls as income rises and falls will follow a somewhat regular pattern. The psychological characteristics of human nature and the general social structure and practices of society, he maintained, do not change readily except under abnormal or revolutionary circumstances. To this general pattern of consumer habits he gave the name "the propensity to consume."

On the assumptions, therefore, that aggregate supply is equal to aggregate demand and that aggregate demand is determined by the propensity to consume and by the volume of investment, and that both the aggregate supply function (because it depends mainly upon physical conditions of supply) and the propensity to consume are relatively stable, what is left but to look for the key to the problem of unemployment in the factor of investment? This is exactly what Keynes did.

In his complicated analysis of investment he gave his closest attention not to public or foreign but to private investment. This latter he took to mean the spending of business concerns for the acquisition of plant and equipment, including repairs, and of inventories of raw materials, partly finished goods and finished goods. As for the question of how much would be spent on these various items, he took it for granted that the volume of investment is determined by "the marginal efficiency of capital" and by the rate of interest on loans. By marginal efficiency of capital he had in mind Marshall's familiar "marginal utility of capital," that is, the schedule of returns anticipated on new investment. Business enterprises, motivated ordinarily by profit considerations, will not as a rule initiate or carry to completion investment projects whose anticipated yield does no more than cover the expected costs involved. The marginal efficiency of capital depends, furthermore, not only on the expectation of profit yields but also upon the replacement cost of capital assets.

Funds for expansion and for replacement of capital assets are normally borrowed funds, however, and thus the volume of investment must rest on some factor other than the marginal efficiency of capital. This other factor is naturally the rate of interest on loans.

Upon what, then, does the rate of interest depend? It depends, in the opinion of Keynes, upon the quantity of money in existence, on the one hand, and, secondly, upon what he termed the state of "liquidity preference." And so we have arrived at a consideration of the essence of the longest, and probably the most important, book in *The General Theory*, namely Book IV, "The Inducement to Invest."

Most writers are agreed that one of the fundamental essentials for economic progress is that capital should increase more rapidly than debt. Capital, to economists, means all man-made means of production. Under capital we include such material goods as tools and machinery, vehicles and man-made highways of all sorts, raw materials, flocks and herds, orchards, stocks of goods on dealers' shelves and buildings used in production.

Capital Growth.—There appear to be five main sources of capital growth. The first is the thrift of consumers, the source of capital upon which the older economists like Adam Smith laid most emphasis. The second is business savings, the turning back of business earnings and especially of corporate savings to surplus. The third is the product of labor rather than of saving and may be characterized as direct capitalization. This source arises, for example, when the owners of buildings and farms paint their buildings or build fences or put in sub-soil drainage. The fourth is government thrift by means of the retirement of government bonds, thus putting into the hands of the bondholder funds which will probably be reinvested in various capital uses. The fifth and final source is new bank money, whether in the form of deposit accounts or bank notes, which permits the borrower, though it does not compel him, to create new capital. Of these five sources of capital no country has ever had an excess of capital created from the first four. Whatever is unsound and unwholesome derives from the fifth source, from an overexpansion of bank credit.

It is part and parcel of the equilibrium doctrine that free prices constitute the great equilibrating factor. Prices tend to equate demand and supply as to commodities, labor, and capital. Rising prices in one field, for instance, constitute a signal for consumers to consume less and for producers to produce more in this field, and for producers in other fields to shift their labor and capital, if possible, to the more productive field. Among these prices is, of course, the rate of interest on loans, the price which equates demand and supply in the loan market and equates saving and investment. According to this conventional theory a rise in the rate of interest stimulates saving and checks investment, whereas a fall in the rate of interest checks saving and stimulates investment.

When Keynes came to the topic of the rate of interest, he threw out of the window the researches in this field of such old-time masters as John Bates Clark and Eugen von Boehm-Bawerk. For Clark the rate of interest is governed by the marginal productivity of capital. Assuming, for instance, that the supply of capital becomes greater in relation to the supply of labor, the lower will then be the utility of capital and the lower the rate of interest. With Boehm-Bawerk the rate of interest is determined by the factor of time preference — by the preference of people for present over future goods of a like quality and quantity. In general it may be stated that the theoretical economists of the past had emphasized the psychological attitudes of savers and the use of capital in industrial processes.

Keynes will have none of this reasoning. Interest, in his opinion, is primarily a monetary phenomenon. As he views the problem, the rate of interest is determined by the amount of money in existence, on the one hand, and by the strength of the community's desire to hold its wealth in the form of money, on the other. There are at least three reasons why people prefer to hold their wealth in money or liquid form: first, money provides convenience in exchanges; secondly, money gives one the readiest means of exploiting opportunities in this world of uncertainties, and, lastly, the possession of wealth in money form enables the holder to avoid losses feared because of an expected decline in the prices of securities. Hence interest, he maintains, is a reward for relinquishing liquidity, for the non-hoarding of money. To the relation between the amount of liquidity desired by the holders of money and the current rate of interest he assigns the name "liquidity preference" (or the liquidity function). The rate of interest in no way correlates the supply of money savings with the demand of borrowers for money funds. On the contrary, the rate of interest is simply the amount paid to induce savers to abandon their liquidity preference and thus to lend their funds rather than to hold them idle. The rate of interest is affected not so much by the amount of money actually hoarded as by the intensity of the desire to hoard, that is, by liquidity preference.

The Level of Employment.—With the volume of investment thus held to depend upon the marginal efficiency of capital by comparison with the rate of interest, what remains to be said on the subject of the level of employment? Simply this, in the view of Keynes, that employment depends largely upon the amount of investment and that unemployment is chiefly caused by an insufficiency of investment. He assumed that the most that can be expected of private investment is that private investment may rise sufficiently during boom times to generate full employment during that period and that period only. In times other than good, private investment fails to take up the slack because people tend to hoard rather than to invest. Their behavior is quite rational even though it tends to bring about results that are highly irrational when the economic system is viewed as a whole. With future profit expectations reduced, the amount of the community income declines. At the same time the rate of interest usually goes up because of the increase in "liquidity preference" on the part of income receivers. The rate of interest may have fallen, it is true, but potential investors are still unwilling to make commitments because of their inability to see any prospect of future profits. Thus investment declines and, as investment declines, employment also declines.

Is there no way out of this stalemate? In the belief of the conventional economists prior to the First World War there was a way and an easy one at that. Unemployment, aside from frictional unemployment, would tend to disappear as soon as people at work accepted wage cuts and those who were looking for work went back to work at wages lower than those previously received. The principal cause of unemployment was held to be a wage scale out of line with prices; the remedy, lower wages. Given what Pigou calls "thorough-going" competition, wage rates fall to the point where it is once more profitable for employers to employ all who wish to and are able to work.

Beginning roughly with World War I, certain phenomena appeared which worked with ever-increasing effectiveness to maintain wage rates above the level favored by the classicists. Chief among these forces were government intervention in the labor market through minimum wage laws, unemployment insurance payments and outright work relief, collective bargaining by labor organizations, and a tendency among the workers to remain idle, rather than accept work at wages which would lower their standard of living. Conventional economists, in general, viewed this new type of unemployment resulting from group pressures as nevertheless voluntary unemployment and refused to modify their positions appreciably.

Keynes refused to go along with the argument that labor is responsible for unemployment. He felt, furthermore, that wage-cutting is both an unsound and a demoralizing practice. A general wage cut would simply reduce consumption and accentuate the depression. Employment can increase, he continued to assert, only if there is an increase in the propensity to consume or if there is an increase in the marginal efficiency of capital or if there is a fall in the rate of interest.

From this analysis, accordingly, sprang his main recommendations for direct action by the government. He urged, first of all, a deliberate state policy designed to force down interest rates and to keep them low by monetary and fiscal means. He favored, secondly, government investment expenditures financed by funds borrowed from the public. Thus he championed the setting up of public works, and to calculate its effects in reducing unemployment he constructed the "theory of the multiplier," a theory designed to show that expenditures for public work often, but not always, increase the national income not only by the amount of the direct government outlay but also by some multiple of this outlay. And, thirdly, he advocated a progressive tax system by which taxes would fall more heavily upon the portion of income that is saved than upon the portion that is spent, in the belief that the decline in the propensity to consume would thus be counteracted.

Reaction to The General Theory.—Hardly had copies of *The General Theory* reached the bookstalls and the hands of reviewers than the beginnings of the Keynesian revolution became apparent. Many of the early reviews, it is true, were vitriolic in their denunciation and not one frankly enthusiastic review appeared until many months after its publication. Yet it was not long until a Keynesian school had formed itself, a school which has no parallel in the entire history of economic thought aside from the Physiocratic and Marxist schools. This school, composed mainly of the younger element in the profession, has assumed such proportions and wielded such influence in economic thinking as well nigh to justify the application of the term the Keynesian period to the years since 1936, much as we speak of the Mercantilist and the Ricardian periods of old. Challenging textbooks for college students with the chief emphasis on the national income approach are more and more exposing the youth of the land to the gospel of the master. The broad essentials of the Keynesian analysis are seemingly being accepted by an ever-increasing number of economists of all schools of thought including many who differ on technical details of analysis.

Receptiveness for Keynesian theory was in great measure created by the great depression of the thirties. With the coming of prosperity attendant upon the prosecution of the Second World War, this receptiveness in the United States apparently lagged for several years. The death of Keynes in 1946, however, occasioned a marked revival of interest. The program of the sixtieth annual meeting of the American Economic Association late in December of 1947, for example, was integrated around two important current economic problems: (1) competition, imperfect competition, oligopoly and monopoly, and (2) the economic and monetary theories of John M. Keynes. The same year was marked by the publication of the first book in the United States devoted to the Keynesian theories, Lawrence R. Klein's *The Keynesian Revolution*. In 1948 a somewhat longer exposition by Dudley Dillard was published, entitled *The Economics of John Maynard Keynes*. These two volumes have performed the great service of rendering the theories of Lord Keynes more intelligible to readers of all descriptions.

Of surpassing significance for students and for the professional economist, however, was the appearance, likewise in 1948, of a stout volume of some seven hundred pages with the arresting title, *The New Economics*. In the belief that no understanding of the economic thought and policies of our time is possible without a grasp of Keynesian economics, the editor, Professor Seymour E. Harris of Harvard University, assembled what purports to be an authoritative analysis. The volume comprises twenty-nine essays written for the occasion, including ten by the editor, seventeen essays reprinted from various sources, several speeches by Keynes, and the nearest approach to a complete bibliography of his writings in existence. About one third of the book is old material. Not only *The General Theory* but the whole of his efforts since 1913 were brought under review. Despite some regrettable omissions, this volume may long serve as a veritable mine of information for both the academic theorist and for student use.

Appraisal of Keynes.—It is, of course, much too soon to offer any final judgment on Keynes and his work, albeit some scholars have already presumed to do so. In order to obtain the grand view of the mighty field that economics is, he climbed to such lofty heights, like Adam Smith and others before him, that he justly laid himself open to the charge of faulty vision and imperfect analysis. With all this in mind, some tentative conclusions may nevertheless be essayed.

That there is little new in his speculations is now pretty generally accepted in academic circles. Every single element in the Keynesian system had apparently been discussed by those who preceded him. To his credit, however, despite an unfortunate tendency at times to disparage his predecessors and contemporaries and even to misrepresent their conceptions, he often gratefully acknowledged his debt to those who had anticipated his views. If there be anything new in what he said, there is some ground for suspecting that this newness may lie in the circumstance that he was, seemingly, the first to work out a system based on the propensity to consume plus the marginal efficiency of capital plus the liquidity preference. That this system is somewhat defective is beside the point. What is significant is that there is really astoundingly little in *The General Theory* of 1936 that is rigidly adhered to today by economists of theoretical acumen. Keynes, it must be remembered, worked within the framework of certain assumptions, preoccupied as he was with the causes of the protracted depression during which he wrote. Thus he assumed a state of perfect competition, giving only fleeting references to the problems created by the enormous growth of monopoly power. Again his analysis is essentially static. He is content to describe the conditions of a so-called equilibrium, as when he assumes that the techniques of production and the amount of fixed capital used in production will remain unchanged during the periods of time which he is analyzing. Although he is writing, furthermore, in terms of relations between aggregates, he makes little attempt to break down these aggregates into their respective component parts. His whole thesis, in short, suffers from a failure to ascertain from careful factual studies the true nature of the phenomena which he is investigating.

As one example, we may note his adherence to the classical conception of the declining productivity of additional units of capital. He seems to have been unaware of the ever-increasing productivity which may result, and frequently does result, from the constant improvement in capital instruments. Nor, as another example, can his fear of the abatement of openings for productive investment be upheld. Many scholars tend to support quite the opposite point of view. Science and invention appear in no respect to be on the point of bankruptcy.

Whether one believes with Keynes that the major cause of unemployment is lack of investment or with others that the real cause is lack of consumption, there can be no disputing the assertion that at long last the problem of unemployment in a capitalistic economy has been put in the forefront of discussion. And whether one agrees or not with the Keynesian analysis, one must agree with Keynes—if one agrees with him that capitalism is worth preserving—that something simply has to be done from time to time to keep the capitalistic ship on an even keel. Granted that in the long run the automatic workings of the system make for full employment, it still remains true that in short periods the powers of general adjustment do not automatically rid the system of disturbances and unemployment. And it is these short run intervals with which he is concerned. Keynes, it must be remembered, never studied the system as a whole, more especially with regard to its historical setting or, if he did, never gave any evidence of such study.

And thus it is in the realm of policy and particularly with regard to short run policy that his influence is most clearly discerned. Probably no other economist in the course of centuries has ever wielded such a potent influence on practical policy in so short a space of time. Curiously enough his proposals met with much greater favor in the United States than in the land of his birth. Although he never fully approved of the New Deal, shot full as it was with paradoxes and gross inconsistencies, and although there is little indisputable evidence of his direct influence, nevertheless the New Deal did conform to the general pattern of his policies in marked degree. A managed currency, low interest rates on government bonds, deficit financing, public works, an increase in purchasing power in advance of production, the world bank, and the international monetary fund testify to the debt of New Dealism to his provocative thinking.

The Keynesian revolution is still with us and to an extent, perhaps, that Keynes himself would hardly have dreamed of in 1936. This revolution, if it can properly be called such, has made its way despite the opposition of intrenched orthodox theory and of subsidized research. Yet in all fairness it must be noted that the revolution is not what it used to be. Current thinking is inclined to the belief that most of the formal theorems of Keynes, where not absolutely rejected, are unacceptable without considerable revision. The gulf between Keynesian and anti-Keynesian economists has narrowed appreciably since 1936 with the growing realization that his theories are, after all, not so much a contradiction as a supplemental development of the work of his teacher, Alfred Marshall. Only the future will reveal the nature and true soundness of his contributions to economic science. Meanwhile the structure revealed in *The*

General Theory will long continue to invite the analysis and criticism of economists. Although *The General Theory* can no longer be regarded as the foundation stone upon which a new science of economics may securely be erected, none can question the strong impulse to further scientific inquiry which this volume has produced. And none can question the influence of Keynes for weal or woe on public policy. Only the passage of time will reveal the proportionate amount of space to which he is justly entitled in the history of economic doctrine.

CHAPTER XX

PRESENT-DAY TRENDS

Books which deal with the underlying principles of economics appear to have had a much more permanent influence, speaking very generally, than those which devote themselves to so-called applied economics. These latter are called forth in response to a demand for realistic treatment of economic phenomena, and serve the purpose of illustrating and enriching the subject matter with which economics is concerned. But although they verify or modify or even discredit the underlying body of principles, their effect upon the mighty sweep of economic thought is apt to be more transitory than enduring. The books which are most pondered, most respected, and longest remembered would seem as a rule to be those which are systematic treatises upon economic theory.

Until the works of the past few decades have been thoroughly scrutinized by the coming generations of students, it would be presumptuous for the most part to assess their value with any approach to fairness. There seems to be some ground for the belief, however, that the twentieth century has thus far witnessed the publications of few systematic works comparable to Adam Smith's *The Wealth of Nations* and to such landmarks of the nineteenth century as the *Principles* of Ricardo, Mill, and Marshall, List's *National System of Political Economy*, Jevon's *Theory of Political Economy*, Menger's *Foundations of Economics*, Clark's *Distribution of Wealth* and Marx's *Capital*. This is not to imply that many significant treatises have not appeared since the turn of the century but simply to state that we are still too close to most of them properly to view them with that perspective which only the passage of time will afford.

To attempt a summary and analysis of the economic literature of recent decades is a task beyond the qualifications of even the most gifted mortal. Changes truly awesome both in their rapidity and their extent have induced such an outpouring of publications that no living man can have read, let alone digested, them all. In all humility what follows is a modest and all too brief account of what seem to be certain significant trends in recent economic theory relating to the vast arena of economic life.

Imperfect Competition.—Down to the decade of the nineteen twenties, most economists from the time of Adam Smith on assumed that competition is the normal state of affairs in a capitalist system, though few went so far as to assume a state of perfect competition. Monopoly, custom, and other limitations were duly noted but not stressed in their analyses of long-run tendencies. Little attention was paid to the criticism of a French mathematician, Cournot (1801–1877), that diminishing unit costs tend in time to make competition impossible, and who therefore took monopoly, and not competition, as his starting point. His concept was revived in 1926 by the Italian Piero Sraffa, a former student of Alfred Marshall, in an article entitled "The Laws of Returns under Competitive Conditions." To him goes the honor of being supposedly the first scholar to construct the outline of an economic system in terms of private monopoly, the roots of which go back far into the nineteenth century.

This outline was soon worked up into book form, although in all cases independently, by scholars from three different countries. In 1933 Professor Edward H. Chamberlin of Harvard University published *The Theory of Monopolistic Competition*, an enlargement of his doctor's thesis of six years earlier. In 1933, likewise, appeared *The Economics of Imperfect Competition* by Mrs. Joan Robinson of Cambridge University. And, finally, in 1934 the late German economist Heinrich von Starkelberg entered the lists with a short volume of a similar tenor. Since then the work of these pioneers has been added to and refined, and the analysis extended into regions for a time believed incapable of theoretical generalization by a host of writers among whom Triffin, Stigler and Fellner in the United States and Jan Tinbergen of Holland must not go unmentioned. Berle and Means in *The Modern Corporation and Private Property* (1934) and A. R. Burns in *The Decline of Competition* (1936) heaped coals of fire upon the discussion of competitive capitalism in volumes which have deservedly had a wide hearing.

In pure competition, as the expression goes, there are so many buyers and sellers of an identical product, and mobility of labor and capital is so perfect that no single buyer or seller has any appreciable control over the price. The product is dumped on the market for whatever it will bring. In monopoly one seller, or a combination of sellers, controls the entire supply and therefore controls the price. In monopsony one buyer controls the entire demand.

The new price theory analyzes the situation intermediate among these three and ties together the apparently unconnected theories of competitive and monopoly prices. Monopolistic (or imperfect, or limited, or partial) competition assumes four aspects on the sellers' side (we neglect the buyers' side because of its comparative unimportance). There is first duopoly, in which there are two competitive sellers. There is, secondly, oligopoly, characterized by the fewness of sellers of an identical or nearly identical product. There is, thirdly, product differentiation in which many sellers offer products which are similar but are either not identical or are represented as not being identical. And there is, finally, service differentiation where the basis for buyers' preferences lies in the services provided by the sellers.

To infer, however, that imperfect competition necessarily means a lesser degree of competition, or less active competition, or even the breakdown of competition, by contrast with pure competition, is to draw an incorrect inference. Competition, it must be remembered, takes five different forms: competition in production, in price, in quality of goods, in service rendered, and in salesmanship. The terms pure and imperfect competition signify, therefore, not degrees of competition but different kinds or different conditions of competition. Hence the contributions of the students of imperfect competition give us a body of material which explains how most of the existing market situations impinge upon what has long been regarded as the orthodox analysis. The new theory supplements and clarifies but does not destroy the old.

In this connection a certain sinister implication has been noted by not a few commentators and must be stressed here. To the extent that imperfect competition results in a lessened production and a higher price per unit for the product, the social gains from imperfect competition tend to wither away. Should this restrictive tendency go far enough, the government may be called upon to eliminate the waste and exploitation caused by the operation of this tendency or even to impose controls upon business adjusted to the degree of monopoly differentials. No economic system has ever been entirely competitive and a satisfactory capitalist system does not have to be. But a system shot through with government controls, on the other hand, is a system where a theory of value based upon an economy of voluntary individual choices has no place. The implication is obvious: capitalism versus socialism or fascism.

General Equilibrium Economics.—Along with the development of the theory of imperfect competition is what has come to be known as general equilibrium economics. This particular brand of economics is a modernized version of the so-called pure type of economic theory first effectively formulated by Leon Walras in 1874. Convinced that the clue to the problems in economic theory lay in marginal utility—he used the word *rareté*—he saw clearly that the price of any one good sold in the market depends upon the prices of all the other goods sold. With this knowledge as a basis, he went on to set up equations showing the amounts of goods which people will buy and sell, all culminating in the equilibrium price finally established for each good dealt in and expressed in a series of simultaneous equations.

This endeavor to make an exact science out of economics was continued by his successor in the so-called Lausanne School, Vilfredo Pareto, who became the first (1906) to attempt a complete mathematical formulation of the theory of economic equilibrium in terms of monopoly and collectivism as well as competition. Scores of economists have since then worked out simplified versions of his theory or have added valuable technical improvements. Identified with this task have been many and perhaps all of the members of the Swedish School, founded by Knut Wicksell (1851–1926); such English economists as Edgeworth, Wicksteed, Allen and Robertson; the Italian Barone, and Americans such as Fisher.

The bible of general equilibrium economics is probably *Value and Capital* (1939) by J. R. Hicks of Oxford University. In this distinguished volume Professor Hicks devotes the first two-thirds of the book to the theory of general equilibrium under static conditions. Upon this carefully constructed foundation is then erected a system of production and prices under dynamic conditions. His starting point is the subjective theory of value in which value is held to be a matter of preference between objects desired. Static theory is regarded as theory which disregards the element of time. Utilizing the familiar concepts of substitute and complementary goods and treating the price problem as an equilibrium between pre-existing prices, he seeks to discover the laws of a price system operating in markets of four main kinds under what he terms "dynamic" conditions. In an analysis which is exceedingly complex, he discusses the nature of equilibrium, concepts of income, theories of capital, interest, money, saving and investment. Certain assumptions, typical of general equilibrium theorists, give pause for wonder, however, as to the usefulness of such a high degree of abstraction. Little attempt is made, for instance, to explain why goods exist, why exchange exists, why the total quantities of goods exchanged are what they are and why money has value. Furthermore, perfect competition is assumed; no attention is paid to the controls exercised by government and by institutions, and there is no discussion, save very occasionally, of how the principles developed might work out in practice. Is it possible that general equilibrium economics, preoccupied with mutual determination and neglectful of causation and of the reasons why conditions change from time to time in our dynamic economy, is all too concerned with abstract functional relationships?

Econometrics.—Of possibly greater significance in the development of a more exact science of economics is the reemphasis in recent years of an old approach to economic principles and problems called econometrics. Quantitative and even numerical analysis dates back to at least the sixteenth century, and has been carried on by some of the most distinguished figures in the ranks of economists, notably Sir William Petty, von Thünen, Cournot, Jevons and Alfred Marshall. Pioneer work in the United States was done by Professors Irving Fisher and H. L. Moore. But of late the rapid growth of a wealth of statistical material, plus the considerable progress of statistical technique, have combined to give us a richer application of statistical procedures to economic analysis. With the organization of The Econometric Society in 1930, econometrics may be said to have come of age. World-famous statisticians and economists have graced its membership, among them Professors Ragnar Frisch of the University of Oslo, Jan Tinbergen of the Rotterdam School of Economics, Joseph Schumpeter and Wassily Leontief of Harvard and Oskar Lange of Poland.

But exactly what is econometrics? The question is more easily asked than answered. In the widest possible sense econometrics is probably the entirety of quantitative economic analysis. In the narrowest sense it may cover no more than pure economic theory mathematically formulated. In a truer sense econometrics is the unification of the theoretical, the statistical and the mathematical approaches to quantitative relations. Involved mathematical processes make the field a rather forbidding one except to those who are versed in the higher mathematics. Typical papers presented at the annual meetings of The Econometric Society have been those delivered on the consistency of the classical theory of money and prices, a theory of stabilizing business fluctuations, and the determinancy of absolute prices in classical economic theory.

Quantitative empirical research, however, is of value only to the extent that unwarranted assumptions are not made the basis for rigorous mathematical treatment of economic data. Such progress as has been made thus far in econometrics has been made mainly by the proper application of mathematical procedures to economic analysis. May that progress continue as scholars everywhere make their contributions both deductively and inductively toward the erection of an ever more genuine science of economics.

Business Cycle Theory.—Of somewhat more importance than general equilibrium economics or econometrics is the problem posed by fluctuations in the rate of economic activity. If by the term business cycles we mean recurrent periods of prosperity and depression, few societies since the beginning of recorded history seem to have been wholly free from them. Hence it is one of the curiosities of the history of economic thought that the founders of classical economics, in general, paid so little attention to business fluctuations. Malthus, Ricardo and Sismondi appear to have gone farthest among their contemporaries in recognizing the possibility and seriousness of depressions. Malthus has even been hailed as the first of business cycle theorists in that he perceived that depressions might arise because of conditions inherent in the capitalistic system and attributed the recurring breakdowns of his era to an excess of saving and a lack of consumption. The rank and file of economists, however, following in the lead of Adam Smith, continued for decades to ignore the significance of business crises, holding with their master that temporary deviations from the equilibrium of a price-regulated economy would quickly iron themselves out.

Attention was focused upon the significance of business cycles, however, by dissenting thinkers like Sismondi and Rodbertus and Marx who drove home the point that depressions are after all inseparable and vital parts of capitalism. By some scholars Sismondi is thought to have been the first to have presented a systematic treatment of the business cycle. Mass production and mass unemployment, phenomena unknown to Adam Smith, have grown apace with the development and spread of capitalism and have catapulted the business cycle into a central position in general economic theory. The fabulous boom of the nineteen twenties and the ensuing Great Depression of the thirties have so multiplied researches and explanations that one is hard pressed to catalog and pigeonhole the scores upon scores of theories now available for one's scrutiny, let alone ruminate upon them.

Business cycle theory appears to have started out as an exercise in logic, as an examination into what might have caused the ups and downs of business in the past and might conceivably produce the ups and downs of the future. Such data as were cited were used merely by way of illustration or support of some particular point in the argument. The newer method endeavors to assemble all possible data on what has actually happened, testing by repeated and systematic observations any course of reasoning which seeks to explain and interpret the mechanism of the cycle. The pioneer in the United States in the description of what really occurs during the successive phases of the cycle has undoubtedly been Wesley C. Mitchell. The work which he so ably and painstakingly began is now being continued in the extensive researches of countless economic laboratories. In the course of time sufficient statistical information may be forthcoming to enable us to deal more efficiently with the complex and puzzling fluctuations to which economic activity is subject.

The key word in most business cycle theories may be said to be maladjustment. Thus underconsumption explanations, historically the first to appear, tend to emphasize the disparities in income and wealth between rich and poor. Total consumption tends to lag behind total production, it is alleged, because the poor are exploited by the rich or because the wealthy classes oversave and thus do not spend enough for consumers' goods. These explanations, currently in vogue under the label of lack of purchasing power, seem to make more sense to the man in the street than any other.

Overproduction would seem in a sense to be but another term for underconsumption, since in the one case consumption is under by comparison with production and production is over by comparison with consumption. Yet overproduction explanations, so-called, do abound, stressing an overproduction of goods that can be sold at a profit as the primary cause of depressions. Increasingly this type of explanation refers not so much to the overproduction of quickly consumed goods as to the overproduction of durable goods.

Of a subtler variety are the investment theories, attempts to explain maladjustments in terms of money or credit. Some lay stress on the presence of too much money in circulation; others, on the lack of enough money. Some attribute the cycle to overinvestment; others, to underinvestment. Some credit the interest rate as the key to credit expansion and contraction; others withhold from the interest rate any real significance. Some theories put in the center of their thinking the changes in the business cycle which occur because some costs and some prices move more rapidly or more slowly than do others. They point, for instance, to the lag between overhead and variable costs, to the lag between farm prices and industrial prices, and to the lag between retail prices and wholesale prices.

Penetrating indeed has been the endless array of analyses of the business cycle, analyses which have won for many of their proponents world-wide fame in at least this special field of inquiry. It would be less than justice to omit mention of Gottfried von Haberler's *Prosperity and Depression*; of the emphasis on psychological factors by Professor Arthur C. Pigou, long time successor of Alfred Marshall at Cambridge; of the enterprise theory of Joseph Schumpeter whose untimely death early in 1950 removed from the ranks of Harvard professors one of the four or five greatest names in the economic literature of his day; of the overinvestment theories of the Austrian born Ludwig von Mises and his pupil, F. A. Hayek—to name no more. The furor occasioned by the Keynesian theory of saving, unemployment and depression still abides, of course.

As a result of the unprecedented researches and theorizing of recent decades, one thing stands out as fairly certain and that is that no single underlying cause appears as the reason for the periodic breakdowns of our highly complex modern economic system. An adequate theory of the business cycle is still in the making and may conceivably never come to fruition.

Growth Economics.—New as to terminology but old as to authorship is a province of economics which in recent years has come somewhat arbitrarily to be known as "growth" economics. The modern era is distinguished from all preceding eras by an idea whose roots go back to the teachings of Christ, but whose practical manifestations became of importance only with the transition of society from feudalism to mercantilism and thence to early capitalism. The idea is simply an optimistic faith in human progress.

This faith is clearly evidenced in the writings of many now classed as classical economists, more especially of Adam Smith, Bastiat and J. S. Mill. The title itself, *An Inquiry Into the Nature and Causes of the Wealth of Nations,* reveals Smith's preoccupation with the question of what really contributes to the progress of society and with the problems of a growing economy. His prime concern was with ways and means of increasing in numbers and efficiency the scarce means of production. True it is that he was among the first to explore and to explain the automatic adjustments which take place in the free market economy. But his interest in the market was merely incidental to his interest in economic development. To him the criterion of welfare appeared to be the amount of the real national product, and an increase in wealth to be occasioned by an increase in the productive power of labor. Prerequisite to an increase in this productive power was an increase in the division of labor. This increase in the division of labor could hardly be expected to take place without the previous and continuous accumulation of capital. This accumulation was held to be the natural result of saving or, to be more exact, of investment in durable goods of a superior quality. With his usual good sense he perceived that the progress of society is neither inevitable nor necessary and that in so-called "mature economies" the process of capital accumulation has indeed ceased. To the extent, however, that capital accumulation did take place it was made possible by technical improvements, or, in other words, by new investments made on the basis of the existence of good investment opportunities. Such is his theory of development, a theory which today would probably be ranked in the category of "innovation" theories, and is the handmaiden of the empirical fact that growth results only from change.

Whether or not the "growth" economics of the present stems in any sense from the picture drawn by *The Wealth of Nations*, we may view with satisfaction the increasing attention devoted in the past few years to this somewhat undefinable field of learning. Hardly anything in economics can be more significant, in truth, than meticulous and carefully documented studies of why change takes place and of the consequences of change and growth upon both the economic system and the attitude of society toward change. The economists of the eighteenth and nineteenth centuries were all too busied with such "laws" as were thought to explain relative values and maintain the economic system in a state of equilibrium. All too little recognition, aside from such notable exceptions as Adam Smith, J. S. Mill, Karl Marx and a few others, was given to the possibilities of innovations and of dynamic factors which point the way to economic development.

The twentieth century, on the contrary, reveals quite a different story. Beginning with *The Theory of Business Enterprise* by Veblen in 1904 and *The Theory of Economic Development* by Schumpeter (first published in 1911 in German) the list of workers in this field has so grown as to include, by now, many of the most gifted economists in this country and abroad. In Great Britain, for example, the publication in 1948 of *Toward a Dynamic Economics* by Roy F. Harrod, now at Oxford University, has elicited a great deal of comment in economic circles. In Canada B. S. Keirstead of McGill University has set the pace with *The Theory of Economic Change* (1948). Leaders in the United States have included such men as C. E. Ayres (*The Theory of Economic Progress*, 1944), H. G. Moulton (*Controlling Factors in Economic Development*, 1949) and D. McC. Wright (*The Economics of Disturbance*, 1947).

The problems of a growing economy are problems which thus far have given rise to little but exploratory work in the theory of economic change. Adam Smith, for instance, apparently failed to realize that an increase in productivity per worker may well entail an increase in unemployment. Moulton's optimism as to the economic potentialities of the century ahead, though in the main sound, glosses over or ignores evidence contrary to some of his findings. Harrod confuses "growth" economics with "dynamic" economics, since it goes without saying that a dynamic or changing economy is not necessarily a growing one. The day of the easy answer, of the casual observation, has seemingly gone forever. There are, unfortunately, no short cuts to the truth in the realm of economics, no royal road to the sources of empirical knowledge. Those who are engaged in the work of exploration must at all costs avoid dogmatic theorizing. As thorough a knowledge as possible of the history of economic doctrine coupled with a discriminating use of such statistical data as are available may well prove to be the foundation upon which a satisfactory structure can some day, let us trust, be erected. And yet all this is not enough. There remains the treatment of institutional problems. Theories of unemployment and employment, of money savings and real investment, of mass purchasing power and the like are all affected to at least some extent by such phenomena as the concentration of economic power in business enterprises, labor unions and the government, and increasing inflexibilities in markets of all sorts. So complex has the modern world become that scholarly evaluation of the factors which are creating and determining the economic growth of mankind has become a matter of the greatest difficulty. Let us content ourselves, therefore, with those conclusions, only, for which the evidence is both ample and overwhelming.

Proof of the current widespread interest in "growth" economics in the United States was furnished at the 1949 meeting of the American Economic Association. Under the heading of capitalism and economic progress papers were delivered and discussion revolved around the topics of an appraisal of American economic progress, capitalism and innovation, and capital accumulation and progress. Agreement was general that capitalism had resulted in tremendous progress in terms of economic growth, and yet that the inadequacy of our knowledge poses a challenge of the utmost importance to social scientists. This challenge, simply stated, is the development of the tools of analysis and the discovery and interpretation of the data which will in time give us answers far more accurate than those which we now have if ever we are to come to a correct appraisal of economic progress.

The Machine Age.—Like it or not most of us live today in the machine age. A myriad of machines of every size and shape has remade the home, revolutionized the shop, liberated mankind from much of the drudgery of life, vastly altered the relations between employer and employee, enormously increased the wealth and income of society in general, and shrunk the world, in terms of transportation, to a small fraction of its former bulk. Never in material matters has there been a revolution to compare with the revolution wrought by the mass production principle of our day.

From the standpoint of the business cycle, the economist observes with growing dismay the impact of this new principle upon the bases of traditional society. The worker still produces, but increasingly less and less by himself. The vast majority of workers in so-called civilized countries and a rapidly growing number in backward countries work only as members of some plant. By themselves they can produce nothing salable. They labor at the pleasure of their boss, be he business enterpriser, labor leader or government official, permanently divorced from the product turned out by the plant.

Hence the specter of chronic mass unemployment in an economy characterized by ever greater integration, interdependence and complexity. Hence, too, the fear of dismissal, the dread of possible unemployment on the part of those currently employed. The situation is without precedent. On the one hand, an unparalleled mechanical equipment; on the other, an antiquated institutional machinery. The gulf between material culture and social institutions was never wider and never more tragic. We have the technology but we do not have the institutions, social, economic and political, to go with this technology. No longer is our economy chiefly one of small enterprises, workers and farmers operating in a highly competitive manner. The economic basis of the philosophy of rugged individualism has been largely destroyed by the seizure of important segments of production by corporations and organized business, by the rise of giant labor unions, and by the promotion by the government itself of practices hostile to active competition. Monopolistic groups now strive with each other for the maximum share of the national pie and in doing so sometimes bring paralysis to large elements of the national economy. In a word, we lack the political and social institutions suited to an industrial age.

The Proper Role of Government.—And thus comes to the fore the age-old issue of the proper role of government in society. On perhaps no other question is mankind nowadays so seriously divided.

The processes of production, distribution, and consumption may be controlled by economic forces operating under a system of personal liberty or by legal authority restricting the freedom of the individual or by both together. Economic forces are those which work through price to guide production into the channels most wanted by consumers, allocate the factors of production among various competing uses, and ration the supplies of scarce goods among those who desire them. The controlling lever is price, an omnipresent lever whose vast control over our economic life is realized by few. In those areas of the world where freedom prevails price determines, generally speaking, what shall be produced and where and when, and directs the flow of savings and of laborers into one field or another.

In striking contrast to control by price in a free voluntary system is control by legal authority. This legal authority, it is contended, rests upon at least two bases. In the first place, human nature being what it is, restrictions upon extreme freedom must be laid by government in the interest of real and practical freedom for all. Old restraints may be altered or repealed and new forms of control may emerge, all to the purpose of assuring the fullest development of all, or at least nearly all, individuals. Under this type of system the essentials of capitalism—control of the economy by the consumer, freedom to choose one's occupation, freedom to own property and to invest one's savings—are preserved. Unless one cares to take a stand, therefore, in defense of chaos and the war of each against everybody else, the argument is closed in favor of some sort of government planning even in an automatic price system. The choice is not between planning and no-planning, as some aver, but rather as to how much government planning there should be and as to when and where it should take effect in the automatic economy.

In the second place, advocacy of legal authority springs from a belief in the superiority of authoritarian control over the principle of free enterprise. This belief is implicit in the philosophy of socialists, communists and fascists. In the greater part of the world the impact of two world wars and the interwar depression have apparently settled the issue in favor of authoritarianism. Not in many decades has the area of economic freedom been as narrowly circumscribed as it is at present. Most of the countries in the western hemisphere are dictatorships; most of Asia is communist controlled; most of the countries of Europe, even, are ruled by socialist or fascist governments. The tendency in recent years for nations of an advanced civilization to abandon the system of free enterprise is startlingly illustrated in the nationalization of large segments of Great Britain's economy since 1945.

The world has thus come a very long way from the conditions which prevailed in nineteenth-century England, cradle of the free economy. Economics, beginning as a branch of philosophy, came to be known as political economy during those many centuries when the government's role was a major one. When economic activity came in time to be only in small part dominated by political considerations, the older term gave ground to a new term, "economics," a name which signified both that this particular field of study had taken on the aspects of a science and that the role of the government had become subordinated to considerations of the individual as a member of society. By now the wheel has turned again. The relation of the government to economic life has once more become the major issue before the economist. "Economics" is giving way nearly everywhere to "political economy," whether we know it or not. Men are no longer the units which they once were. Voluntarily or under compulsion they are being coagulated into groups. More and more mankind demands and depends upon group action and shifts to groups the burden of individual cost and responsibility. What is happening is more than mere changes of an economic or political nature. What we are witnessing is a shifting in mass attitudes regarding life, work and the functions of government. These psychological changes would seem in part to be the result of the inability of unregulated private enterprise to cope with the problems raised by recurrent booms and depressions, and in part to the disruption created by the Second World War. Most of the globe is still in bondage to the forces of fear, suspicion, greed and hatred. The postwar years have brought no real peace nor hardly, in truth, the making of peace. Labor unrest, mounting inflation, huge bureaucracies, bankrupt governments, iron curtains, mass hunger, overpopulation and dread of the possibilities residing in the newly discovered forms of energy are but a few of the problems which agitate the minds of most peoples.

What then of economists in these trying days of transition? As has been the case for many decades past many economists, by preference or otherwise, remain aloof from the market place in their ivory towers. The profession has the most urgent need for this type of economist inasmuch as nearly every significant forward step in the development of economics as a science can be traced to the abstract thought of closet thinkers. Economists are still struggling against the weaknesses and imperfections of their discipline in their endeavor to discover what may some day be looked upon as eternal truths. Free scientific inquiry is of the very essence of economics. Rarely in the past has it been more successfully carried on than in academic halls of learning. With them we may place the researchers.

On the other hand there are those economists who are doers rather than ivory tower philosophers, economists who utilize the thinking of others as they wrestle in the market place with the problems of the day. And finally there are those rare individuals in the fraternity who are both thinkers and doers.

The legacy of destruction bequeathed to the present generation by World War II is almost beyond comprehension. The specialized knowledge and training of economists is needed as never before to aid in the bolstering up of what is left of western civilization. Against the background of world devastation the responsibilities and obligations of economists loom increasingly larger. In a universe once more shaken to its very foundations by the heavy hand of dictatorship, economists must not fail to lend their undivided support to the production and execution of effective economic policy.

Histories of economic thought, together with books of selected readings, serve the useful purpose of acquainting the reader with the broad historical picture of the past. The significance of present day theory, needless to say, can in no way be appreciated without some knowledge of the ideas and conclusions of the pioneering thinkers who have gone before. Some of these histories, like the present volume, have as their object the very modest one of removing the student from a state of total ignorance in a field of learning whose boundaries are limitless. Most readers of these textbooks have neither the time nor the inclination for more than a gaining of a fairly adequate picture of the landmarks of economic thought. Other histories ambitiously endeavor to present what purports to be a fairly complete and critical narrative of economic doctrine, and are especially valuable for those who are specializing, under pressure or otherwise, in this giant field of learning. In strict logic these histories, whether of one type or the other, should be written by scholars who have devoted a lifetime of reading and meditation to the history of economic thought, and who thus bring to their task a maturity of judgment usually associated with old age alone. For some reason or other, however, those scholars in the United States, speaking very generally, who would seem to have been most qualified have departed this earthly scene without putting into book form the notes from which they lectured to their students. An immeasurable loss to scholarship was sustained, for instance, in the failure of Professors Bulloch and Taussig of Harvard, Seligman of Columbia and Hollander of Johns Hopkins to leave in printed form for posterity the ripe reflections of decades devoted to the course of economic doctrine. The burden of authorship has thus fallen upon younger shoulders, like those of the present writer, with the result that serious students would do well not to confine themselves to the perusal of any one textbook. The vision of authors is furthermore limited by the scope of their own interests, not to mention other limitations.

All in all, therefore, students should look upon histories of economic thought as mere guides to further reading and wisdom. As has been so many times remarked, books about great books are but a substitute, and at times a wretched substitute, for the great books themselves. Whether one follows the chronological or ideological approach, or attempts to combine these two lines of approach matters little so long as students come to regard textbooks as merely points of departure for further inquiry. And in recent years periodical literature has come to rival in significance the contributions to economics made in book form. Many of the outstanding economists in the United States as well as in other countries have attained their present stature as scholars through the sole medium of their articles in economic journals or in journals closely allied to economics. Not the particular findings and doctrines of thinkers of the past and present so much as the institution of free systematic research exemplified in their writings is the one heritage above all bequeathed to us of today which we should most jealously conserve. As Karl Pearson sagely observes in his *Grammar of Science*: "Every great advance of science opens our eyes to facts which we had failed before to observe and makes new demands on our powers of observation."

The Future.—Economists, like the vast majority of other people, are often, and perhaps usually, out of touch with the most important issues of life. Economic analysis has thus unfortunately tended merely to scratch the surface of things inasmuch as economic issues are ordinarily but secondary phenomena in the general scheme of the universe. Moral, religious, social and poltical planes, rather than economic, are those which normally touch human beings closest and create problems for whose correct solution economists are all too ill prepared.

At the half way mark in this present fantastic century the biggest question in the world is whether there shall be peace or war between Russia and the United States. World War II, it is realized, was but the prelude to a possible World War III. That

there is a widespread desire for peace among the great masses
of people the world over seems incontrovertible. Yet on the
other hand there are countless millions who welcome the prospect of another war either because they can see no peaceful
way of effecting a change in conditions which they consider to
be intolerable or because such a war, if in their favor, would
redound, temporarily or permanently, to their personal advantage. It must not be forgotten that a veritable revolution is
sweeping over the non-white world, a world in which, for the
most part, life is still lived on its lowest terms. What the people
of Asia, for instance, want above all else is apparently freedom
from all oppression in all its forms, native or foreign. The
Soviet Union has cleverly framed its policy in line with these
aspirations, operating until June of 1950 with a certain amount
of camouflage. This mask was dropped with the electrifying
invasion of South Korea by Russian trained troops. The determination of the Kremlin to achieve world mastery by the even-
tual exhaustion of its opponents is at last in the open. In order
to prevail in the global war that seems inevitable the West must
not alone rid itself of the creeping rot which is infesting its
boasted civilization but must furthermore whip up a culture for
the non-white world superior to anything offered by Russia. The
decline and fall of the West is otherwise a foregone conclusion.

The keystone to the entire capitalistic system of the West is
undoubtedly the private enterprise system of the United States.
In his endeavor to effect the collapse of America's capitalistic
economy Stalin seized the initiative at the Teheran Conference
in November of 1943 and has never since relinquished it. The
Soviet strategy apparently calls for one war alarum after another
on the far-flung front to which America is committed. Enormous
appropriations, ruinous taxation, ever-increasing demands on
the United States by countries dependent on America for the
building up of armaments, runaway inflation and national debts
rising to staggering totals are counted upon by the Russian
rulers to topple the capitalism of the United States in ruins and
with it the whole economic system of the West. Direct war with
the United States is seemingly to be avoided until precipitated
by America herself or unless the cold-blooded members of the
Politburo believe that their chances for victory in a direct war
begun by them are overwhelming.

In a war jittery world economists for the most part thus become mere bystanders. The homage which they pay in so-called civilized countries to the ideals of international co-operation and their efforts in behalf of global organization, highly praiseworthy though they be, will be of no avail should the third World War result in the collapse of western civilization. The fate of the history of economic thought trembles in the balance as mankind girds itself for what may prove to be the most destructive and decisive conflict in all of recorded history.[1]

[1] For some of the opinions expressed in these concluding paragraphs, the author has drawn upon the stimulating book by Ferdynand Zweig entitled *Economic Ideas* (Prentice-Hall, 1950).

APPENDIX

MERCANTILISTS

Value Varied and confused theories. Some accepted a labor theory. Natural and market values recognized as separate entities.

Rent No special concept, but land recognized as an assisting factor of production.

Production Commerce given first rank, manufactures second, agriculture third. Immaterial services not productive.

Wages No consistent theory followed. Low wages favored.

Profits Conflicting views. Began to see that some payment of interest is due to productivity of capital.

PHYSIOCRATS

Value Equals cost of production, i.e., sum of material in commodity plus subsistence of workers on it.

Capital Arises only out of *produit net,* hence from extractive industry ; not related to interest and profits.

Rent The surplus resulting from the subtraction from gross product of the sum of annual advances plus interest on primitive advances, i.e., *produit net.*

Cost of Production See "Value."

Wages Approximation to subsistence theory ; not clearly stated.

ADAM SMITH

Value (a) Labor cost : labor the real price and measure of value ; (b) labor command ; (c) money the nominal price ; (d) cost of production the natural price ; (e) demand and supply.

Capital Stock includes goods intended for consumption and capital (goods intended to yield revenue); distinction not maintained.

Rent Monopoly price, therefore effect of cost ; also part of cost ; not consistently treated.

Cost of Production	Includes wages, interest, and rent.
Wages	(a) Subsistence the minimum ; (b) demand and supply in general.
Interest	Part of profits ; paid for use of capital.

MALTHUS

Value	Depends on relative estimation in which goods are held by the parties, based on desire to possess and difficulty of possession. Money value ; labor command.
Rent	Ricardian ; a part of price.
Cost of Production	Wages, interest (rent part of price).
Wages	Necessary price of labor ; subsistence.
Interest	Profits not distinguished. Rate limited by powers of worst land in use. Money wages do not regulate profits, because of price level.

RICARDO

Value	Determined by cost of production (labor plus stored-up labor) of least favored producer ; demand and supply ; monopoly price ; comparative costs in international trade.
Capital	Stored-up labor.
Rent	Difference between product from given land and that from poorest land in cultivation.
Cost of Production	See "Value."
Wages	Standard of living the minimum ; wages fund.
Interest	The marginal profit.
Profits	Part of cost ; vary inversely with wages.

J. S. MILL

Value	Limited-supply commodities, supply and demand ; otherwise, entrepreneur's cost of production.
Capital	A fund to provide food, maintenance, and materials for workers ; fixed and circulating.
Rent	Ricardian, modified by Jones' distinctions ; emphasized influence of custom.

Cost of Produc-tion	Principal element, quantity of labor ; also considers profits and interest in long-run cost.
Wages	Temporary wages dependent on supply (number of workers) and demand (wages-fund) (later retracted but not in his book); natural wages on cost of rear-ing worker.
Interest	Rate dependent on demand and supply of loans ; loanable fund limited by taste for business of fund-owners and amount of annual accumulation from products of labor.
Profits	Surplus remaining to capitalist after replacing capi-tal ; resolvable into interest, risk insurance, and wages of superintendence ; dependent on cost of labor.

JEVONS

Value	Ratio of exchange ; reciprocal of ratio of final de-grees of utility of quantities available for consump-tion after exchanging.
Capital	Labor sustenance.
Rent	(James Mill source): difference between return to worst-land capital and to other capital.
Cost of Produc-tion	Varies inversely with productiveness ; determines supply ; final degree of utility ; value.
Wages	Ultimately coincident with what laborer produces after deducting rent, taxes, and interest.
Interest	Determined by ratio of new product to capital which produced it ; rate of produce increase divided by whole produce.

AUSTRIANS

Value	Determined by marginal utility.
Capital	Aggregate of profits destined to serve as means of acquisition.
Rent	Ricardian.
Cost of Produc-tion	Sanctioned by marginal utility of product.
Wages	Productivity.
Interest	Marginal productivity ; time-discount of successive returns to capital.
Profits	Residual claimant.

KARL MARX

Value	Labor is measure, cause, substance of value ; value of every commodity is the crystallized human labor it contains ; exchange value less subsistence of workers equals surplus value, stolen from workers by exploitation.
Capital	Variable (for subsistence of worker) and constant (machinery, tools, etc.). Variable alone produces surplus, for surplus comes only from labor.
Wages	Kept at subsistence level by exploitation of capitalists.
Interest	Part of profits, not distinguished from profits proper ; all contained in surplus value fund.
Profits	That part of surplus value kept by employers for own use ; like rent, differential revenue ; amount dependent on quantity of labor employed.

MARSHALL

Value	Subjective and objective value co-ordinated through supply and demand. Temporary market value features demand, and long run natural value follows cost of production.
Wages	A standard of living theory.
Rent	Ricardian analysis. Introduces quasi-rent.
Interest	Demand and supply.
Profits	Fourth share. Return to organization or management.
Contribution to Economic Terminology	Consumers' and producers' goods ; demand and supply schedules ; elasticity of demand and supply ; the representative firm ; quasi-rent ; consumers', workers' and savers' surplus ; equilibrium price ; marginal dose ; marginal purchase.

INDEX